US ARMY INSIDER MISSIONS 2

UNDERGROUND CITIES, GIANTS & SPACEPORTS

To Yumi

Michael Salla

Oct 20, 2023

Also by DR. MICHAEL SALLA

US Army Insider Missions
Underground Cities, Giants & Spaceports – Vol 1 (2023)

Galactic Federations, Councils & Secret Space Programs (2022)

Space Force: Our Star Trek Future (2021)

Rise of the Red Dragon
Origins & Threat of China's Secret Space Program (2020)

US Air Force Secret Space Program
Shifting Extraterrestrial Alliances and Space Force (2019)

Antarctica's Hidden History
Corporate Foundations of Secret Space Programs (2018)

The U.S. Navy's Secret Space Program & Nordic Extraterrestrial Alliance (2017)

Insiders Reveal Secret Space Programs & Extraterrestrial Alliances (2015)

Kennedy's Last Stand
Eisenhower, UFOs, MJ-12 & JFK's Assassination (2013)

Galactic Diplomacy: Getting to Yes with ET (2013)

Exposing U.S. Government Policies on ET Life (2009)

Exopolitics: Political Implications of ET Life (2004)

US ARMY INSIDER MISSIONS 2

UNDERGROUND CITIES, GIANTS & SPACEPORTS

MICHAEL E. SALLA, PH.D.

BOOK NINE OF THE SECRET SPACE PROGRAM SERIES

EXOPOLITICS TODAY

TENNESSEE, USA

US ARMY INSIDER MISSIONS 2

UNDERGROUND CITIES, GIANTS & SPACEPORTS

Exopolitics Today
PO Box 946
Dandridge, TN 37725 USA

Printed in the United States of America

Cover Artwork: Adam S. Doyle

ISBN 979-8-9891404-0-4
Library of Congress Control Number: 2023917688

Table of Contents

Table of Figures

Preface

In Volume 1 of *US Army Insider Missions*, I described the history of my communications with JP going back to July 2008 and his contacts with Nordic-looking extraterrestrials. These unique meetings quickly led to him being approached by operatives from the US Air Force. Due to JP's unique abilities and relationship with the Nordics, the USAF operatives arranged for JP to be taken for a variety of off-world encounters with ancient technologies to assess his capacity to safely interact with them. Previous attempts to expose military personnel to such technologies had led to severe injuries and death, as discussed in Volume 1. After concluding that JP had the right consciousness and DNA to enable him to safely interact with and even activate these exotic technologies, the Air Force operatives intensified their efforts to recruit him into the covert world of secret space programs.

Two incidents came to weigh heavily on JP's mind and ultimately influenced his decision to join the military. He had twice been denied further access into classified programs due to his civilian status, thus missing an opportunity to learn more about what was really happening behind the scenes, and ultimately to make this information public. The subsequent creation of the US Space Force and Space Command in late 2019 inspired and convinced JP that his future lay with military service, an honored family tradition, and he immediately enlisted in the US Army.

In Volume 1, I covered JP's missions until August 2022, when he traveled to an underwater city complex populated by a tall Nordic-looking aquatic race in the Bermuda Triangle region. Prior chapters described a combination of off-world missions to the Moon, Jupiter, and Ganymede, and terrestrial missions to various exotic locations, including a submerged space ark in the Bermuda Triangle adjacent to the underwater city. Volume 2 of *US Army*

Insider Missions picks up from his August 2022 mission and covers all his new missions up to July 2023.

What has become clear in JP's mission updates is that he is being exposed to a wide variety of classified projects related to extraterrestrial life and technology, along with the tacit understanding that he will continue to be allowed to reveal them publicly. A senior military officer is advising him on which missions to release to me and when to do so. JP refers to this process as getting the "green light" or "red light," as he waits for this officer to signal what he can safely reveal. JP has been told that as long as he sticks to this process, he and his family will be protected. In March 2023, my wife (Angelika Whitecliff) and I traveled to the military base where JP is currently serving, and he showed us the specific location where he regularly meets with this senior military officer, whose rank he did not disclose. I could guess the rank from the officer quarters adjacent to the well-hidden meeting place, but I have been asked not to reveal more about the officer and the base at this stage.

It has also become clear to me that JP is part of a covert disclosure initiative to expose the public to the diverse projects involving "non-human intelligence" and associated technologies that are known to the US military, but doing so in a way that maintains plausible deniability. It's worth noting that within the Unidentified Anomalous Phenomenon Disclosure Act for 2023, which has been incorporated into the National Defense Authorization Act for 2024, there is much emphasis placed on "non-human intelligence," which is defined as:

> … ''non-human intelligence'' means any sentient intelligent non-human lifeform regardless of nature or ultimate origin that may be presumed responsible for unidentified anomalous phenomena or of which the Federal Government has become aware.[1]

This broad definition of non-human intelligence is very helpful to understanding the scope of JP's missions as he has encountered both extraterrestrial visitors, and ancient underground or underwater civilizations that have been here for centuries or even millennia. All possess different types of antigravity spacecraft that have been sighted and photographed as UFOs by surface humanity. As you will discover in Volume 2, almost all of JP's missions have involved "non-human intelligence" based on Earth in underwater or underground locations. This is a marked shift from Volume 1, which contained an even mix of off-planet and Earth-based missions.

Among the non-human intelligence that figures prominently in JP's mission updates (Chapters 1, 2, and 6) are an underground civilization of "Ant People" which have been described as humanoid, but with large bug eyes and two skin-like antennae protruding out of their heads. These Ant People have a monarchical system of governance and have long given refuge to surface humans in times of calamity on the surface. The Ant People appear in the legends of Hopi Indians and other Native American tribes. A noteworthy function this group is playing today is protecting a sleeping giant associated with the ancient gods Thoth, Ningishzida, Quetzalcoatl, and Viracocha (chapter 3), who is expected to awaken soon from his stasis chamber.

JP has also been taken to a number of underground spaceports where he has witnessed hundreds of spacecraft in various stages of parking, landing, or taking off (Chapters 7, 10, 12). These spaceports belong to Nordic-looking extraterrestrials who have either established colonies in underground locations or worked closely with ancient underground civilizations. Nordic spacecraft are now conducting more overflights of Earth's surface, allowing themselves to be photographed and filmed to help humanity's planetary awakening process.

Among the most intriguing missions of JP's missions presented in this book is one to the Grand Canyon, where he encountered ancient Egyptian and Far Eastern artifacts, and an abandoned ancient spacecraft, all in a secluded cavern (Chapter 8).

The cavern JP witnessed has many similarities to the famed mystery cavern sighted by G.E. Kincaid during two expeditions conducted in 1908 and 1909, which were reported by a major newspaper at the time.

After the publication of Volume 1 of this book series, JP reported that several officers approached him privately to congratulate him on the good job he has been doing and even asked for his autograph. Given that JP is only an enlisted serviceman, such recognition speaks volumes about the covert disclosure initiative that the US Army/Air Force is conducting through him. JP has been told that more whistleblowers will soon be coming out with evidence of UAP-related projects, who, like JP, have been green-lighted to do so. Former USAF intelligence analyst David Grusch is an excellent example of this new breed of whistleblower. Through interviews and Congressional hearings,[2] Grusch has been able to reveal what he has learned about Unacknowledged Special Access Programs involving non-human intelligence. Importantly, he gained this critical knowledge during his official duties as the representative of the National Geospatial Agency to the UAP Task Force, which was created on August 14, 2020, by the US Navy.[3]

It can be anticipated that as this new crop of whistleblowers come forward, they will share documents, photos, and locations concerning various projects that will eventually corroborate JP's revelations as reported in Volumes 1 and 2 of *US Army Insider Missions*. I'm looking forward to the opportunity to compare these forthcoming whistleblower testimonies with what JP has revealed. JP's mission updates are essential first-hand eyewitness accounts by an active military serviceman describing what is happening in some of the most highly classified projects being conducted by the US concerning non-human intelligence and exotic technologies.

Michael E. Salla, Ph.D.
August 29, 2023

Chapter 1

Mission to Underground Civilization in Florida and a Gift for Humanity

In late September 2022, JP led a covert mission of eight military personnel to an underground facility in Florida guarded by a strange race of insectoid-looking humanoid custodians known as the Ant People. His team was taken to a massive underground garden and distant temple where they saw advanced technologies such as antigravity craft and a very large tree that absorbed water from an adjacent stream. The tree emitted filtered water from its branches that was highly rejuvenating and impacted all of the surrounding vegetation. JP's description of the large tree with the rejuvenating waters could be compared to the mythical "Tree of Life" mentioned in religious texts or the "Fountain of Youth" as described by sixteenth century Florida explorer Ponce De Leon.[4]

In addition, JP witnessed a bioluminescent plant that could emit sufficient light to illuminate a large area at night. JP says that seeds from the rejuvenating tree and the bioluminescent plant were given to him by the custodians of the underground garden/city, which he was allowed to take back to his military command as a gift to humanity. In addition, JP and his team were shown a 12-foot-tall white-haired giant with a very long beard who slept in a stone sarcophagus. The Ant People protected the giant and regarded him as a god who would soon wake up.

In an interview, first released in audio form on October 6, 2022, JP discussed the mission he led, the TR-3B antigravity craft that took him to the vicinity of an underground Florida cavern, the long journey deep into the underground civilization that they found there, the fear his team felt when they saw the sleeping giant, and the gifts given to surface humanity by the custodian Ant People guarding the underground civilization he visited.[5] What follows is the transcript of the interview with grammatical corrections and my own commentary.

Interview Transcript

Key: MS – Michael Salla; JP – Pseudonym for US Army Soldier

> MS - I am here once again with JP [who] has just completed another mission. So welcome, JP ...

> JP - Thank you, Doc; it's a pleasure to be here ... sharing my information. It's information that everybody wants, and let's give it to them.... I think the people should hear about this ... I'm being pushed [by insiders] also to give this information, so I'm kind of protected inside the [military] branch.

JP's reference to "being pushed" by insiders to reveal details of his missions is highly significant. It shows that he is working with a covert branch of the US Air Force/Space Command that is in favor of disclosure and has taken the unprecedented action of having an active-duty serviceman reveal details of classified missions. In addition, JP's statement suggests that the agreement reached between the USAF and Nordic ETs (see Volume 1, Chapter 6) involved a condition or requirement that he would be allowed to reveal the truth about extraterrestrial visitation and secret space programs from his point of view. My interview with JP continued:

> JP - Yeah, I'm gonna share a mission that I recently [had] been in. You know, I joined the military, the Army, and I'm really happy that I joined the military. I'm learning a lot about different things that I kind of knew, but now I know more in-depth, more

information. It's really interesting being in the military, you know. I support the military 100 percent, and I really want people also to understand that in no way am I trying to put the military down ... in a negative way. I totally support the military.

MS - But you support the US Army more than the Navy, right? Like, you know, you root for the Army at the big football games, right? You don't go for the Navy?

JP – Yeah, for sure [laughs], but we're all one team.... We all work together, and we all, you know, share information, so it's one big team.... Other governments in the world understand that, and we do work together in space, on Earth, in the sea, and anywhere that there's a government or military. We all do work together, so if you want me to share, I'll share.

MS – Please, yes, tell us about your last mission.

JP - So, this last mission is quite interesting. They have me in charge. It was a group of eight guys; we had different weapons. We came in on a TR-3B. I know a lot of people are familiar [with] what kind of ship that is. I actually talked to the pilot a little bit. I let the guys bring down whatever equipment that we had into the TR-3B and I was talking to the pilot about how the TR-3B works, and he was telling me [about] its ionized technology. The military has been working on this since the 30s or 40s, and they made the current ionized using a massive amount of electricity and some sort of quantum movement using mercury that goes around and using some type of magnet to create this massive surge of electricity that creates an ionized [effect], I don't know if you understand what I'm trying to say ...

MS – Well, it's creating an ionizing effect, and that's what is part of creating an antigravity wave.

JP - Are you familiar with that?

MS - Just a very basic understanding of the way the TR-3B operates with the plasma going around at a very high pressure and ... high temperature, and that generates an antigravity effect that lessens the weight. Now, I think the plasma is ionized ...

JP – Oh, the ionization makes a ship glow, and it ... was kind of interesting how he was explaining [it] to me that it's ionized technology now they're using ...

MS - So the craft is ionized, there's... some sort of glow to the craft when it's operating. Is that what you're saying?

JP - Well, the glow [is] because it concentrates on where the magnets are, so those lights that we see on the TR-3B is because it's ionized, but when it ionizes like so much that it condensed those three magnets, condensing to one, and that's what makes the whole ship glow and go the speed it does, and it can just rapidly move easily using this ionization technology. I wrote it down somewhere. One day I'm gonna share it with you. There's more to this technology because it could time travel as well, and I did not know that. When he told me that, he said that this technology could take you to the future but not to the past, so it was quite interesting when he told me that.

In Volume 1, I described how the first TR-3B prototypes were deployed by the US Air Force in the late 1980s and respectively sized at 250 (76 meters) and 600 feet (183 meters). The first whistleblower to expose the TR-3Bs was a retired USAF engineer, Edgar Fouche, who provided a detailed schematic of them when he first came forward in 1998 and revealed that Lockheed's Skunkworks had built them.[6] Over time various sized models of the TR-3B were developed according to subsequent whistleblowers.[7] JP has photographed some of the triangle-shaped antigravity craft he has witnessed or been taken on, whose diameter he estimated to be as little as the length of a standard school bus in the US which is 45 feet (14 meters) long. JP's habit is to refer to these smaller flying triangles as TR-3Bs, even though they are much smaller than the prototype craft first exposed by Fouche.

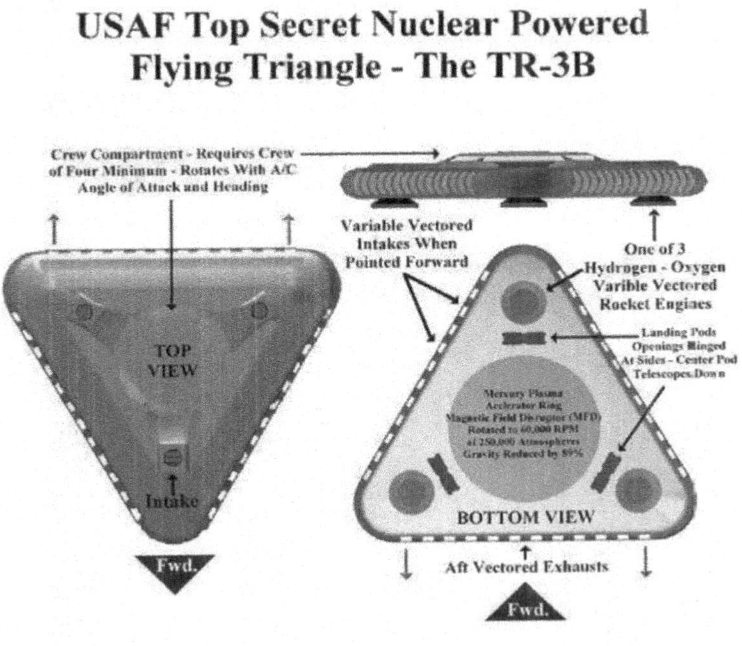

Figure 1. Illustration of TR-3B. Courtesy Edgar Fouche.

MS – Okay, so you get on this TR-3B, you're leading the mission with ... eight guys ...

JP - So we get off, we land, we flew like 10 to 15 minutes, we landed. The guys were taking down the equipment. I was talking to the pilot. There were actually two pilots. One got up and was by the door of the ship that went down, and I was talking to him. I was asking [him] to explain, you know, the technology because everybody was asking about it and how it worked. So, he left us in Florida somewhere ... We came into this cave [entrance the] size of a garage door, and we went in, and it was a total of eight guys. We had our PVS 14s and 31s [night vision goggles], and it was almost night. We went into this cave, and we saw writings right from the back...

Figure 2. US Army soldier with night vision goggles

We got in and it smelled like somebody has done a fire or a type of barbecue, you know, that smell that you get when you do a barbecue.... So, entering the cave, we all started smelling that and we were joking because we were kind of hungry. It was like, "Wow, it's almost like, you know, barbecue, oh yeah.' So, we kept walking in. We were met by two beings that looked different, and I talked to the guy that was right next to me. I asked him, "Do you know about these guys that are here?" They're like holding a stacked-looking thing, and they're like protecting the entrance. So, one of the guys in the back said, "Oh, hey, I got a paper to do that, I [should] have given it to you before the mission, but I forgot to give it to you!" So, I got the paper, and it said, "Do not open it. Give it to the people that are standing guard!" So, we gave the paper to the people standing guard.

MS - Can you describe more about the people standing guard? What did they look like?

JP – Well, these people, their faces are weird, their eyes are on the side like. It's not like ours. Their eyes are more to the side, and their face is wider. Their mouth is wider, but their body structure is the same. I remember seeing a total of probably four fingers instead of five. They were wearing like a robe type of thing. It was like a pearl color robe. And they had on their head ... a hair type of thing, like two [antenna], coming out from their heads, but it looked like skin, and they had it to the side.

After our interview was completed, JP said that the insectoid-looking humanoids are generally known in the covert military as the Ant People. He said that he felt reluctant to openly say it in the interview because he thought listeners would find it hard to believe. In subsequent interviews presented in later chapters, he refers to the underground insectoid-looking civilization as Ant People. This is highly significant as there are legends from the Hopi and other Native American tribes about the Ant People giving shelter to the ancestors of Native Americans who fled catastrophic Earth changes.[8]

Figure 3. Ancient Hopi petroglyph found in the American Southwest.

JP - So we approached them. We gave them the paper, and their eyes were black, so it was different. They look different, I had never seen this type of person before. And they're talking with clicks, similar to how certain tribes in Africa talk—talk with like clicks with their mouth. But they also speak the English language as well, but with a heavy accent. So, we give this paper to them, and one opens it up and closes it up, and then he lifts up his staff, and he says in a low voice, "follow me." So, we start following him. You know, a lot of things go through

> our heads. You know, it could be that these people are getting ready for Halloween. What the hell's going on? ... They're dressed up ... but ... our job is just to go there and to do our mission. Our mission was to go in and to investigate what was this place that we were dropped off to investigate, and why it was connected to the ark they told us [about]. I don't know if you remember the last story, the guy that had the suitcase was the one giving the information and the locations where to go. I'm sure there was another group that went to the ark that same day that I went to the cave, yeah.

Here JP is referring to the Atlantic Space Ark discussed in Volume 1. He next reveals that one of his mission objectives is to find the connection between the Atlantic Space Ark and this underground civilization of Ant People in Florida.

> JP - They were talking with clicks, and we were following them, a total of four [Ant People]. We were in formation [eight soldiers]. We don't know what the heck was going on, but we were in formation, you know, locked and loaded, because you never know ... Nowadays, you just never know. You can't trust anybody. So, we started following them, and when we followed them, it was really steep, like if you trip and fall, you will probably roll all the way down. You can't stop it, you know, you have your heavy kit on your [back], and you have your ACH [Advanced Combat Helmet], and you're like, you're heavy ... and you're wearing your boots, so any kind of trip, you can really bust your ass and roll down that steep hill in the cave. But the walls were squared out, and it was steep. Sometimes there were steps.

I was doing my pace count. My pace count was like 74 to 76. So, every 76 or 72 steps ... I felt stairs, like for 15 meters, and then it kept going steeper. There was a time that it went so steep that we did a [human] chain. We took our ... elbows to elbows, and we did a chain going down. But these guys [Ant People] they were just walking like [they're] familiar with [all] this, you know, walking down. So, we kept going down and down. Man, ... we walked like for maybe 40 [minutes] to maybe an hour. I was checking my time; it was like maybe 45 [minutes] to an hour. We were walking down the steep hill inside the cave. So, the smell was different. And then, once you get to the bottom, it straightens out ...

MS - JP, so you mentioned that some people were sent to the Atlantic Ark, and you ... and the eight guys were sent to this tunnel. Now what's the connection between the ark and this tunnel?

JP - Well, that's the thing that we were checking. So, we get to the bottom. There's a big door.... It looked like a hanger door. So this guy, he touches this round looking rock, and I'm talking about the different looking being [an Ant Person]. He touches this brown rock, and he just swipes it to the right, swipes it to the left, and then it starts glowing. And this hanger starts opening up. It's super bright in there, and you see a lot of vegetation, and we were like, "What the heck is going on? What is this?" So, we entered with caution. But once that [hangar] opened up, the light bounced off and started shooting up to the cave. That's how bright it was. But you can clearly see the vegetation, and there's a source of light that we cannot see. And in the distance, we could see like a fog. We had a guy with us that was part of our group. He knows about plants; he went to school on plant biology, so he was with us on a mission.

MS - A botanist.

JP – Yeah, so whoever put this team together knew what was going to happen, that's what I'm trying to say.... We had different people with different kinds of specialties and all that. So, he [the botanist] says, "Wow, look at these plants!" Then he started talking and saying ... some of these plants have been extinct for hundreds of thousands or maybe millions of years, and he kept talking about ... these plants. He was going crazy.... And these plants were different. A lot of different-looking plants that you wouldn't see on the surface. These plants have different types of flowers and ... we were noticing ... [that] the type of trees that they have it looks similar to the trees that they have at Madagascar. Those trees that bleed, that are red, look similar to these trees.

JP is here discussing the Rosewood tree that bleeds a blood red sap known to have "analgesic, anti-inflammatory, antipyretic, antimicrobial, antidiarrheal, anti-ulcerogenic, anti-spermicidal, larvicidal and mosquito repellant properties used in traditional medicine."[9] In addition to Madagascar, the Rosewood tree is found in Africa, Central and South America, and southern Asia. JP continued to describe the expertise of the botanist on his team.

JP - I remember seeing those trees but hanging from these trees, there was like a nest of some sort of bug ... He knew about these bugs as well. These bugs they come out and pollinate everything in there ... These bugs, they look like a beetle, and they look really silver. But when they open up their wings, they look like a butterfly and the light bounces off these bugs. It was kind of interesting because ... [in] hard-to-reach places, you can see these bugs going in, and they were reflecting light to these plants. So there they had a connection.

It was kind of cool. There's different kinds of insects ... that we saw looking inside ... purple [ones]. So yeah, they have different kinds of insects. There're different kinds of animals also. We saw something that looked like a rabbit, but the ears were shorter—they were rounded off, and they had a long tail. So that was kind of cool. The eyes were humongous, it looked just like a rabbit, but it had bigger eyes, rounded ears shorter, and had a long tail with white fur at the end of the tail. So, it was kind of cool we saw that, and it was not running away from us. It was trying to get close to sniff us, similar to domesticated squirrels ...

So, we kept walking in, and in the distance, we saw a temple-looking thing. And it was embedded in, more into the ground, surrounded by vegetation, right—vines, and all that. It was a tropical-type of location. It looked really tropical. And it was foggy, like our clothes got wet [from] the mist that it had. I don't know if the mist was artificial or there was a type of tree [causing it]. I know that there was a tree there that was dripping water. So, this tree has straws that suck the water up, and it drips water. It takes water from the river, and it drips water to the plants that surround it. So that was an interesting tree that the [botanist] dude was studying. And he was trying to get seeds of this type of tree because he said this tree could help a lot of villages in different parts of the world with farming because ...

> it sucks the water, and it drips the water into their surrounding. It is a huge tree, and the water that comes out of it is drinkable and is filtered, and it's healthy to drink. It's like drinking pots of honey. It's really interesting this type of tree.
>
> MS - Well, that raises a very interesting question... In the Book of Genesis, it talks about the Tree of Life. So, I mean, this tree you saw, it sounds unlike any other tree I've ever heard of.... But the fact that water is an important nutrient and that it filters it and ... can be used for the plants or for drinking.... That raises a very interesting question: any relationship with the Tree of Life in the Book of Genesis?
>
> JP – Well, I'm not sure. But it could be that this tree is part of that because it was protected by these [Ant] People that were there.

The Tree of Life appears in the Book of Genesis as follows:

> Then *Adonai Elohim* caused to sprout from the ground every tree that was desirable to look at and good for food. Now the Tree of Life was in the middle of the garden, and also the Tree of Knowledge of Good and Evil.... From all the trees in the garden you are most welcome to eat. 17 But of the Tree of the Knowledge of Good and Evil you must not eat. For when you eat from it, you most assuredly will die![10]

What this biblical passage suggests is that Adam and Eve were allowed to eat from the Tree of Life, thereby indefinitely prolonging life. But they would remain in a state of ignorance. After they ate from the Tree of Knowledge, they were banished from

Eden and then lost their access to the Tree of Life. The Eden-like garden paradise JP had witnessed, with the Ant People protecting it, does raise an interesting question about the watering tree and its connection to the biblical Tree of Life. I will return to this later. JP continued his update as follows:

> JP – Once we entered, we saw a lot of these people walking around, and they were dressed in robes, and they were just taking care of these plants. It was a huge place ... like 15 football fields big. Bright, I don't know where the heck the lightning was coming from. It looked like it was emanating from the walls, but it was like white. You could see vegetation, green vegetation, and you can see all these types of animals. I'm sure they had pockets of these places and different places that you can go to that have different types of plants from, I guess, every nation or something like that. That's what one of the guys was telling me about this, [the] historian type of dude. His job was to see the writings or see anything that this culture had. He said that somewhere around Nevada, they talk about these, the Indians, they talk about these [subterranean] people, and it's kind of interesting.

JP is here referring to Hopi legends of the Ant People who rescued their ancestors and gave them refuge in their underground realm until cataclysmic events on Earth's surface had subsided. Our conversation continued:

> MS – Well, very interesting because ... you mentioned Florida, that this is some cave in Florida [with] that tree that emits water through its system.

> JP - Well, it has a straw that sucks the water from the little rivers, and it drips water or the [filtered]

substance onto the other plants around it. Everything around it flourishes.

MS - It raises ... the story of Juan Ponce de Leon, who was one of the Spanish conquistadores. He explored Florida, and one of his missions was he sought the Fountain of Youth ... in Florida.... That tree that you saw could be the Fountain of Youth that Ponce de Leon was searching for?

JP - I don't know. Wherever I went, it was beautiful. I know that it was different. You felt, just by breathing the air, you felt stronger, you felt healthier. It was amazing, the feeling that you feel when you go into this place, and everybody felt the same way, everybody felt happy, like amazing.

Once again, the Eden-like garden paradise that JP and his team were witnessing raises the intriguing possibility that it is the source of an ancient legend. Rather than the Hebrew Bible depicting a Tree of Life somewhere in Mesopotamia, it is the mythical Fountain of Youth hidden somewhere in Florida. In a later chapter, where I discuss the physical location that JP traveled to, I will return to this possibility. We continued our discussion:

JP - We saw an oval type of flying vehicles as well, that were flying left to right, and we were asking them all about those vehicles, how they just use it. Yeah, they use it for transportation. So it also leaves there really fast, like it blinks out of existence, and then they blink back into existence. So they probably have the technology to teleport these ships anywhere they want. It's kind of cool, using a type of quantum entanglement technology of some sort. They're really advanced in agriculture, and I'm thinking these people taught a lot of different indigenous people or Indians how to do vegetation or how to plant, or how to use certain kinds of foods, what to eat, what not to eat. So, it's kind of interesting where we went. And [as] we kept walking down into this temple-looking thing, we started seeing writings similar to the Indians in Mexico.

MS - You mean the writing was similar to what was in the Atlantic ark that the Mexican Aztec people saw and started singing?

JP - A Kuria Matte, exactly.

MS - Okay, and now we know what A Kuria Matte means: it's an activation code.

The meaning of A Kuria Matte was explained by Quetza Shah, a Mexican Aztec shaman I met online in the run-up to the 2022 Galactic Spiritual Informers Connection conference that was held in Orlando, Florida. In a Skype interview, Quetza Shah explained that the words "A Kuria Matte" had profound significance in the Aztec language.[11] The words were used to create a portal from heaven to Earth. This was a surprising validation for what JP had witnessed in the Atlantic Space Ark when the Aztec Mexican team members sang and danced the words "A Kuria Matte," which allowed them to walk deeper into the space ark, while other members of the multinational team were unable to follow.[12] My interview with JP continued:

JP – Yes, so these people that went to the ark, it was probably that tunnel that it went to, and they went through that time change. You remember the Chinese were mad because they went in there and time changed. So, I think that the tunnel is connected to this place that we went to.

MS - Okay, so just to remind the listener, you're talking about the mission to the Atlantic Space Ark where there was a kind of time dilation effect that people would slow down movements, would slow down, you know, if you waved your hand ... it would be like a very slow wave where you see like multiple, hands. But the Aztec Mexicans were able to walk through the space ark there under the Atlantic because they were singing and dancing "A Kuria Matte," as they went through. Whereas you mentioned the Chinese members of that expedition that they got stuck. They couldn't move. They couldn't follow the Mexicans even though they wanted to.

JP – Oh, the Aztec guys [went] into the caves and remember that we left them behind, and when we came back to pick them up, they were different, you know, it was kind of interesting.

JP here gives a vital piece of information about what happened when the Aztec Mexican Indians separated from the rest of the multinational team in his first mission to the Atlantic Space Ark.[13] JP said that two weeks had passed before a rescue mission was sent to bring back the Aztec Indians. In the interview, JP revealed that the Aztec Mexicans had portaled from the ark into the underground cavern system of the Ant People civilization and spent two weeks there before returning to the space ark, where they met their "rescuers." My interview with JP continues:

JP - So we started going into the temple, and we saw these writings, and we saw at a distance like a sarcoph ... how do you say it?

MS – Sarcophagus.

JP - There you go, yeah. My language is messed up, Doc, I don't know what to do, I don't know how they can hear me in the Army, you know. But I know a lot of Spanish-speaking people in the military, you know, that understands me. So, it was huge, I have to tell you that. And they were protecting this type of tomb, whatever it was. And then the guy that could read the writings he said that what they had in that tomb was a type of god that they were waiting for ... to come back alive.

MS - So, looking for a god to come back alive, to return.

JP – Yeah, we went in there, and there were candles. But these candles were made by a vine. It looked like a vine, and you could see fire coming up from this vine. So it was actually a plant that could create the fire that they had hanging in the temple. And this plant, every couple of seconds, it does like a puff, and it creates light like ... a candle. And I think it's the same way, I guess, it uses like an acidic kind of thing and it does a puff, and it creates like a fire, but it doesn't burn away. It just keeps doing it. So, they had dozens of these plants around the temple. The smell ... was like vanilla. Amazing smell, it's beautiful ... It looked like a vine that swings up, and then it has a beautiful flower here, like a reddish yellow flower. And this vine, ... it puffs up, and it gives like a little smoke, and then it turns into fire, and it lights up. I think this plant does that to attract insects at night. So that's what the plant biologist was talking about. He says, "Wow, I didn't know plants can do that!" They could attract insects by the little flame and also by the smell that flame [emits]. So, these plants were kind of interesting because now this makes me understand how the ancient people probably lived inside these caves on Earth and how the lighting ... [for what] they ... painted came from these plants that probably lit up.

MS – Now, you just described the vine that had kind of like ... a firefly [effect]... It lights up kind of like, I guess, a firefly.

It's worth pointing out that fireflies produce a chemical reaction that creates bioluminescence. This is how *Scientific American* explains it:

> When oxygen combines with calcium, adenosine triphosphate (ATP) and the chemical luciferin in the presence of luciferase, a bioluminescent enzyme, light is produced. Unlike a light bulb, which produces a lot of heat in addition to light, a firefly's light is "cold light" without a lot of energy being lost as heat. This is necessary because if a firefly's light-producing organ got as hot as a light bulb, the firefly would not survive the experience.[14]

A similar chemical reaction appears to be happening with the bioluminescent plants that JP witnessed. I return to our discussion:

MS - Now, is that plant or the vine that carried these little bulbs that were just, kind of like, lighting up like a firefly? Is that similar to what you saw on the Atlantic Space Ark? You said there were these plants that were covering the writings and that they were luminescent, is that the same?

JP - Yeah, but it was different; it was quite different. These plants, yeah, it's similar to those plants. But those plants in the ark they glow, they were glowing.... It does not emit fire like a real flame.... The name that he [the botanist] was giving me [was] "atractores de insectos." That was the name he was giving me, "attractors of bugs" in Spanish. The [Ant] People ... they look different. Remember, I was telling you they were there with us walking with us and they said "atractores de insectos," attractors of insects. We saw a lot of ... Venus fly traps also, but different. They look so different. They look like drums, and they open up like, they just open their mouths, and they close. And they have this seed on top that when it closes it hits them, and it makes a noise like a little drum. So that was kind of interesting.... So every time they catch a bug, they have seeds that hit the top of it, and it makes noises at night. So you hear all these types of Venus [flytrap] kind of plants, closing and opening at night, similar to what frogs do. So, these plants were different back in the day. They were more communicative with each other ... like regular mammals or insects. The plants back in the day, they were more communicative with each other and they did a lot more different stuff than what we have now.

MS - Okay, so you're seeing all these exotic plants down there at the bottom of this very large cavern that has antigravity craft that fly around, and this mysterious tree, and these vines that would have ... some kind of organic fire breathing or fire emitting plant. So what else did you see?

JP - We saw these [Ant] People bringing a type of food to us. We sat in a circle, and they [JP's squad] were asking me, "Hey, how long [do] we have to be down here?" I said, "I don't know. They [the Ant People] have to give us something back after we're here. We have to bring something back with us." So, we were just waiting. We didn't want to be rude and say, "Hey, give us whatever you need to give us, and let's get the hell out of here!" We don't want to be [rude], you know, so it was pleasant. It wasn't like it was not pleasant. We didn't have any bugs biting us. We have nothing bothering us. Our OCPs [Operational Camouflage Pattern uniforms] have bug repellent regardless. So, a lot of military people would know that. So it was a pleasant trip.... We were just waiting for them to give us something in return, and we had to protect whatever they gave us and take it with us back to the base and give it to whoever was asking for it.

They brought us this type of food. I can tell you what kind of food they had. The food was ... like beans, but it was mushed up. And they had plates that looked really steep ... [and] made of clay. This [food] you eat it, and you feel a little bit dizzy eating it, but it's good food. They give that kind of food to us, and we ate it, you know. And then they took us into the temple, and they showed us the being that was in there. I don't know how to describe this, but it was—he was huge, big, and he looked asleep. And he did not look like these creatures [Ant People]. He looked humanoid to us. We looked at it and he looked ... [like] he was asleep, and they were just waiting for him to wake up.... I thought that he was going to wake up while we were there. I didn't want to be there when he woke up because I didn't know what the hell was gonna happen.

MS - How big was he?

JP - He was like the sarcoph ... how do you say?

MS – Sarcophagus.

JP - La caja, that's how you say in Spanish, like the box, was like facing in a ... slant, so all you can see is ... the skull. The skull was probably four times bigger than my skull. Big head, big eyes, and ... his hair was different. His beard was like ... wrapped around his neck. And it looked like he had a long beard because it was wrapped ... around his neck and laid behind his head, and I think that he was like 11, probably 12 feet [3.7 meters tall], humanoid [i.e., a giant].

MS - Red hair, white hair, black hair, what kind of ... hair?

JP - White hair.... He had white specks in his face like freckles, and his skin was like a type of white grayish. I don't know if it was like that because he was pale or he hasn't woken ... in a long time. It was a white-grayish color. And his lip was blue as if he was lacking oxygen or something like that. But he was in this box, and we got scared when we saw it, because we were talking about how the [Ant People] ... [will react] when he wakes up—like [for us] to take him out or what the hell is going on?" Why would they show him [to us]? Like one guy [a soldier] was so negative there, he was like, "Why would they show this to us and what's going on?" I said, "Bro... just follow up and just keep [to] the mission!" You know, we were kind of scared when we saw this [giant] because we don't know why they were showing [him to] us. And then we were asking one of the [Ant] guys. He says they were showing it to us to make us feel welcome in their culture...

MS - Earlier, you mentioned something about they were waiting for their god to wake up. So they talked about this being ...

JP – Yeah, they told us about [how it would be] if he would have woken up, like right there, like right away. So we didn't want to be there when he woke up because what reaction would he have to us being there, you know? ... I didn't really care, you know, if he woke up. "Let's communicate with him, and let's do whatever we need to do." But we were waiting for something then, so they took us out.

MS - But before you said that ... the sarcophagus that he's in, you said it was at a slant, and you could only see his head. So what did the sarcophagus look like? Was it made out of metal? Was it stone?

JP - It was like a stone ... it looks like a door type of shape, but it's slanted into the ground. It looked like it was put in there, so I don't know how they moved that stone. But it probably weighs more than four thousand, probably five thousand pounds. It's like a marble type of stone, like it's heavy. It's a heavy stone and it had handles, big handles, that it looked like other big humanoids can move it, you know. So, whoever put him there was ... they were big as well, and they kept these ... other humanities [Ant People] that looked like different from us, to protect this place.

In a 2016 article, I cited several sources discussing the existence of giants in stasis chambers awakening or hiding in underground locations.[15] US Special Forces were seeking these giants on behalf of a worldwide organization desiring to capture and imprison the giants due to their ancient knowledge and capabilities. There are also many legends about giants, both good and bad, and their significance to humanity. In a later chapter, I will reveal what was learned about the identity of the giant being protected by the Ant People. Our discussion continued:

> JP - There ... was a step pyramid.... In the distance you could see the Aztec step pyramids.... You can see it was made of really bright gold. The edges of every step were made of gold, and you could see the reflection of the steps coming back toward us. We saw that in the distance coming out from the temple. So we kept walking. They kept showing us around. We saw a lot of different kinds of animals.... We saw something ... like ... a small elephant, but it had tusks in the bottom and legs like the ears. But it was not [an elephant but] it was like an elephant. It was kind of interesting, really friendly. It looked, it felt like ... a pig, you know. It was snorting around ... smelling our feet and all that. And it had tusks. So, it was a size up to like my knees. I'm six foot. So to my knees, would be like, what, three feet tall, like in between my thighs? So, we saw those creatures.
>
> We saw a cat that looked like a saber tooth [tiger] as well.... But it was [a] small type of saber tooth ... kind of cat. We saw a lot of different reptiles. We saw a type of reptile that looked like a dinosaur, but it looked like a chicken. It had scales instead of feathers. It still had a beak, and it still had a tail, and then at the end of the tail [it] had these feathers that closes and opens, closes and opens. So it was kind of cool. We saw ... bees that looked like blue honeybees.... Their honey is like whitish honey. It's not golden honey. I think it's because of the plants that are there, the color of the honey. Their honey, we tasted it... The honey tasted like pear, like a really

ripened pear.... It had that texture as well. So it was kind of a really good type of food. There was also different kind of fruits that we've never seen before. We were there like for five hours, Doc.... It was a really tiring day for me. We walked a lot with our kit, you know. They actually asked us to take our kit off, you know, and leave it, but I didn't let any of my guys take that off.... We kept our kit on at all times and kept our weapons with us at all times because we were just waiting for that moment.

And then, in the end, he [the Ant Person] comes in with this box, and I asked him, "What is this? What are you giving us?" He comes in with an elder now. I'm slightly taller than him, but [he] looked the same way as them. He says these are ... a different type of seed that the people upstairs [on the surface] were asking for.... and we made a deal—and this is for you guys. I said, “what is this?” He pointed to that particular tree that we saw that was ... drinking up the water, and he said ... also those vines that give out like fire, and he said that it was time for them to give them the seeds of this garden. They also gave us tubes of eggs of some sort. I don't know if they were insects or probably the silver insects that we saw, but they were frozen, and they kept them inside ... this clay, but it's like a gel inside. And they kept it inside like that, and they give it to us. It looked like a ball of clay, but it had like a cap that you can open. And it had like a gel that they keep these capsules in it and they gave us that. So, we make our way back ... We start walking out. We said goodbye, and then I asked, "We're gonna see you guys again?" They said, "Yes, we'll go to the surface soon!" So, they were saying that they would come to the surface soon, and they said, “tc start rebuilding." I said, "Wow, rebuilding what?"... I asked them, "How many of you guys there are?" He says billions, millions of these types of humanoids [Ant People] that live inside the Earth in different pockets.

MS – Okay, can you be clearer than that? ... Millions or billions?

JP - Millions it could be, but he said that there was a lot. So I don't know if it's billions or millions. And we kept walking up the cave. We were tired once we stepped out, they closed the door, and it was dark. So, we put our flashlights on, our red flashlights, and we kept walking up the caves. We got to the TR-3B, and then we came back. We ... [took] this box to [where] they told us to drop it, in this particular location, and to leave it there. Well, I don't know who picked it up, who got it, but I know that we left it inside the base. So whoever got the box was part of us, but [at] a higher level. And that was our mission, Doc. It was kind of interesting. It was fun, and we learned a lot about that culture.

MS - Were you ever given a name for that garden or that culture?

JP – No.

MS - Did the guards of the temple, of the garden, did they ever say anything about, you know, who they are, their names?

JP - They just look weird. They never told us their name.

MS - Okay, and people within the military, within the covert branches of the military, want you to share this information. Can you say anything about that?

JP – Yeah, I asked prior to sharing this information. They said, yes, I can share it, "just don't give your name, and don't tell people where you were at."

MS – Okay. Well, I want to thank you, JP, for sharing your latest mission; definitely fascinating and raises a lot of questions about the history of Florida and connections to space arks ...

JP - It's funny that Florida in Spanish is flowers. So that's quite interesting, you know, the purpose. Why was it called flowers? Like you said, that guy that found that beautiful garden, you know, the Garden [Fountain] of Youth, Ponce de Leon, so that's kind of interesting....

MS – Very fascinating; well, I guess we're going to find out eventually more about all of this. Thank you for sharing that, and we look forward to more updates from you.

JP - Roger, I appreciate it.

Once again, we see that JP is being allowed and even encouraged by his superiors in the chain of command to share details of his classified missions. Clearly, there is a major disclosure initiative being pursued by senior military officials through the information being leaked by servicemen such as JP in a manner that maintains anonymity and plausible deniability. In the next chapter we learn what happened to the seeds that JP took to the surface, and what transpired in a return visit to the underground Ant People.

Chapter 2

Second Mission to Underground Civilization in Florida

On October 11, 2022, JP completed his second mission to an underground civilization in Florida belonging to an insectoid-looking group of humanoids that have been called the Ant People. JP was again part of a squad of eight soldiers drawn from different military services that met with representatives of the Ant People. JP was in charge of security for the mission while two members of the squad conducted negotiations with the Ant People, who were very upset that a gift given during the first mission had been taken overseas, out of the USA, contrary to what had been agreed to.

The missing gift contained seeds from a tree that could filter water and provide rejuvenation and life-extension properties associated with the mythical Tree of Life and Fountain of Youth. In addition, the gift included seeds from a bioluminescent plant that could light up large areas at night. JP said his primary mission was to see and learn more about the giant sleeping in a large sarcophagus, but the Ant People denied his squad access due to what transpired over the missing gift. The transcript of the interview follows, with grammatical corrections and my commentary.[16]

Interview Transcript

Key: MS – Michael Salla; JP – Pseudonym for US Army Soldier

MS - [JP] had a mission recently ... tell us about your mission.

JP – Hey, how are you doing, Doc? We had something going on yesterday; we were out for a couple of hours. We went back to that cave system and we went down.... They were doing [a] type of exchange. We did not ... [go] all the way in, but we went next to the door where we could see the garden, and we went down ... It was eight of us, the same people, but we had two different people with us, pulling a type of security. So we tried to go in, but the two guards from the garden did not let us in. They were saying that ... the person that they gave the seeds to that he was having a bad heart about giving it to somebody else.

MS - Can you explain what you mean by bad heart? Do you mean bad faith?

JP - Well, not like necessarily by faith ... usually when something of [a] big magnitude is given out like that, a lot of people have second thoughts and all that. So, they sat us in ... this big like oval type of waiting room. And we sat down on these granite rocks, and we were just waiting for one of those humanoids [Ant People] to come in and to talk to us.... What I was understanding is that they [US authorities] were taking these seeds overseas. But they [Ant People] said that they wanted us to keep it here and they don't know why they're trying to move overseas what they gave to us. So, they were kind of confused over who was making the decision of taking care of the things that they were giving to us. One of the guys [in JP's squad] that were there, he was one of the guys that they [Ant People] gave the seeds, but

> one of the other guys [from the first mission] ... was not there. They did not want anything to do with him [the guy that was present] ... because [of] something about a bad vibe about him. So, they wanted us to ... find him [the other guy], to bring him down, but he's overseas now, and he's doing another mission.

I later learned from JP that the missing seeds had been taken to England on the orders of the new British monarch, King Charles III. It's clear that the two members of the first mission that were responsible for taking the seeds out of the US were agents of the British crown and/or an associated organization such as the Freemasons. King Charles became the new head of state immediately after his mother, Queen Elizabeth II, died on September 8, 2022. She was buried on September 19, 2022, and Charles' coronation was planned for 6 months, 6 weeks, 6 days later on May 6, 2023. The occult symbolism involving the number 666 in planning the coronation is not accidental. According to remote viewing of Charles' coronation conducted by Dick Allgire and four other remote viewers, the coronation involved a secret ceremony involving a blood sacrifice and different occult objects with various powers.[17] This is where the real power was formally transferred, according to Allgire. The missing seeds taken from JP's team were apparently used in some way in the planning or the actual performance of the coronation for some unknown occult purpose.

As far as the missing seeds and the Freemasons are concerned, it's well known that many prominent members of the British royal family have been Freemasons and achieved the high rank of Grand Master.[18] It is publicly known that Charles' father, Prince Philip, joined the Freemasons in 1952 and maintained a life-long connection, so it is very likely that Charles is also involved though this has not been publicly acknowledged.[19] The Freemasons are a worldwide organization that has agents inserted in all major world governments and militaries, who closely monitor classified programs, and step in to take control of extraterrestrial technologies or ancient artifacts, which would include the missing seeds. The most accurate description of how the Freemasons operate and quickly step in to take control over newly discovered ancient or extraterrestrial artifacts is found in a book authored by Radu Cinamar called *Transylvanian Sunrise*.[20] It is clear that the Ant People were very upset over what had transpired and distrustful of one of the members of JP's eight-man team who apparently was an agent for a third party - either the British Crown, the Freemasons, or both. I will return to the stolen seeds later in this chapter. My interview with JP continued:

> JP - When we were waiting, they brought out another box, and inside this box, they had tubes of different colors of water. These tubes had a red color; they had a blue color, it had a lighter blue color, and a grayish color of water. These little tubes ... looked like science [test] tubes, and they were saying this needs to go up there because this is part of what these plants give, that this type of like liquid it comes out from these particular plants that will help these seeds grow. And I think it will help the ground or make it ... like to grow faster, something like that. So, they had us bring that up, but they're not scared. They're like, "Should we or should we not?" because they see so many things happening on the surface that they don't want really to happen. They're still like, "Should we or should we not?", and we told them that we're trustworthy, that we're gonna take this information out to where you need us to and we're gonna make sure we get this information to the higher-ups that you feel like that... So, they want to give us more stuff, but they're being hesitant now to give us more things.

MS - So with the original box and the seeds that were inside, these humanoids ... are they humanoids or are they Ant People? Maybe you can talk a little bit about that? How did they know that these seeds were taken out of the country and were not being used in the right way?

JP - I guess they have a way of tracking them. They have a technology that can track where these seeds go. I think they have the technology to track any biological living thing through a type of GPS or technology that they have, that they can track things that they give to us. They have a way to track anything that they give to us. It's connected somehow; everything is connected, Doc....

MS - The person that they felt ... had a bad vibe. I mean, that person ... did he take the seeds? ... I think you explained ... he took the seeds from the last expedition out of the country ...

JP – Yeah.

MS - Was that because the seeds were supposed to stay here to be used here in some way?

JP – Well, what was explained to them was that the seeds were going to stay here. But now they know that the seeds are not here no more, and ... they [want to] know where the seeds are. They didn't want to give a specification ... where the seeds are or ... they already know where it is. They [Ant People] don't want that information to come out. I think there's a higher mission in our end with these particular seeds and the things that ... are given to us, that are coming out from the [Atlantic] Ark—

from those people that are coming out from the under the ocean city that we went to, because they're also giving us different kind of things and technology to prepare the ... surface population, they say, "upper side." We're getting bits and pieces of different cultures and different people that live inside [the ocean city].... They're all connected to each other, and they know that they're getting us ready for something. It's gonna happen.

JP is here pointing out that new technologies are being handed over to military authorities running the classified missions that JP has participated in, i.e.: to the space arks, the underwater cities in the Bermuda Triangle, and the underground Ant Civilization. There is an expectation that the newly acquired technologies will be responsibly used for the benefit of all humanity, rather than hidden away for the exclusive benefit of a minority or to empower manipulative secret societies such as the Freemasons or the new British monarch.

MS – Okay. And how did they communicate? And with whom did they communicate? I mean, you were leading this eight-man squad?

JP - I did not lead this mission. Somebody else was leading. But the last mission I was, well, leading in a way—as the security portion, Doc, not the negotiation or not the ... [receiving of] the different things that they're giving to us. Just the security portion because you know everybody [in the mission has] got a thing that they're in charge of, you know. [JP is referring to the MOS or other specialty each person in the eight-person team had]
MS - So six of you were providing the security, and two of you, the two new guys, they were the ones doing the negotiations or the dialogue?

JP – Yes. And, well, you know, when we pull security, we're just making sure everything is looking good; making sure [we're] looking around, taking notes with our mind, and making sure that there's a good vibe. Because, you know we're good in reading people ... and we like to make sure everything goes as planned, as like what we have to do.

MS - I see. Now, with these humanoids, can you talk a little bit about them and their relationship with the Ant People? I mean, are these Ant beings, these humanoids that were guarding you?

JP - Well, they look like us, but ... their mouth is more closed, like in circle form, like a V circle form. Their nose is like slits. Their eyes are bigger, and they have this skin that comes out of their head that looks like two antennas, but they don't look like an antenna. It looks like hair, but it looks like a type of skin that comes out, and their skin is like that bluish-grayish color.

MS - So you wouldn't call them Ant People; you would describe them as something else?

JP - They kind of look like ants if you look at them ... They have two hands, two arms. They wear robes. Their feet are longer than ours. Yeah, it's like if I have a size 10 they have like a size 13 or 14. If they're my height, you know, they got long feet, but you can still see ... their toes and all that. Their fingers are slightly longer, and their nails are slanted down. They're not straight out. They're slanting down so their finger has the nail protecting the tip of the finger ... slanting down like they could do ... this to any ... surface [tapping a surface]. You could still hear their nails and all that. It's not like ours ...

MS - How many fingers did they have?

Figure 4. Illustration of an Ant Person by Adam S. Doyle

JP - They have five fingers. We asked to go back to that giant being that was there, but they did not want to give us the opportunity to go there again. They kept us in that room sitting down. This room had different kind of lights that was glowing around the room.... There was an orb that was going in and out, the size of a tennis ball, and it was just going to each one of us and going back out, coming back in, going to each one of us. And you can feel the vibration of this tennis ball flying to us. And you can feel the hairs of our body like if it was a type of electricity, you know.... It was intelligent, whatever this orb was. And it was just checking. We asked what it was, and [the Ant guard] said, "Oh, no, it's just checking you guys," like checking the aura to see if we're [in] good faith, you know. We're telling the truth and all that.

MS – Okay, so they can tell if someone is there under some kind of deceptive agenda?

JP - They can tell using ... these orbs [that] were all over the place when we went last time.

MS – I assume then that's why the military needs people like you, people who ... don't go in with some negative agenda and ... were sent in on the missions or lead the missions because ... your intention is very pure. And these beings recognize that.

JP - You know, most people, if they go to these missions, their heart rate goes up. I think I've... developed, since when I was in the civilian sector, to see these different beings. And when you see a different being, you know, ... you got to be calm. They teach you that, you know. You have to be calm.

> You have to talk [with] a straight face. If they telepathically talk to you, talk to them back. If ... they're talking to you, you talk to them back telepathically because they don't know [if] you [are] just making eye contact. If they talk to you telepathically, you tell them the same thing ... what you're saying inside [your head]. It's like you're talking without moving your lips, but they're nodding their head, and I'm nodding.... They talk telepathically as well. So that was quite interesting because when you get used to that, and they talk to you, right, and you don't see them move their lips, but you're understanding each other.... It takes time to train to do that, to get used to doing that.
>
> Maybe in the next two to three years, us humans, we're gonna have the capability to talk to each other without using vocalization, ... just nodding our heads and understanding each other. I'm sure it's a type of technology that they have or is a type of consciousness that we haven't developed, but we do have. I'm sure that we do have that [ability].... That was quite interesting, Doc.... I know there's a lost history of a lot of things that we used to do that we don't do any more, and that's one of them - to communicate telepathically with each other.

According to Paul Wallis, author of *Escaping from Eden*, the Tower of Babel incident described in the Bible referred to humanity as once being a telepathic society that challenged the authority of the Elohim (aka extraterrestrials or Anunnaki) who controlled the Earth at the time.[21] Consequently, the Elohim/Anunnaki intervened by changing humanity's DNA, removing the ability to telepathically communicate, and instead making humanity solely capable of vocal communications. Thus the origin of verbal communication was devised as a means of punishment and the further subjugation of humanity.

> MS – Well, while we're on the subject of history, I know that there are legends, Native American legends, about the Ant People protecting the Native Americans during cataclysms, periods of cataclysms. So from what you saw in that underground cavern and the passageway and ... in their kind of main garden area and the ships that were flying around, do you think that was kind of a place where you could actually have like lots of people finding refuge during surface catastrophes?
>
> JP – Yes, it could totally be a place of refuge, yes. But it's protected because they have so many varieties of different things there.

JP has here confirmed that the large cavern space, the abundance of vegetation, animal life, etc., would be sufficient to host a large population in a time of cataclysmic changes on Earth's surface. This corroborates Hopi Legends about Ant People giving refuge to Native Americans during cataclysmic Earth changes. Our interview continued:

> JP - I found something interesting [about] the place that we went [to]. I think it's right in the [natural] springs in Florida, so that is quite interesting. It's in that area that the guy that ... [searched for] the magical tree of life [i.e., Juan Ponce de Leon].
>
> MS - So you're saying the area in Florida that he explored, that's the same area where this cavern system is located?
>
> JP - I'm sure it's around there.

MS - I know there's a [natural] springs in Florida. Is that what ... you're referring to?

JP - It's somewhere around there....

MS – Interesting. Well, there's a Florida [Ponce de Leon Springs] State Park, so is it under the Park?

JP – Yeah. You can see the radius of it, how big it is. And the good thing is that it's in front of everybody's face. It's right there. The name is there, you know, and I found that I could share that with everybody, the location maybe if you drive by there ...

MS - Were you given permission to do this to reveal the location?

JP – No, but I feel that, yeah, [it's okay] to give the location of that [park].

MS - Well, last time you said that you were taken there by a TR-3B. So what happened this time, again from your base? Were you taken by [a] TR-3B, or did you go there some other way?

JP - No, we drove there.

MS – Oh, okay. So then you know the precise location, and you're telling us it's somewhere near that [State] Park there in Florida?

JP – Yes.

MS – Wow. And, of course, this [natural] springs park it ... actually says that ... visitors can regain their youth by taking a dip in the cool, clear waters of these immaculate springs... The question is, well, those immaculate springs do they have anything to do at all with the underground water system that you saw and the tree that you saw?

JP - It's connected.

Figure 5. Screenshot of Ponce De Leon Springs State Park website

MS – Wow, okay. That's interesting.

JP – It's really pure.

MS - All right. So people should go there and have a drink from that park?

JP - I don't know about a drink, but a swim or something. It's really interesting, Doc. Maybe if you come down to Florida, we can probably visit together and go down there. But, yeah, I just wanted to share that. And it's around there, the cavern is around there.

Figure 6. The author with JP in March 2023.

The website of the Ponce de Leon Springs Park explicitly refers to the Fountain of Youth and the underground springs that flow into the Park:

> This beautiful spring is named for Juan Ponce de León, who led the first Spanish expedition to Florida in 1513 - as legend has it - in search of the fountain of youth. Ponce de Leon Springs' water temperature remains a constant 68 degrees Fahrenheit year-round. The main spring is a convergence of two underground water flows and produces 14 million gallons of water daily.[22]

While authorities at the park might claim that they don't really believe their own promotional material linking their park to the mythical Fountain of Youth, it nevertheless would be a good way of hiding the truth in plain sight. My October 11, 2022, interview with JP continued:

> MS - That's great. Thanks for sharing that. I think people would love to know more about the giant. Do you know anything more about who that was? I mean, there are questions some people are speculating [about] who that could be? Do you have any idea?
>
> JP – Well, when we were there last Doc, he was sleeping in stasis, his long beard wrapped around his neck ... and they called him a type of god. So [until] he wakes up, nobody would take him out of that stasis [before then]. When I say stasis it's similar to what a bear does in winter. It's a type of hibernation, but for hundreds of years instead of a winter.... Nobody knows why it's like that. But there are dozens of these guys [giants] in stasis around the world.
>
> MS – Well, I guess the question is, though, are they actually sleeping or hibernating for long periods of time, or are they just lying down having a short nap in some kind of space-time capsule? ... For them, maybe only a few days pass, or a few hours pass, whereas hundreds of years, or even thousands of years [might] pass on the surface because the sarcophagus that they're in is actually a kind of technology where time is dilated in some way.

Another possibility to consider is that the stasis chamber holds an avatar body that becomes activated when the host consciousness or soul returns. This would mean that the soul/consciousness of the sleeping god-king could go to his home world or spacecraft or even incarnate as a human when he enters the stasis chamber until the avatar body is needed again.

> JP – Well, we went into the temple, right. And there were vines that were giving [off] fire, right. I remember me telling you that there was a feeling of vibration around it.... But I'm not sure if it's time, we didn't get close enough to feel that, but I'm sure it could be that type of technology with the way that they were protecting it, and the way that the symbols were on that type of temple. It was similar to the ones we saw in the ark where we left the Mexicans, the [Aztec] Indians—time slowed down where we saw these symbols, and they kept walking. And the Chinese, they tried to go behind [to follow] them, but time was really slow [dilated]. So, I'm sure it could be that same type of technology when the Mexicans came back. We don't know how long time was changed when they went in through ... the ark because you can see them [moving] different, like more alert. But I'm sure it's a type of technology that keeps them in a stasis condition. I believe it could be one of the gods that comes down to teach and to know when something is wrong; to wake up.

> MS - I think one of the Egyptian gods, Thoth, who is known for having prolonged life and having taught the secrets of human longevity, I recalled that he traveled to Florida. There are stories or rumors. I think it might come from The Emerald Tablets or some sources say that he traveled to the Americas. So I'm wondering if that [sleeping giant] could be Thoth?

JP - ... His hand is probably like six times bigger than my hands; a big guy. His skull is probably like also six times bigger than my skull, you know. You can see his jaw, his beard, like if he was alive, it would be really intimidating looking, you know. He's there ... inside the box. There's like a staff ... a golden staff that he has there. But other than that, I could [not] tell you more about that. Oh, I know these [Ant] beings are protecting it and they're just waiting for the moment for him to wake up—and I guess for all the other ones to wake up at the same time. I think it's gonna happen during the same time the arks probably will come out, and everybody will see. So everything is going to happen in unison.

MS - Well, thanks for keeping us up to date with what's going on and these missions that you're doing. And I'm very much looking forward to these beings waking up and the arks becoming active and being seen.... And you're going to be able to give us the information we need to ... understand it all.

JP - Roger that. Thank you for having me.

MS - Thank you JP.

JP's second mission to the Ant People's underground colony shows how they are no longer trusting but instead cautious because the technologies or gifts they shared with human authorities were not properly allocated, as specified in their agreements. The Ant People have the means of being able to detect those individuals harboring ill will or a deceptive agenda, and to deny them access to precious knowledge or technologies. It is clear from JP's account that the Ant People have much knowledge to share that can help surface humanity's progress. This appears to be part of an ancient practice of protecting portions of humanity, as depicted in Hopi legends. The relationship between the Ant People and the sleeping giant is clearly one of reverence and protection. From the Ant People's perspective, the sleeping giant carries immense knowledge that has almost certainly helped the Ant People in the past and predictably can one day assist in surface humanity's development.

The fact that the Ant People refused JP’s team further access to the sleeping giant shows how cautious they are now in working with surface humanity’s representatives because of their conflicting agendas. This situation is exemplified in what happened to the seeds from the 'Tree of Life" and other exotic plants, which had been gifted to humanity with precise conditions. While JP himself is very transparent and has no deceptive agenda, the Ant People clearly recognize that others sent with him, or those exercising some unknown authority over the missions, may have mixed motives and loyalties. In the next chapter, I discuss how the identity of the sleeping giant protected by the Ant People was discovered.

Chapter 3

Sleeping Giants & Return of the Gods

The Awakening of Ningishzida and Return of the Feathered Serpent

On October 23, 2022, in a roundtable discussion recorded after the conclusion of the Galactic Spiritual Informers Connection conference, Alex Collier, Elena Danaan, JP, and I sat down to discuss recent developments involving the sleeping giant in Florida, the missing seeds from a Tree of Life, and the return of Quetzalcoatl.[23] JP had earlier revealed that the missing seeds were taken to England on orders of the new British sovereign, King Charles III. The roundtable then discussed the connection between the sleeping giant and legendary figures in the Americas, such as Quetzalcoatl, Viracocha, and Kukulkan, who were predicted to return one day. Danaan presented information that the sleeping giant was awakening because of an activation ceremony held at the conference that was led by Quetza Shah, an indigenous Aztec/Mayan shaman. Grammatical corrections have been made and commentary has been inserted into the transcript.

Keys: AC – Alex Collier, ED – Elena Danaan, MS – Michael Salla, & JP

> MS - I am joined by three very special guests. This is at the end of the Galactic Spiritual Informers Conference. I'm joined by JP, Elena Danaan, and Alex Collier, and we are going to be talking about something that was announced at the conference, as well as some activation ceremonies that

happened at the conference... that concern the giant that JP saw in an underground location in Florida. JP has conducted two missions there. During the second mission, he says that the Ant People denied his team access because there were some missing seeds, so he wasn't able to see the giant. So JP, maybe we can start with you just going over that part of the second mission where you meet the Ant People at the entrance to this cavern, and they say they are upset about something. What did they say about the giant?

JP - Nice to be here... an amazing conference.... The mission that we had to the cave system to meet up with the Ant People? As you said in the last interview we had [see previous chapter], they are really pissed off with us ... taking the seeds somewhere else because the seeds were supposed to [remain] here [in the USA]. Now the seeds are not here as well as the [other] things they have given us.... I know about the location. We were talking about this earlier.... We know that Europe has a new King [Charles III]. That is where these things went. So, I guess when the King asks for something, he gets what he wants.

MS - So the British crown somehow had that kind of influence and authority to have those seeds transported from the US?

JP - You know that being a king is a generational thing.... The bloodline goes back a long time. They know about these things that the Inner Earth population and the Ant People have. They know about the sleeping giants... which are the sleeping kings. In their eyes, these sleeping giants are kings.

So it is understandable that another king would want something that comes from a 'sleeping king'... that is not awake yet.

MS - Interesting. The Divine Right of Kings [doctrine] somehow translates to human kings having some kind of rights over sleeping giants that are kings as well....

JP – Yes.

MS - So your mission was to find out the identity of this giant in Florida. How far did you get asking the Ant People about his identity?

JP - I did not get that information from the Ant People. They told me that 'he was really important'. Maybe you can show the picture that I drew. Maybe Elena can explain what she felt about this magnificent [sleeping] king that the Ant People are protecting ...

MS – So you were told by the Ant People that it was very important ...

JP – That they were protecting him in stasis ... and that is the reason that we could not go back after we took the seeds.

MS - So that was what you found out in the first mission. In the second mission, you said you were supposed to find out who the giant was but you did not get that far because they were so upset about the seeds.

JP: They put us in a room that had a marble seat. We sat in that room, and I remember telling you that these orbs came in and 'read' us, and feeling what we were feeling.... And they knew who was genuine... who was trustworthy, who had bad will.... So the orbs were coming in and out of the room that they had us in. We were doing a negotiation, and it [an orb] was not allowing anybody to come in.

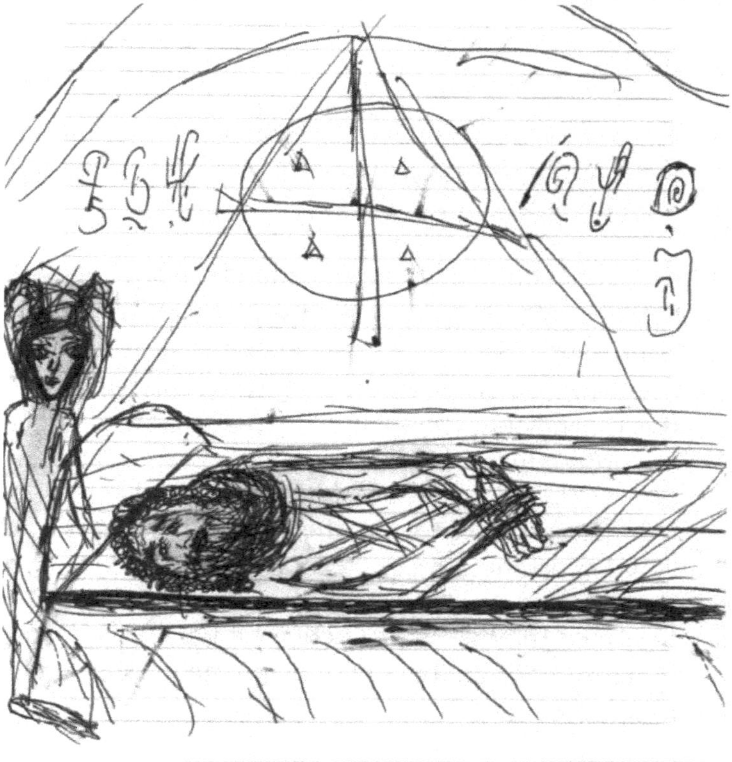

Figure 7 JPs drawing of sleeping giant]

MS - So the negotiators did not have the 'right vibe'. So the Ant People said, "Go away!" So that mission did not find out anything more about the sleeping giant. Now we will move forward to a conversation that I had with Elena Danann while we were in Tennessee.... We were visiting a cave in eastern

Tennessee... the "Lost Sea Cave,"... and you had a communication with Thor Han. So tell us what happened?

ED - Yes, we were having a conversation about the mysterious sleeping giant that is somewhere under Florida ... when I received a communication from Thor Han... which happens randomly.... I never know when it is going to happen. I told you that I make connections through my implant ... a device.... I offered to ask him questions. So you [Michael Salla] asked him, "What do you know about this sleeping giant?" First, he told you that he [the giant] is one of Enki's scientists. When Enki left, he left some scientists on Earth to take care of humanity... and to make sure that certain knowledge would be hidden... in sacred places. I think we can safely call these places the "Halls of Records."

This particular scientist had come from Atlantis. He went to the Americas, both North and South, to hide knowledge and technology. Thor Han said that, and you [then] asked if he could tell us the name of this scientist. I asked Thor Han to repeat it several times because it was difficult to hear, and I wanted to share. And I told you I heard something like Ningish-da ... something like this. I wasn't sure. When I got home I checked with research on the internet.... I told you that I said, "OMG! There was an Anunnaki named Ningishzida"... who was a scientist... and his name means, "The God of the Good Tree" or "The Tree of Life." And in the name Ningishzidda, you have the word 'vine'. So when I heard about the 'red vine', I thought, I heard that already.... I remembered that in one of your recent interviews with JP, he had mentioned vines that were related to this tree.... And the sleeping giant underground in

Florida is beside the Tree of Life ... —the tree that gives life and drips water on the plants below it, and regenerates DNA.... And JP described that the roots were 'like vines'.... So everything was like 'OMG!".

MS - So one of the things that Thor Han said was that this sleeping giant was one of four remaining Anunnaki scientists... who had gone into stasis... after the Great Flood and after Enki left. I think we asked Thor Han... "Why didn't the scientists just leave with Enki?" Explain what Thor Han said to that.

Figure 8. Sumerian Tree of Life with Ningishzida

ED - Thor Han said the scientists were left to look after humanity. Enki had lost the battle with his brother Enlil.... Enki was a scientist, and all his friends and colleagues were scientists as well. Their ships were not warships [they were designed for scientific inquiry], so they could not fight with them. Enlil was the chief of armies, so he had all of his armies with him. So these scientists stayed on Earth to help the people... but also... to preserve this ancient knowledge and technology... hiding them in some secret places. So they put themselves in stasis... hoping for the moment when humanity would evolve and raise its frequency and kick out the regressives [negative extraterrestrials].... And then Enki could come back when the faction of Enlil was defeated... And these sleeping scientists would be able to 'reconnect to their soul'... and wake up ... and bring this knowledge to the world. That's what Thor Han said.

MS – So this is the time when these sleeping scientists will be awakened, and they will bring back all of this ancient knowledge?

ED – Yes.

In a subsequent communication with Enki/Ea, Danaan was told that there are actually seven surviving Anunnaki scientists in stasis chambers hidden around the world who will be awakening with the return of Ea and 'the Seeders' (a group of 24 extraterrestrial civilizations).[24] She was told that originally there were twelve stasis chambers housing the scientists, but four of them were destroyed, and one was captured by the Enlil Anunnaki faction and their Deep State minions. Of the seven remaining stasis chambers, four are currently activating, while three remain dormant. I will elaborate on this new information in Chapter 4.

MS - Now Alex, ... with these giants or Anunnaki that were left behind that were geneticists, ... you were given information from the Adromedans about the Anunnaki. Did you hear anything about them leaving behind some of their scientists in stasis? What do you know about these Anunnaki geneticists who were working with Enki? And, of course, the power struggle between Enki and Enlil that led to this departure and some staying behind.

AC - They were not specific about them being on Earth, but they did say that they were in our solar system, and that several moons and crafts were left behind. There is a very large 'mining craft' in the 'A-Ring' of Saturn... and it is maintained by automatons. Apparently, the original crew is in stasis there. I do not know if they are some of the scientists, but I was told that there are at least seven onboard that ship. Now, this goes back quite a few years. Nobody can go near the craft because it has a defense system, and the automatons will protect it as well.

The automatons are like 'human robots,' but they are made of a polymer... so they can move very well.... They have agility and athletic skills. They are the ones that do the maintenance, who make sure everything is running. The only reason they left [the mining craft] there is because at some point... they expected to turn it on and wake up the crew. And that would be the only reason to leave it here. Just as it would be for them [the Anunnaki scientists] to go into stasis underground somewhere on the Earth, because they expect at some point to be awakened. There is no other reason to stay here. If that was not true, then they would not be here.

MS - One of the things that Thor Han said ... which takes us to something that happened at this conference that was very meaningful... was that this Anunnaki scientist Ningishzida... was also known in the Americas as Quetzalcoatl... and Viracocha... and Kukulkan.

ED – Yes, when we were having this Q & A with Thor Han, ... you asked him, "Was he also named Viracocha?" Thor Han said, "Yes," and I went, "Okay." Viracocha is Kukulkan and Quetzalcoatl; they are the same. So it was very important to find out they are all the same person.

AC - And there is another possibility. Maybe the reason they stayed here was because Enki left prematurely, and Enlil refused to let the scientists go on his ship and leave with the rest of the Anunnaki. In other words, they were intentionally left behind... by Enlil... because if they worked for his brother as geneticists, then they would have helped Enki... and Enlil would have resented their presence, especially after the fallout with Enki.

MS, JP, ED - Yes... makes sense.

AC – So they had to go into stasis as that was the only way they could stay.

JP - The way that the Ant People are protecting the temple and the giant, it was like really sacred. They were protecting him, waiting for him to wake up. And the guy in the box could be thousands of years [in stasis], but to him, it might be like only two or three days that pass by. And I know that soon something might happen that is really interesting.

MS - Let's get to that and talk about it. Something happened at this event. And to give people an idea [of the context], when we were doing one of the pre-conference panel discussions with Dani

[Henderson], there were a number of speakers. One was Quetza Sha ... and I asked him about the phrase that JP heard... that was repeated... when the Aztec Indians from Mexico went into the Atlantic Space Ark. They were singing and dancing 'A Kuria Matte.' We did not know what it meant. So at this interview before the conference ..., I asked Quetza Sha, and he said that it means a "portal from the Heavens to the Earth." So, what was it that we did with Quetza Shah at the conference that you found interesting in terms of activating this giant?

JP - We all felt something beautiful... a type of 'activation'. I remember I had a download at that particular moment when almost 1,000 people were singing "A Kuria Matte" at the same time. It was opening up a portal of some sort... to a location or to a place... to activate something. And hearing how he was doing it on stage... it was the same way that the little Mexicans were doing it going into the ark. The Aztec Mexicans—Indians—were shaking and singing it... 'A Kuria Matte.' ... And they were dancing into the ark. It was hilarious. We were like, "Oh shit. Look at the Chinese [Spec Ops]" who were going really slow ... while the Mexicans were going inside of it.

The Chinese got pissed off because they could not go inside. But now we understand.... In order to enter a portal... or to enter a realm, ... you also need to 'be with it'.... And say it in order to activate it. If you are not saying it, ... you won't get shit.... I am sorry, but you are going nowhere. Maybe Elena will know more about the spiritual part of this, but we, as soldiers, don't give a shit because we are just there to do our job. We are sent to do a mission, and we complete our mission. But that is what I saw, and that is what I felt. It was the same thing I felt on the ark. It was amazing.

MS - Yes, it is interesting. The Aztec Mexican shaman was dancing and singing 'A Kuria Matte' ... exactly like what you saw on the ark. Now, Elena... you had an experience; you saw something and had a communication when that ceremony was happening with 900 people. Tell us what happened.

ED - As a Druid myself... this was very similar to the Druid practice of opening portals. Later on, I had a discussion with Quetza Shah ... I was quite receptive to what he was doing.... I was conscious that he was opening a portal. When I heard the words, I felt like JP said ... and I thought, "OMG, that Quetza Sha is really opening a portal." And there were almost a thousand people in this room ... repeating all together... 'A Kuria Matte'... and we raised our hands to sky... and it was absolutely powerful.... Something happened.... I could hear the ground vibrating. Now we are in Florida as we speak... today ... so this is around in Florida somewhere....

JP - Close enough.

ED - Yes, close enough. Now while I was feeling these things... my implant went 'PING'.... Thor Han tuned in... and he showed me powerful visions. It was like I was there. It was like my consciousness was transported there. And I saw a body... from the trunk up to the elongated skull ... a white person with wide cheekbones... straight nose... and a long beard that was wrapped around his neck.... And his clothes on his chest were glittering white ... and the sound was ongoing 'A Kuria Matte' ...

The sound was connecting to something.... There was a soul connection that was made... and he was coming down to the body. So, what I was shown is what is going to happen.... It is in process. The giant opened his eyes. I remember they were beautiful and magnificent ... a clear blue... like aquamarine. Then the vision vanished. Later we had a conversation all together with the Shaman. He said, "Something has activated. Quetzalcoatl is coming back. It is in the process." Then Thor Han said the same as well, "It is in the process."

JP: So, if you go to science.... that box is really controlled by time.... Maybe a blink of an eye could be months in our time.... As he blinks, his time runs differently there.... So this could happen at any time.

AC - Here is another idea. The body is the avatar body.... It was designed to live and exist on Earth. But the soul is not in the body. The soul is somewhere else. And I have the feeling... I feel pretty strongly about this... Enki has already made arrangements for boots on the ground to go and retrieve the seeds... and return them to where they are supposed to be.

JP - Holy shit.

AC - What I mean by 'boots on the ground' is other extraterrestrials who understand the significance of it. But the body itself is an avatar, and the soul is not there. So the soul is somewhere else, but it is coming back. And that particular body was designed and created for here (Earth).

This is a critically important point that Alex Collier has raised. The atmospheric, gravitational, and microbial conditions on

Earth would be very different from the Anunnaki homeworld, and particularly on the Nibiru mothership they use to travel to our solar system. It's very unlikely that the Anunnaki could stay long on Earth using their own natural bodies. This is where the creation of avatar bodies would be necessary as a host to a transferred Anunnaki consciousness or soul. Sumerian texts describe how the Anunnaki scientists, Enki and Ninhursag, created the first homo sapien prototypes using the early hominids then in existence.[25] In addition, the Anunnaki created giants, which would become the avatar bodies for the Anunnaki. This scenario is reflected in the *Book of Enoch,* where the offspring of human and Anunnaki [aka Fallen Angels] DNA would be giants [aka Nephilim].

> MS - So, what do you think about this giant being Quetzalcoatl or Kukulkan?
>
> AC - It has been prophesied that he would return. It has been prophesied forever. And all of the indigenous people say that the giants would return. That has been known for a very long time. I believe that even Edgar Cayce said it... that the giants would return... would wake up.

In a compelling synchronicity, the release of the latest Marvel Comics superheroes franchise at the time, *Wakanda Forever,* was released on October 26, 2022, three days after our roundtable discussion and the conference events that led to the activation/awakening of Ningishzida (aka Kukulkan/Quetzalcoatl). *Wakanda Forever* includes the return of Kukulkan to surface civilization where he wages a violent campaign to prevent humanity from gaining knowledge of the fictitious rare metal called "vibranium." Kukulkan is depicted as a traumatized child survivor of the Spanish conquest of the Americas who partook of a sacred plant that bestowed upon him incredible powers and enabled him to create a flourishing underwater civilization with those he took with him. The symbolism in *Wakanda Forever* is highly significant given what we know about Ningishzida (aka Kulkulkan/ Quetzalcoatl) being the god of the good tree and vine.

> MS - One of the things that we covered in the conference was the idea of alchemical practices [aka holistic medicines] coming back. And these giants, and in particular Ningishzidda, the God of the Good Tree... and the vines.... and he was an alchemist. Enki was an alchemist. So, what do you think that means for the common person?
>
> AC - I think they are going to teach us the ancient holistic medicines... the Earth medicines. That is what the indigenous people practiced for thousands of years. A lot of that was lost because governments were trying to kill them off. So, I think they are coming back to teach us the old ways, that is, from the Earth. And they were the ones who taught us that in the first place.
>
> JP - That could explain that these seeds are probably extinct seeds that we used to have on the Earth.
>
> AC - They could even be medicinal plants, for all that we know.
>
> JP - Maybe that is why the King [Charles III] wants them. It makes a lot of sense.
>
> AC - Well, Charles is in a lot of trouble anyway, so the seeds would be leverage. He could leverage the fact that he has them... to try and cut a deal. The Deep State operates like that all of the time.

ED - You mentioned in one of your interviews that the 'Fountain of Youth' was sought after in Florida by ancient explorers.

MS – Yes. Ponce de Leon is known to have searched for the Fountain of Youth ... and the myth was created because there was some knowledge that there was a tree somewhere.... The mythical 'Tree of Life' ... he heard about in the Indian traditions. So now we know, based on what JP saw, that the tree is real.

JP - That tree was amazing! That tree had straws that fed from the river, ... and the sap is so RED, ... which is similar to the trees in Madagascar.... When you cut them, they 'bleed'...

As I explained previously, JP is referring to the Rosewood tree, which emits a red sap that looks like blood and has a number of medicinal qualities used in traditional medicine.

AC - Now that is interesting. They said there were four giants, right?

MS - Still alive, yes.

AC - Let's look at the indigenous people of South America. What other cultures are that old and did similar types of healing? The Indian culture. The Indians of India use their Ayurvedic medicines. And we know that the ancient gods all practiced that.... In many ways, they were the exact same people, but they had different names because of the different languages and cultures. But the medicines are very similar. It could very well be that another of the giants is in stasis somewhere in India... with seeds. And the other might be China.... The giant could be inside one of those pyramids that they will not let anybody near, with seeds. So then, we might be looking at either the United States or Indonesia ... where they practice the same kind of medicine. They would scatter them around to make sure that they would all survive. You would never put them all in one place.

MS - So what do you think is going to happen now that this giant has been activated? Whether he's Quetzalcoatl, Viracocha, or Ningishzida, what do you think is going to happen?

JP - Boots on the ground... like Alex said.

MS - So you think there is going to be an intervention here with some of the Enki faction?

JP: Well... not sure.

AC - It would make sense that Enki would not want to come down here on Earth ... because it would cause a massive rift in the family.... But ... that does not mean he could not ask for a favor from the other extraterrestrials who are here and working with the Alliance.... Here is what you need to do and here is how you do it. They have already done things like that. They are here to help us anyway.

And it could be they [friendly ETs] are there when the giant, Quetzacoatl, wakes up ... and say [to him], "Hey, here is who we are. We understand what you are doing. We need to move you from here and take you to someplace where you will be safe." The first thing the Giant is going to do is say, "Where are the seeds?"

JP - Hmm. So far, the Ant [People] messed it up.

AC - He went to sleep with the seeds, and he is going to want to know where they are.

JP – And so I think there was a deal between King Charles and the ...

AC - And the Freemasons?

ED - I was thinking about that.

AC – Probably, and Charles needs leverage to protect his family and himself. He is who he is. You know, that is how they operate. They have always operated that way. Leverage could be children... blackmail... that is all they have done. For a thousand years, they've done this crap.

MS - So when Enki left, Enlil took his own people with him and he left behind a few people to manage things. One of them was Enlil's son, Ninurta. And I believe that he is still around.

AC - I would bet he is in India.

ED - I have been told that he is still around.

JP - We also have Brazil. They are going through a situation right now that is political... something is going on over there...

AC - That is a better choice than Indonesia ... Brazil is being forced.

JP - They have a space ark over there in the middle of Brazil.

AC - My guess is that Enki left because there was going to be a 'shit storm'... and Enki assumed that the rest would be lifted off [the planet] ... and that is not what happened at all. Enlil, being Enlil, pitched a 'shit' ... and just said, "You are on your own." The only thing they could do was go into stasis because they ... were probably concerned that the humans would hunt them. Because that is what they were doing to the Nephilim... because the Nephilim were cannibals.

JP - There was a situation when they were dropping MOAB [Mother Of All Bombs] in Afghanistan ...

AC - And that woke up the other giant.

JP - I remember that Doc wrote an article about that.

MS – Yes, Afghanistan and giants.

JP is here referring to my April 15, 2017, article, "Is Pentagon Using MOAB Bombs against Giants Hidden in Afghanistan?" In it, I discuss several sources familiar with giants living in the mountain caverns of Afghanistan that were being hunted by US Special Forces who experienced great difficulty in finding and apprehending these giants.[26] Casualties were so high that the Pentagon decided to deploy the MOAB to flush out the giants from their hiding places. It's no coincidence that the bomb acronym, MOAB, can be linked to the ancient Moabites, a tribe of giants that lived in Palestine during the Old Testament era, as JP next refers to.

JP: And the Moabites...

MS - Yes, and the MOAB... the Mother of All Bombs was cover... while they were seeking Moabites... in Afghanistan.

JP: And the term "Moabites" means.... Giants!

MS – [Elena], you covered this in the communication with Thor Han... that the son of Enlil [i.e., Ninurta] was left behind, ... and that he is operating behind the scenes. He is in his full body. Do you want to tell us what that means?

ED - Yes. I was surprised to hear that from Thor Han that he is not in a human form—that he is in an Anunnaki body. They can live that long because they can 'swap bodies,' clones of themselves.

AC - He is awake?

ED - He is awake.... He is operating behind the scenes at the deep root, at the top of the Deep State pyramid, working with the Freemasons. He is behind the scenes, and he is still here [on Earth].

AC - Is he here in the United States, or is he in Europe?

ED - On the planet. I was not told where on the planet. He is on the planet physically, and he is hiding... he is hunted.

AC - Yeah, I would think so. That is 'leverage'. He would be leveraged.

MS - That is interesting. Ninurta is the son of Enlil [the warrior]... and Marduk is the son of Enki [the scientist]. And they competed with each other for dominance.

ED - Yes.

AC – It was a family thing.

MS - So to what extent is this family feud going to reemerge?

JP - In what book does Zechariah Sitchin talk about this?

AC - What is the Indian book with the history of the gods?

MS: The Mahabharata.

AC – Yes. The very same story is in that book that Sitchin writes about, but the names are different of the players because they spoke a different language.... It was Sanskrit.

ED - The fight between the two brothers is a common world myth you will find in most of the older cultures— ... like Zeus and Poseidon... Thor and Loki... Osiris and Seth... —everywhere.... [also Cain and Able]. They must have had contact with everybody.

AC - And not just here on Earth. That argument would have carried on wherever they went.

MS - So what do you think lies ahead now with the awakening of this giant in Florida ... and being told that the Deep State is on the run because it is about to collapse? Does this herald a good thing? And what should we make about this remaining son of Enlil operating behind [in] the shadows? Is he a spanner in the works?

ED - They are going to find him.

MS - What do you think will happen? Will they find him?

ED - Probably. The Deep State is losing power.

> AC - They are relentless. They will not stop. But as far as I know... them coming here and playing games... there are too many witnesses. And with all of the other Star Nations here... he is not going to do it with all of them in front of him. No way. He is going to have to capitulate. It might resume itself at another point in time... but it won't be on the Earth, ... you know, between him and his brother.

The eventual appearance of Ancient Anunnaki scientists connected to the Enki/Ea faction of the Anunnaki, who are associated with ancient legends of god-kings such as Quetzalcoatl, Viracocha, Thoth, etc., who have remained in stasis chambers for thousands of years, is going to be a momentous occasion for the entire planet. A majority of the global populace will predictably embrace these benevolent giants/returning god-kings who will be willing to share with humanity their ancient wisdom, technical knowledge, and advanced technologies to resolve a range of global problems such as hunger, pollution, disease, etc. There will nevertheless be a minority of the global population who will have great difficulty embracing such a promising development. This will be due to ingrained religious belief systems established by the rival Enlil faction of the Anunnaki long ago, which negatively portray giants (aka god-kings) as the progeny of 'fallen angels,' whose knowledge and wisdom is not to be trusted. It's clear from JP's repeated missions to the underground Ant People civilization in Florida that the identity and locations of the sleeping giants is highly sought-after information.

Chapter 4

Recovering Stolen Seeds and Awakening Anunnaki Scientists

Recovering Stolen Seeds from a Tree of Life and Activation of a Sleeping Giant in Iraq

On the evening of November 1, 2022, JP told me about another giant in a stasis chamber that had been discovered in Iraq who was a king in ancient times.[27] JP explained that the Iraqi giant has a significant connection with the giant in the stasis chamber found in Florida, who was also a former king. JP made a further connection to a third sleeping giant in an underwater city in the Bermuda Triangle that he first visited in a covert mission in late August 2022.[28]

JP also said that the seeds from a Tree of Life located next to the sleeping giant in Florida, later identified as Ningishzida, which had been stolen from US military control and taken to England on the orders of the new British sovereign, King Charles III, had been found and would be returned. The seeds, however, needed to first be taken to Iraq for activation of the newly discovered giant there. As discussed in the previous chapter, the activation process for the giant in the Florida cave took place at the recently completed Galactic Spiritual Informers Connection event in Orlando. What follows is the transcript of the recording of the conversation I had with JP on November 1, 2022, with grammatical corrections and my commentary.[29]

Interview Transcript

Key: MS – Michael Salla; JP – Pseudonym for US Army Soldier

MS - I'm here with JP who has an update about the missing seeds from the Florida underground cavern civilization that he visited on two occasions with missions. He has some more information about the missing seeds that were taken out of the US to England ... Welcome, JP ... tell us what have you learned.

JP - How are you doing, Doc? We learned that we caught this person.... People are not saying that it's human.... They were interrogating him and they're going to bring him back to the States. We're taking the seeds.... Somebody else is going to be with us.... I don't know if they got an ... agreement with England about the seeds and catching this character. They're going over there ... with people that are in charge of the Kingdom, so I don't know if we came into an agreement or not. I don't think we're working with them, but I know the seeds are in our possession again. The place that we're guarding over here in Florida, the [Ponce de Leon] Springs, it's open again. They're guarding it. But now it's open again, ... so they're actually taking these seeds to Iraq—in the middle of Iraq—to do some type of ... ritual. They have to, like, take it somewhere. They're saying that there's another sleeping king over there that is in stasis.

MS - So just for those that maybe aren't quite clear what seeds we are talking about, these are the seeds from the Tree of Life that is located ... in Florida ... and there's a sleeping giant there that we've identified as Ningishzida who is also known as Quetzalcoatl, Viracocha, and Kukulkan. So these seeds and that giant [in Florida] ... there's some kind of connection with the other giant king in Iraq somewhere between the two rivers. Well, that whole area of Mesopotamia is the land between two rivers [in] Iraq. So I guess we're talking about the Euphrates and the Tigris Rivers.

JP - I know somewhere in the middle of Iraq, in between two major rivers that run through, they're gonna take these seeds over there.... I don't know if there's an ark there. I'm getting a feeling that there probably is an ark there, but I'm not sure until ... I get more information and we probably do a mission. It's kind of warming up right now, you know ... the Ark in Brazil is [also] warming up right now ...

MS - Well, that's interesting. I know you've mentioned there are nine arks that you know of. You identified one in Caldas Nuevas.... That's not that far from the capital, Brasilia.

JP - It's not that far from the capital. Right now ... something is happening to the ark over there that is warming up. But going back to the seeds over there in Iraq, ... they're gonna take these seeds to a machine and activate them. I think there's an activation process and I think that's what [was happening] over there in England ... They were trying to do that and explain that to us but we ... wasn't getting it. So they're gonna do an activation. This is also going to activate certain things around the world ... When these seeds are activated in a certain way, it's going to activate some arks around the world....

MS - You're saying that there's some connection between these space arks that have been activating around the planet because these ... [Intergalactic Confederation] fleets have arrived in our solar system, middle of last year. And that these seeds from this Tree of Life that were taken from Florida to England and are now on its way to Iraq. That somehow those seeds are connected to the arks? Can you explain more [about] the connection?

JP - They're connected to the arks. These seeds are connected with the ark somehow. When I say seeds, Doc, it's not only plants; it is also blood, or how can I say this in the proper way? This might sound strange, but semen. It [semen] is considered a seed. Remember I told you that they're also giving us a tube filled with a liquid ... that went with the seeds. So that's actually how I know this. Probably sounds far-fetched, but people would understand that bloodline is really important in any situation. It's actually semen. I don't know how people are gonna get this, but you probably understand what I'm trying to say.

MS - Now, this is genetic material from the giant himself?

JP – Yes. It's also his genetic material. When I say seeds, it's not only the Tree of Life type of seed. It's also genetic seeds as well, biological, you know, any kind of seed. I know they gave us certain animal species and plant species... I don't know what's gonna happen from there. But yeah, it's semen ... You asked me how this is connected to the arks. The way people activate the arks is ... when you enter into the ark, a certain person can activate it ... like

> the Aztec Mexicans that entered the ark, or a person like myself, or a person ... like Jean Charles [Moyen] or Elena [Danaan]—a person that has [the right] DNA to activate arks. So by taking these seeds [semen], I'm going to call them seeds to be polite, if you also take these seeds with you to the ark, it'll activate it. That's quite interesting.

In this interview, JP is talking about the different gifts given to his eight-man mission to an underground civilization discussed in Chapter 1. He is also suggesting that biological material such as semen can also play a significant role in the activation of the arks. Medical studies show that semen produces the highest quality clones, which avoids many problems encountered in other cloning methods.[30] We also know from many thousands of abductee reports that Gray extraterrestrials are extracting semen and ovum for their biological experiments involving cloning and hybrids.[31] Clearly, the Grays know that semen is the optimal genetic material for cloning and other purposes. Consequently, creating clones from the semen of the stasis giant is therefore not only a way of reproducing optimal avatar bodies for Anunnaki souls, but also could be used to access or activate ancient technologies. This enhanced cloning application may be why members of the Deep State connected to the British Crown took the seeds, including the semen, out of the US to England.

> MS - I know Elena has said that activating the arks has been a high priority for the dark alliance when they find them, but that they need both the genetic material of the crew as well as the soul vibration.... It's not just a matter of cloning a body and sending it in there but the soul vibration as well.

> JP - But now they're trying to activate these seeds over there in Iraq with some other sleeping giant. I don't know who's protecting that particular giant. I

don't know which civilization is protecting that giant, but I heard that the people that protect the giant over there in Iraq are really aggressive. They're really protective and they will die before anybody gets to this giant. So, they only let certain people with [the right] bloodline in. So I think they came [with] an agreement to go with whoever is in England to Iraq to activate these seeds. When these seeds activate, the weather is going to get crazy. It's going to be insane because the arks are activating as well. They're turning hot, so right now....

MS - What do you know of those protecting the giant in Iraq? I mean, you described Ant People ... protecting the sleeping giant in Florida. What about in Iraq? You said that they were ferocious.... Are we talking about a non-human race, [some] kind of secret society ... protecting the sleeping giant in Iraq?

JP - I can't tell you because I do not know who it is. All they told me is that they're aggressive, and if anybody that does not have the [right] DNA to get into those chambers or those caves that are over there [try to get in], they will retaliate, and they will protect the king that is in stasis over there, because this king over there, he's really important as well Doc. He is as important as this king in Florida.

JP here gives us a clearer idea of why the semen of the Florida giant was stolen and taken to England on behalf of the British Crown. Given the advanced nature of cloning and soul-transfer technology possessed by the Deep State, a cloned giant inhabited by someone with the right consciousness could potentially gain access to other facilities hosting sleeping giants, because they would possess the right genetics and consciousness to do so. Our discussion continued:

> MS - You said something about the seeds—after being taken to Iraq—would be brought back to the United States.
>
> JP – Yes. They will be bringing [them] back. I don't know if they're going to leave some over there just to get access to whoever's protecting [the sleeping giant]. I think they need to show a type of proof to enter [the protected caverns] like a passport, like you're entering a place that needs proof that you are valid to be in there. After they do that, they're going to bring the seeds back to the United States. And now, in this particular moment, they're doing a type of negotiations with the Ant People to have access again into the cave system over here....

JP's statement here is very significant. It suggests that US authorities that recovered the seeds/semen from England understand the significance of genetic material that can be used to clone giants, which can enter areas that would otherwise be off-limits to normal humans or Special Forces personnel. This scenario is not unlike what was depicted in James Cameron's Avatar movies, where 9-foot-tall blue giants were cloned for normal humans to gain access to areas that they would normally be unable to access.

> JP - Also interesting what's happening over here as well. I guess they're keeping everything up to date now [with] what's happening with the seeds and with the Ant People. They're giving them a time-by-time [account of] ... the mission and what's happening. They [the Anunnaki] left different types of ETs protecting each sleeping giant that is in stasis. So each one does not know about each other but

they do know about the king that is in stasis that they're protecting. There's also somebody that is sleeping inside the [submerged] Atlantic [Ocean] city that's protected by these tall ET looking humanoids that ... we went to. The Atlantic [Ocean] Navy ship over there [used] to go down to the city as well. So now everything is coming together ... I'm understanding this.

MS – Okay, now you said during your first mission to this underground cavern in Florida that the seeds were taken by two guys to England, and one of them is an ET and was caught.... Can you say more about the two that took it to England and ... one being an ET and being caught?

JP – Well, they're interrogating this guy that they brought—that ET—back to the United States. They were interrogating him until we got access over there, and we got [the] seeds back. But they left a person in charge as well over there to be with the seeds ... because they're quite connected to the seeds. They said that they have the right to be wherever these seeds are because they're connected to these seeds.

MS - Who's saying that the ET that took them to England says that he has the right [to be there]?

JP – No. The people in England, you know who I'm trying to say?

MS – Right. The new Sovereign over there [King Charles III].

JP – Yeah....

MS – I guess we'll get a little more clarity when you do your new mission. But as you were saying, there seems to be a lot of connections now between the different missions you've done.... There's a connection now with that underground city in the Bermuda Triangle you visited [with the] ET-looking beings down there. Anything [else] you want to finish off? ... When can we expect these seeds to be returned to the US, and who's going to be in control? Will it be the military? Will it be a corporation [or] the Freemasons? Who is going to be in control of those seeds?

JP - The military is going to be in control. What happened was that this person was contracted to do these missions with us.... There are always contractors ... There are always smart people out there, but we contracted the wrong person. They happened to be a double agent.... So shit hit the fan, and we fixed it. We got it back. But we're still doing that process of activating the seeds in Iraq in between these two rivers over there.

The presence of double agents is a perennial problem with covert missions to facilities belonging to either ancient civilizations or extraterrestrials. This problem is best explained in Radu Cinamar's *Transylvanian Sunrise* book series. The series describes how Freemasons have infiltrated senior levels of government and military institutions in all major nations, and have placed their people in key positions when it comes to the investigation and exploitation of advanced technologies and artifacts found in covert missions. This divided set of loyalties leads to covert missions where military personnel will go to great efforts to find advanced technologies and artifacts, only to have the double agent controlled by the Freemasons take the discovery away when the opportunity presents itself.

> MS - I know there are some people that always say for you to say a little bit more about yourself or to describe more about your military service. So anything you want to kind of finish off in terms of your military service?
>
> JP - I really respect this country. I'm serving because I love this country, and I believe in what this country was built on. I'm over here in Florida, and I'm serving Doc. I don't know like what you want me to say ...
>
> MS - Just reaffirm for people ... needing to hear more about your background that you're currently serving with the US Army and ... you do these missions and ... they're part of ... a temporary[duty] assignment TDY [where] ... you're called away from your regular position and taken into these covert missions.
>
> JP – Yeah, it's a lot of people.

JP is here confirming that many of the military personnel he serves with in covert missions are in a similar position to him. They have their normal duty within the military branch in which they serve, which is called a "Permanent Duty Assignment" and can be called away for up to 180 days for what the Army describes as a Temporary Duty Assignment (TDY) or what the Navy calls "Temporary Additional Duty" (TAD).[32] Clifford Stone said that this was the process used to have him work with covert UFO crash retrieval teams under US Air Force-led projects Moon Dust and Blue Fly throughout his 22-year Army career from 1969 to 1991.[33] JP finishes our interview with his views on how people can prepare for the full extent of what lies ahead as disclosure unfolds:

> JP - I think people need to understand more about the spiritual part of all this ... and start getting into

their spiritual path in life and meditate, and do whatever you need to do to get closer to ... whatever positivity [you have] in this beautiful world that we're in. If I could tell people something, it's to get more spiritual. Be careful what you eat and try to meditate more. Meditation is key. Find a spot around your house, or if you live somewhere beautiful, go and take 30 or 40 mins or maybe one hour, two hours and meditate. And use your body to bring all this positivity to your way [of life] and to always be happy, and do good to others.... Look at what's happening in a spiritual way. That's how I see this, you know. I'm not here for no reason, you know. I started getting my experience, and I started taking videos and pictures. And these ETs started connecting with me, and I started connecting with them. Some ETs connected telepathically, and the experience was really awesome. I believe if people start getting more spiritual, they will have these contacts the same way I've been having Doc. That's why I really want to tell people to see this in this spiritual way, you know. It's a war that we're not seeing, but a lot of people are feeling [it]. So I want to leave it on that, Doc.

MS - JP, that's very wise words to finish on that mission.

JP - Thank you.

JP is making an important point here insofar as extraterrestrials are very interested in working with individuals that have the right consciousness as well as genetics. While individuals may have a genetic connection to one group of ETs or another that opens the door for contact to happen with that group, it is an individual's state of consciousness that is all-important for when the contact actually happens.

Thor Han Eredyon on Sleeping Iraqi Giant

After informing Elena Danaan about JP's latest update, I asked her if Thor Han Eredyon had any additional information to share about the sleeping Iraq giant. This is what she wrote to me:

> I asked Thor Han about JP's intel, and he replied that he believes that this Iraq giant is another of Enki's scientist team. He said this Iraq "giant" guards the Hall of Records linked to the Bucegi [Mountains] and Tibet, and that there is an ark there as well with highly advanced and powerful technology. He employs the term: "quantum holographic" for some of the tech there. The Earth Alliance military has it secured only recently.
>
> Thor Han added that the war in Iraq was about it. He said that more "giants" should come to our awareness soon, but he does not have clearance to disclose precise locations. ... Thor Han just added that I need to tell you that this place in Iraq is "the center of the web."

Thor Han's information corroborates key aspects of what JP was told about the importance of the newly discovered sleeping stasis giant in Iraq. Significantly, JP was given the geographic coordinates of the sleeping giant in Iraq, which are 32°07'35"N 45°14'0"E. Google Maps shows that this is adjacent to the ancient Sumerian city of Nippur, which was known as a center for the worship of Enlil and his son Ninurta.

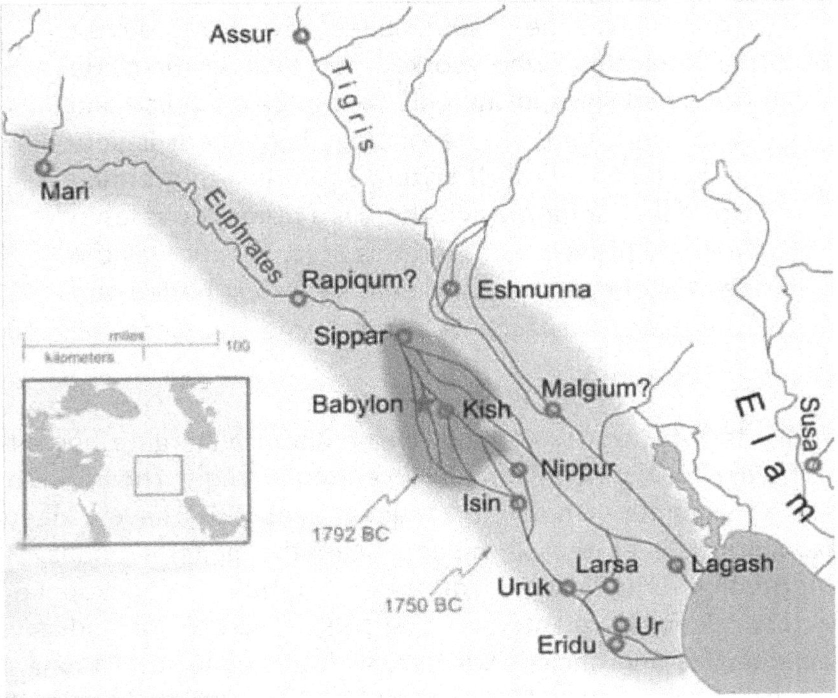

Figure 9. Nippur geographical coordinates: 32°07'35"N 45°14'0"E

This Nippur location would mean that any technology hidden there would have been among the most sophisticated and advanced possessed by the Anunnaki at the time since Enlil was commander of their space fleet. The geographic coordinates given to JP corroborate what Thor Han said about the place in Iraq being "the center of the web."

Thor Han later revealed that there was a total of seven Anunnaki scientists that went into stasis chambers to await a new cyclic era or the return of their leader, Enki (aka Prince Ea). It is possible that one of them was previously associated with Enlil and had defected to Enki's faction, thereby choosing to go into a stasis chamber located in the hub where the most advanced Anunnaki technology was located. My analysis was subsequently confirmed by Thor Han, who gave the name of the sleeping Iraqi giant as "Arunna", and gave the following information about him as relayed through Elena Danaan:

> [Arunna was the] chief engineer for advanced craft technologies, who worked for Enlil at first. He switched sides in the end, to join Enki's cause and work with him. The technology kept there is very important and much prized. There is also a buried stargate not far [away]. There is a tremendous lot of military presence around this area. Nippur was the center of operations for Enlil for a long period and there was a spaceport there. Some ships are still there.

In February 2003, I first wrote about a stargate being the real cause for the US military intervention in Iraq.[34] The Iraq war is a good example of how conventional geopolitics have a deeper exopolitical layer that is hidden from the general public. JP's information brings to our attention another deep exopolitical factor: sleeping giants holding the secrets of advanced technologies and ancient wisdom. It does appear that humanity has arrived at a critical historical point where the stasis giants are being secretly discovered and activated. The scientific, alchemical, and historical knowledge possessed by these Anunnaki scientists is highly likely to make a very significant contribution to humanity's development and integration into the galactic community.

Seven Sleeping Anunnaki Scientists are Awakening

After JP revealed on November 1, 2022, that another giant king in a stasis chamber had been found in Iraq, it was learned that the giant was part of a group of twelve scientists left by the departing Enki faction of the Anunnaki. JP gave details of the location of the sleeping giant as somewhere under the remains of the Sumerian city of Nippur, which was the ancient capital of the leader of the Anunnaki space fleet, Enlil, and his son Ninurta. The location of Nippur as one of the places where a sleeping giant could be found was highly significant as it meant some of the ancient

Anunnaki space technology was almost certain to be found hidden in the buried ruins.

As mentioned earlier, Thor Han Eredyon had revealed the identity of the giant to Elena Danaan as Arunna, one of Enlil's offspring. In order to learn more about Arunna and other sleeping giants, Danaan asked Enki (aka Prince Ea) about the identity of the sleeping Anunnaki that had been left behind when he left Earth after the Great Flood (ca 9700 BC). What follows is Enki/Prince Ea's [EA] responses to Danaan's (ED) questions, where he discusses a total the twelve Anunnaki scientists that had been left behind, each possessing unique esoteric knowledge and technology secrets:

> EA - My crew decided to stay. Well, indeed, most of them. Some others decided to leave Earth with me. They wanted to go home. But those who stayed took upon the mission and responsibility to be the Keepers of the Knowledge. Each of them, you see, are key activators for the technology. Not only their body's genetic frequency key is necessary, but it must be coupled with their personal consciousness. You see, consciousness is the key.
>
> ED - How many are they—the sleeping Anunnaki in stasis?
>
> EA - They were twelve, but four bodies have been destroyed, and one is in the custody of the enemy. Seven remain untouched. Four are in the process of activation.
>
> ED - Kukulkan is one of the four?
>
> EA - Ningishzida, yes.
>
> ED - Who are the others?

EA - Knowing their names is part of the activation process, so I cannot disclose their real names. Do you understand? Some are not ready yet.

ED - I do understand. Thor Han told me that the one [located] under Nippur is named Arunna. Is that right?

EA - How do you know about him?

ED - Our friend that is in the Earth's secret military programs told us. He may go on a mission there.

Danaan is here referring to JP, who was the first to be given details about a new sleeping giant located in Iraq and had passed on the geographic coordinates of where it was found.[35] JP had previously witnessed a sleeping giant in a Florida cavern whom Thor Han identified as Ningishzida, also known as Kukulkan, Quetzacoatl, or Viracocha. Ningishzida's activation process was initiated when he was identified at a major Orlando conference with over 900 attendees who participated in an activation ceremony led by an Aztec shaman Quetza Sha. Danaan next brought up the question of technologies that could be found in Nippur, and Prince Ea (Enki) went on to elaborate on their advanced nature and sophistication:

ED - Thor Han said that Arunna is a scientist engineer specializing in spacecraft.

EA - The master ship-maker. The technology he is guarding has great power. With the ships are also the core engines and a far greater technology: power energy sources. The containers are still there, but no one on planet Earth knows how to activate them. Terrans are even scared to handle these containers. So they are waiting for the keys to understand how it works. The key is Genome-Consciousness.

ED - Can anyone incarnated on Earth, who has the same genetics, activate this technology?

EA - How do you think they chose the soldiers and the people for these missions? All have the genome. And you know, otherwise, they couldn't access the places. The frequency shields would stop them.

By "Genome-Consciousness," Enki is referring to individuals such as JP and Radu Cinamar, described in the *Transylvanian Sunrise* book series, who carry the right genetics to access locations where ancient technologies are hidden, pass through sophisticated protective frequency barriers, and activate these ancient technologies. In previous articles, I explained how JP would activate technologies when he entered buried space arks.[36]

Over the last two years, JP has been given more responsibility for missions to hidden space arks and other ancient extraterrestrial technologies. He has been leading missions and instructing others, which corroborates what Ea/Enki revealed about those with the right Genome-Consciousness being the keys to finding and activating such advanced ancient technologies. Similarly, Radu Cinamar has been allowed to go on missions to examine various ancient technologies associated with a buried Hall of Records in the Bucegi Mountains of Romania, which is linked through underground tunnels and portals to similar halls in Egypt, Tibet, and Iraq. In his books, Cinamar explains how Genome-Consciousness is the key to accessing ancient technologies—either extraterrestrial or human in origin.

In response to another question from Elena, Ea/Enki next describes the existence of a stargate hidden under Nippur in Iraq and its centrality to a more extensive network that connects to the rest of the galaxy.

EA - Thor Han mentioned a stargate.

ED - There, under the Nippur area outside the ancient city, is the main gate that once connected this planet to the network of the great routes of this galaxy. It is deactivated, but it is the central key linking all the other gates together. This central portal links minor portals in other ancient places where records and technology are secretly kept.

As mentioned earlier, I began writing about the Iraq stargate in 2003 and its presence being the real reason for the Iraq invasion by the Bush administration. Since then, there has been much written by multiple authors about the existence of stargates and efforts to control them.[37] Enki/Ea's responses to Danaan's questions have given many more details about the incredible technologies and information that can be found at the locations where different Anunnaki scientists have been preserved in stasis chambers. According to JP's accounts, these scientists were giants in physical stature and were regarded as kings by early humans. As the Anunnaki scientists awaken, we will learn more about the technology and knowledge that lay buried with them for millennia and how the release of this will help propel humanity into a new golden age.

Chapter 5

Nordic ET Supply Missions to Ganymede and Europa's Secret Underground City

In earlier chapters and Volume 1 of *US Army Insider Missions*, the covert missions JP participated in had been disclosed with the approval of more senior officers in a secret space program (SSP) run by US Space Command. Contrary to such SSP missions as an active-duty US Army soldier on temporary duty (TDY) away from his regular assignment, he was next picked up by Nordic-looking extraterrestrials in one of their spacecraft that was part of a space convoy to Jupiter's moons: Ganymede and Europa. The spacecraft's crew included the same three Nordics who he first met back in 2008 during his contact experience in Brazil.

Arriving at Ganymede first, JP was asked to observe a resupply mission where a base belonging to another extraterrestrial group was given supplies by the Nordic convoy. JP said that the base he visited there was not one he had seen before when he was taken to Ganymede in late 2021 by another convoy that was organized by US Space Command.[38] In addition, JP was taken to Europa, where the spacecraft flew into a cavern located inside a crater on the surface. Inside the huge cavern, he witnessed a large crystalline city and a vast ocean adjacent to the city. JP made sketches of the underground city, the Nordic space convoy and the ship that picked him up (shown later in this chapter).

JP says that the Nordics allowed him to take his mobile phone with him, which is currently not the case with his SSP missions organized by US Space Command where all personal electronic devices must be left behind. After he was returned home by the extraterrestrials, JP immediately took photos and video of the departing Nordic spacecraft. One of these photos is also included at the end of this chapter. What follows is the transcript of the interview, with grammatical corrections and my commentary.[39]

> MS - I want to welcome JP back to Exopolitics Today. Thank you for coming and sharing some really interesting information about some contact experiences you had with some Nordic extraterrestrials ...
>
> JP - How you doing Doc? I'm glad to be here to ... share this information. Let's go, let's do this!
>
> MS - All right. Well, we first began communicating back in 2008 when you told me about a group of Nordic extraterrestrials that you had a contact experience with, and you've had experiences with them on and off over the years. So, you just recently had another experience with them where you had a telepathic communication. So why don't you tell us what happened?
>
> JP - I live really close to Alabama and there are open places around here that these particular ships ... come in and out, and they land. There's a lot of farmlands here where I live. I was driving back from work and in the distance, I saw a ship, and it landed behind this fence.... I looked behind me and I saw no traffic. I look in front of me, and there's no traffic. So I'm like, wow, they timed it really good. So, I parked my car on the side, locked it, [and] I ran across the road. And I was looking at the ship. Then my mind just went blank.... I opened my eyes, and I was on the ship already.

Figure 10. JP's drawing of the Nordic ship which landed near the road

MS - Can you tell us about the shape of the ship? ...

JP - It looks like a particular [saucer shape] UFO that people all around the world ... see. It was bluish in color but metallic. It had a hatch that comes down like a ramp. And yeah, it looks like one of those regular UFOs that people see. But when I crossed the road, and I closed my eyes, and I opened my eyes, I ended up inside the ship.

MS - And what do you remember about being inside the ship?

JP - I remember being strapped on sitting down. I remember seeing a Nordic looking being dressed up ... with a military kind of jumpsuit, but really tight.... I think it was a couple of years ago that I showed you a picture of a being, a Nordic with a symbol that they had in their chest. They had that same symbol....

MS - You described in 2018 ... a meeting [with] that Nordic in Orlando that wanted to take you up. And you didn't go on the ship. Is it the same one [Nordic] or a different one?

JP - This is that same Nordic, but [there was] also a Nordic that picked me up in Brazil that I remember. There was a total of three [Nordics] inside the ship ... I don't know their names, [but] I know [them] by face. I remember the 2018 Nordic, and I remember the Brazilian Nordic that also picked me up. So, they were sitting down. The one that had the military uniform was in the middle of the ship, moving his hands around. I think that's the way they maneuver ... the ships and all that. You can clearly see everybody in the room telepathically talking with each other....

There's something I want the public to know, okay, telepathic communication.... If people study ... how quantum entanglement works, right? And the study of that and understand that our brain is made of neurons that flash on and off ... I don't know if I could say this, but I'm gonna say it. There're certain military people that ... have a technique of telepathic communication that they already used—[that] we already use. There's a technique that we use for telepathic communication Doc, and I think people should know this technique. So, I'm going to share with you also a certain technique on how to telepathically communicate with each other. You can try it with your spouse. You can try it with anybody you know that you trust.

This technique that they telepathically communicate with is [where] you look eye-to-eye.... Once you have eye-to-eye contact, you shut your eyes; you open up; you shut your eyes; you open up; and you picture—when you shut your eyes—you picture what you want to send to the other person. So, you close your eyes [envision] your picture, and then you send it to the other person. The other person will receive it and automatically will turn it into whatever words their brain will pick up by pictures. So there's something about this technique [that works], but you have to have a meditative state of mind. You got to clear your mind so fast, but it works. I want people to try this at home, this technique. You close your eyes hard, you picture it, you open it, and you have eye contact. Once you have this eye contact with the other person, people can pick it up.... It's like any other exercise, you know. You got to keep doing it until you receive it, receive the message and all that. So, yeah, telepathic communication.... It's kind of interesting that type of communication. I really want to share [with] the public different techniques [for] how to develop that, because I think people can develop it like fast if they share that technique. And we use it in the military sometimes.

So, we went up and I could see Earth [looking] really small. And there were more ships with us. The same shape followed us. And when I looked, I closed my eyes. I opened my eyes, and we're already out of ... our, you know, Earth and Moon [region].... We started heading out from Earth and the Moon right, and I started seeing ships that looked the same, and these ships were following us. Then, in between these ships, there was a large ship that looked similar to a ... submarine shape—a cigar-shaped ship. Then, from a distance, I already can see Jupiter. You can see Jupiter getting bigger and bigger, and that was that. That is really good in my memory that I saw that.

Figure 11. JP's drawing of the Nordic ET convoy to Ganymede

So, we visited Ganymede, and we started dropping off these types of instruments that they have for communication, and also ... types of medicines.... I don't really know what kind of stuff they were taking to these certain places that we were going [to], but we also went to the moon Europa. That was quite interesting.

MS – Well, before you tell us about Europa, maybe just explain a little bit more about Ganymede because I know you told us about a mission you had with the [US] Space Command to Ganymede where there are different extraterrestrial visitors and bases there ... You went with the Nordics as part of their convoy ... of craft that were dropping things off to who? Who were they dropping the things off to? Was it to Space Command up there on Ganymede?

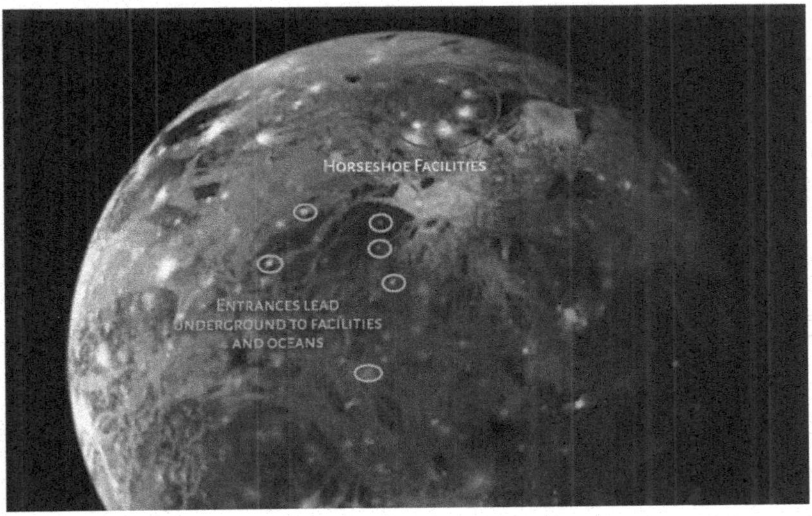

Figure 12. Facilities JP revealed after his 2021 mission to Ganymede organized by US Space Command.

JP - It was out to other ETs. So, yeah, we were dropping off to an area of Ganymede that I never went to [before]. It was the bottom part [of the moon], I think. I sent you a map of these parts that I went to like a year ago [see Figure 11]. We visited, but I stayed inside the ship. I saw the hatch go down. They [the Nordics] went down, and I was just feeling numb.... Everything was cloudy ... I was looking around and analyzing the ship.... [to see] what was happening. I was saying to myself, "What's going on," you know, "why am I here?" I was getting flashes in my eyes when I was in space and all that. I got ear problems now. My eyes hurt sometimes at night. But it was quite interesting.

MS – Okay, so they wanted you to see this. They wanted you to see that they were dropping off supplies to some other ET group on Ganymede. Did they give you a reason for why they wanted you to see that?

JP - They want me, I guess, to understand that the Nordics are working with us, and they're doing what they're doing because they want to help in our solar system and other solar systems that are going through ... the same situation.

MS - Can you describe the situation that our solar system is going through from the perspective of the Nordics?

JP - They know that the giants are awakening, and they had a type of relationship with these giants. The way I see it is that they used to work with these giants as messengers of some sort. So, they were a type of messenger to people, similar to ... [my role now as a messenger]. So I started putting that in perspective, and I was like, wow! ... probably the angel that visited Samson's mom or angels that visited different people in the Bible, can it be that these were Nordics? ... Different Angelic beings that visited different people to guide them, to talk to them, to give them a message of what to do next [were Nordics]. I thought about that, and ... they're like ... guiding me. Also, while I was there, I was

> getting information telepathically they were communicating with me that there was another giant waking up in Slovenia. So they told me that information during ... this trip back and forth. I want people to understand that this is what happened with me [and the Nordics]. It has nothing to do with the US military.... This experience happened separately. So not a lot of people in the military know about the situation that happened with me [with the Nordics].

This is what makes JP unique and valuable to the covert branch of the US Air Force and Space Command involved in collaborating with extraterrestrial visitors to acquire advanced technologies and ancient artifacts. Not only does JP possess the right genetics and consciousness, which allows him to interact with and activate ancient technologies, but he is also a contactee being shown space events by his Nordic friends. Thus, JP is providing the USAF/Space Command with indispensable intelligence on Nordic activities in our solar system. Our interview continued:

> MS - We know from your military missions that you went to that location in Florida, and you saw the sleeping giant there in Florida. But now the Nordics are telling you that there's another sleeping giant that's awakening in Slovenia, and that they used to work with the giants many thousands of years ago when the giants, I guess, were ... openly interacting on the surface of the planet.
>
> JP - They used to pick up people and ... show them things that [they] didn't understand. They'd pick up leaders of different tribes or different places, and they used to help out ... humanity—how to move forward. It was quite informative and interesting what happened because they told me about this ...

other giant that was awakening over there in Slovenia. I mean, they were telepathically telling me that, “Hey, there's going to be another place. There's going to be another giant awakening. You might be going there and it might be part of a mission. I might be going somewhere else for another mission. So they're already preparing me for what I was gonna be doing.

MS - Now, I think it's helpful to point out here that you've been having contact with the Nordics since 2008, and you ... joined the US military and signed up at the end of 2019. I was going over some of our old contact notes when we were talking, and in 2017, you actually said that the Nordics were telling the US military to ... look out for you... To make sure that you weren't in any way harmed or mistreated because they were working with you, and that this is one of the reasons the military wanted you to join.

JP – Yeah, the Nordic that is dressed in that [military] uniform— ... he was really protective of me. He was saying, “Stay in the ship, don't come out. We'll do this but keep observing!” ... I kept observing what they were doing, how they're flying, the ships.... It's kind of interesting because they never give me their names.... And, you know, I've been having this contact for the longest time with these guys.... [Two] of the guys I used to work with in these missions were Shien and Lovent. I don't know if you remember these guys, but they used to come with me in some of these missions. And Shien, I remember telling you that he passed away, remember?[40] Lovent kept, you know, visiting me and ... we kept doing [missions], but I haven't heard about these guys ... in a long time. They used to go on these missions with me. But now [on] these missions to Ganymede ... they're telling me about Slovenia. They said that these giants and the soldiers that are in Slovenia have this technology that is really different that they're going to share soon with the Earth. So that was also quite interesting, them telling me that information.

MS - Can you say a little bit more about this army protecting this giant in Slovenia?

JP - It's a different race. They're from the Inner Earth, and they're there to protect this particular king. And they told me ... that this is near the Peca Mountain. That's the only place that they told me.... This giant also has a beard that wraps around his neck and wraps around his body, and he's going to wake up soon. I don't know when he's gonna wake up, but they told me that soon he was gonna wake up. But the [protection] army is already woken up, and it's already like doing the recon of the place ... and making sure that it's ready for him [the giant] to wake up.

After JP told me about the sleeping giant in Slovenia that is going to awaken, I learned about a Slovenian legend of a King Matjaz (aka Mathias) going inside Mount Peca after suffering a crushing military defeat. He and his army retreated into a large underground cavern system where they would hide until a good time to return would occur. Here's how one website describes the legend:

> Kralj MatjažKralj Matjaž/King Mathias is the mythical king of the Slovenian people. The stories of Kralj Matjaž are many, and go far back into pagan times. He represents the mythical ruler, the king

> who is just and a defender of his people, and a golden age of prosperity in a similar way as the Arthurian legend of British tradition. He sleeps with his warriors in a mountain cave and will rise when the need of his people is great.[41]

The legend also tells of King Mathias having an extremely long beard that winds around his neck. While the legend of King Mathias is most often associated with a 15th-century Hungarian king who fought the Ottoman Turks, it is very likely that the origins of the legend go much further back in time. We know from the revelations of Radu Cinamar, author of *Transylvanian Sunrise*, that an antediluvian civilization flourished in the area of the Carpathian Mountains, but vanished during subsequent cataclysms in the region.[42] The similarities with what JP was told, including the long beard that winds around his neck, and the protective army, suggest that King Mathias is actually one of the giants from an earlier era whose body has been preserved in a stasis chamber, along with his protective army, and is now awakening—just as JP was told by the Nordics. It's also worth mentioning the similarities with the sleeping giant being protected by the Ant People in an underground Florida cavern. Another giant, according to JP, is also sleeping within the underwater city he visited in the Bermuda Triangle.

This is where Elena Danaan and Alex Collier's information in Chapter 3 about Enki/Ea's defeat at the hands of his brother Enlil/Yuh just before the global cataclysm around 9600 BCE becomes quite relevant. Enki/Ea was forced to flee our solar system in his Nibiru command ship, but he left behind some of his scientists who found places of refuge all over the world, and preserved themselves in stasis chambers for an extended period of time. At this moment, because of the return of Ea and the Seeder/Intergalactic Confederation motherships, the sleeping Anunnaki scientists, who were also giants and regarded as god-kings, are awakening. My interview with JP continued:

MS - Can you say a little bit now about Enki? You had something to say about what the Nordics were telling you about Enki. Can you say anything about that?

JP – Yes. The reason why these giants are awakening is because when Enki came to the solar system, he also activated something with these giants. Now, I'm not sure if it was because of the situation that happened with Elena, but when these giants wake up, they're gonna have a type of power that people won't understand how they have it or why they use it. People are going to see him as an authority. And a lot of people are going to say, "I told you so," you know. We also have the arks that are activating around the world and around our solar system. It's not only our solar system going through this situation. So yeah, that's the information I have, Doc. I don't know if that's informative, but I'm trying to be careful what I'm saying ...

MS - I just want to ... to clarify. When it came to Enki, ... the Nordics, they communicated with you while you're on the ship that these giants are waking up because of Enki.... They told you that on this ship. Is that when you learned about it from them?

JP – Yeah. They told me that.

MS – Okay. Well, that's very important because that supports what Elena Danaan was saying that Enki has returned, and that because of his return, he's having an effect on these sleeping Anunnaki scientists that are waking up.

JP - It's a communication that everything has with these beings.... They were telling me that the activating of these giants is because there was a force, there was a strength that entered the solar system. I'm sure that strength, that force, was Enki when he came in and he addressed his presence Doc. His presence is overwhelming. So everything feels, it's hard to explain. It's like; it's everywhere. It's connected to everything. So, everything knows. But I don't know why it's like that, but everything knows about his presence. So that's kind of cool.

MS - That is really important ... just acknowledging that the Nordics have been working with the giants and presumably with Enki for thousands of years. And so it's no big deal for them to, kind of like, work with these beings that are now waking up.

JP – Yeah. And these Nordics were probably the angels that everybody was talking about. That's what I'm trying to get to. I don't know how people are going to see this in different religions or, you know, see this in different ways.... These Nordics were around thousands of years ago helping people out. And they were getting ordered by Enki to do these different, you know, tasks.

In a July 7, 2023 communication with Thor Han Eredyon, relayed through Elena Danaan, the history of the relationship between Pleiadians (Nordic-looking Errahel and the Taal) and the Anunnaki was explained.[43] Thor Han described how the Anunnaki allowed fleeing Lyran refugees to establish colonies in the Pleiades constellation, which comprised such newly formed suns as Taygeta and Alcyone. Planets were created and terraformed, and colonies were established by the two major Lyran refugee groups, the Errahel and Taal.[44] The Anunnaki became protectors of the new

Pleiadian colonies, and the Errahel, who had settled in the Taygeta star system, worked closely with Prince Ea in subsequent Anunnaki colonization projects, including Earth. Thus Danaan's information matches what JP learned in his interactions with the Nordics.

> JP - There's a lot of them [Nordics] because when we went, when we left, I saw dozens of these ships following us. So I don't know if they're carrying more people [contactees] with them that has the same ... [compatible genetics] that I do. It's not only me. I know deep inside that it's not only me.... [There are] all these people coming out with these beautiful stories about these beautiful experiences. There's going to be a lot more coming out; I know it. These people are coming out with their experience in the programs.... It's quite interesting when people have these experiences, Doc. They change people.... You change; you see the world differently. You see the world in color [rather than black or white] when you have these experiences. I know people can relate to that when they have these experiences and when they telepathically communicate with these beautiful beings. They go into the ship, and you're physically there. It's like entering your car, turning it on with your key, turning on the radio, and you're there. You feel it. You are there.
>
> So when people have these experiences, and then sometimes when you have these experiences, people know and they will visit you. And they will tell you, "Hey, do not share this story. We know what you're going through. You get threatened. That's what's happening now, Doc. A lot of people are getting threatened not to share these stories. But people are not giving a shit anymore. People are gonna start sharing these stories, and this is gonna

get out. And the world is going to know about what's happening and what's hidden, and why we are hiding this, you know? Why are we still hiding what is a UFO or UAP? If everybody knows already what it is, you know, this situation is gonna get fishy. It's gonna get nutty, you know.

I had a friend that texted me. He told me that this situation is gonna get nutty. I really believe that because a lot of people don't want this information to come out, but it's coming out, Doc. It's coming out on the news, it's coming out in different sources. And people are really getting into it right now. People are understanding what is happening. They're feeling it, you can feel it. You can go outside and meditate for two or five or ten minutes, and you can feel the presence of all these beings. If you've been through these situations and these experiences and even people that haven't been through these experiences, they're going through different dreams. They're having more dreams. They're having more communication. And it's going to come a time that everybody's going to be connected, Doc. That's what I believe.

MS - Exciting times, definitely, we're living in.... After the Nordics took you to Ganymede and you witnessed stuff being transferred from this convoy of Nordic spacecraft ... the next moon was Europa. Do you want to tell us what happened there?

JP - So when we were in Ganymede, and we were dropping [off] the equipment and this stuff, right ... we got picked up, and we left.... We kept going around, and then I saw Jupiter. And you could feel the magnetic field of Jupiter. You could feel the press—the gravity of Jupiter, you know. And we went around Jupiter. Then I thought we were going back home, but then we went back.... I saw a bright moon, and I asked, "Hey, which moon is that?"... They said, "It's Europa." They talk with an accent. I don't know what language ... they speak, but the Nordics speak with an accent ... between Spanish and Jamaican accents. It's kind of cool. They spoke back. They didn't telepathically talk to me.... We circled around the moon, and they told me that [it] was Europa.... Everybody knows that Europa is an icy moon. I'm like, "What the hell are we doing here? What do we have here?"... That really interested me. And I saw that ... all the ships lined up, and they were facing this crater. But this crater that Europa had, it goes in into a slant, and it keeps going into like a big cavern or like a tunnel type of thing. And it's surrounded by ice. [As] we started going into the crater, gravity got stronger and we sat down.... It curved up, and we saw the ocean—the beautiful ocean that Europa has. Then in the distance of the ocean, it was so bright and beautiful, you could see cities of white icy-looking skyscrapers. You can see the roads that are ... made of golden sparkly gold. You can see different kinds of flying craft going left to right ...

You see the city in the distance and you see the skyscrapers of ice.... You can see ships going left to right of the same kind. We stopped, and they parked [on the surface].... It looked like grass, but it was white grass—like it's a plant that looks white. So, I don't know if they were a type of fungi or whatever, but it smelled good. It smelled like roses and mint

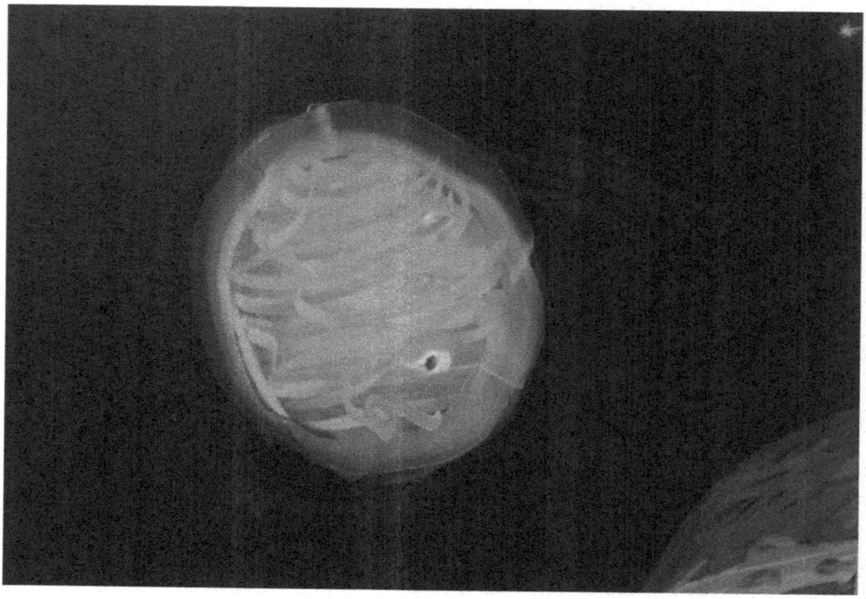

Figure 13. JP's drawing of the craft approaching Europa

mixed together ... It smelled like you could taste honey in the atmosphere. You could taste, like when you breathe in. You could taste the ... honey. So that was really pleasant. It was really amazing. And you see all these ships coming down [and] parking ... [as far as] you can see. One by one, they were like parking next to each other.... They told me to step out from the ship, and I thought I was gonna die with coldness, ... you know, freezing. But no, it was around 70 degrees, in between 65 and 70 degrees. And you can feel the wind coming from the tunnel and coming from the cavern.

You can hear the ice of Europa moving like a boom, boom. I think they use the ice that moves on the surface ... as energy to help the city lighting. They use the movement of the ice of the moon to create energy to give power. That's what they're telling me.... This sound that I was hearing was like a deep [boom].... I'd probably go crazy if I lived there and heard that [all the time], Doc. But yes, that's what I was hearing. You lived in Hawaii. I don't know how those [sounds]...

MS – Coqui frogs, roosters ...

JP - You get used to it, right? So, I imagine that, you know, they get used to that sound. It's like a deep whoomp sound. So I was hearing that, and it was dazing me up. It was meditating me.... It was a low tone that you feel on the inside. It was like 'whoomp, whoomp,' when you feel it. And everybody is like feeling it. And the Nordic looked at me.... He smiled, like, "Do you feel that?" I'm like, "Oh yeah, I feel that. That's kind of cool!" Then I was feeling the taste of the honey of the atmosphere, and I was smelling the rose with mint, and everything was like feeling good ... Oh yeah, it was awesome. So we went into this.

MS - So you saw the city in this giant cavern under the ice. So then the ship went into the cavern, under the ice. And there's this huge city there, and you got the ice [all around]. So where's the ocean? Can you see the ocean from the city?

JP - You can see the ocean [in the] distance. The ice goes down into the ocean but you can see the ocean moving. The ocean is like a dark blue, beautiful color.... In the distance, it turns dark, like [when] the ice meets the ocean, and it just turns dark. The cavern is so big, so huge, that you don't feel it. Everything is like when you wake up at seven o'clock

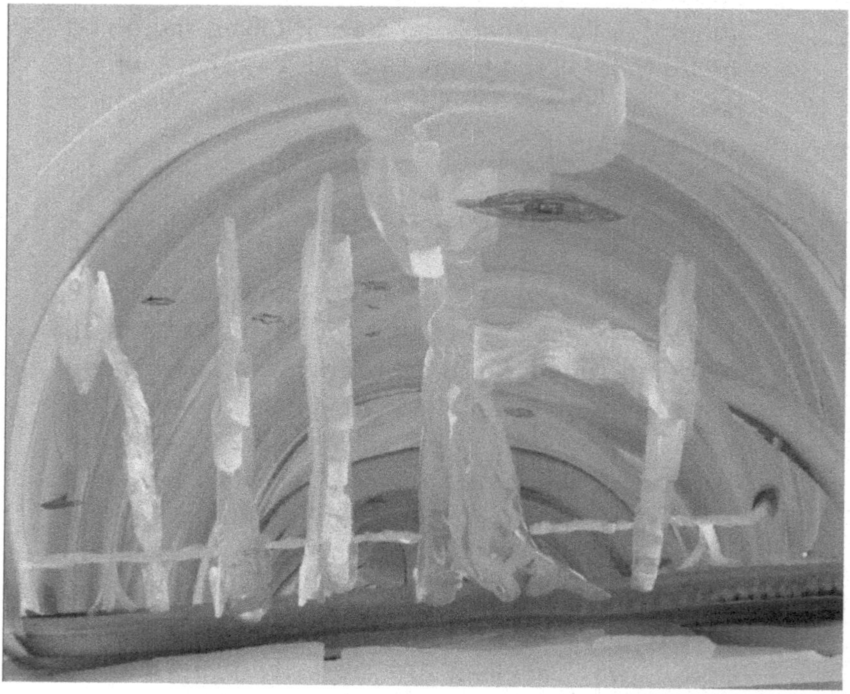

Figure 14. JP's drawing of the city, skyscrapers, and spacecraft within the cavern on Europa

in the morning, and you see the sun rising. Like that type of light. The cities were really bright. So that energy that the cities were receiving was from the ice moving.... That movement creates ... the energy that they receive.

I asked the Nordic, "Hey, was this always here? What is this place? I never heard about this place?" He said that, "Yes. This place was always here, but it just got activated now." He also brought up Enki again, [saying] ... "it got activated when Enki came." So, I was like, "What the heck? Like this shit was always here?" He says, "Yeah. You guys are one of the first humans in thousands of years that have come here!" So, I'm like, "whoa." I felt special. I felt like that's awesome. I said ... "Did other humans ... used to visit here?" So [he says], "Yeah. We had a lot of humans that used to visit here. And we used to share information and bring it back to Earth." I'm like, "Whoa, okay, so that's interesting." And they told me also that this moon moves. It's only been around Jupiter for about a couple of hundred thousand of years. And... this particular moon is like our Moon. It can move ... anywhere. Using the same movement of the ice [for energy generation], it moves the moon wherever they want.

MS - So they just wanted you to see this giant city that was activated by Enki's return?

JP – Yeah. It's beautiful. [On this moon] they had a major library, Doc, that had information on our solar system and other solar systems that are close. On this moon they ... were telling me that they had a library that had information on the solar system and other systems ...

MS - So anything more you want to share about Europa? ...

JP - It was a peaceful place. That's one [thing]. I felt that they'd been there for a long time. If you see these skyscrapers that connect to the cavern all the way up, they connect to the ice on top. So it looks like ... a beam that [starts] ... from the ground going up to the cavern. You see all these ships going in and out from these skyscrapers. And you see these bridges that look like glass and [are] made of ... something that was really different.... This cavern ... looks like a crater right when you enter it. And then when you enter, you curve in. And then you fly through this, like, cavern tunnel-looking thing. And then you see the city—the bright city. It's beautiful. And the smell was like ... rose with mint. I remember that ... the oxygen, you can taste [it] like it was honey. Then you felt the [whoomp] sound, and it put you like in a meditative state. Everybody at once. It's similar to what happened when we went to Ganymede, and everybody's heart starts [beating in] ... the same pattern. And everybody's intertwined. Everybody's in the same zone. So that felt really beautiful.

After that I closed my eyes. I felt my face hit the floor and my body could not take it, Doc. They told me that what I was feeling was so supernatural that I couldn't take it. I couldn't. So I just blacked out. They put me back into the ship, and they put me into this liquid tube.... I opened my eyes and I could breathe in this liquid, but it was different. It was like breathing in slow motion. But you could still feel yourself in the liquid. So, I was breathing in slow motion inside this liquid, and ... I blacked out again.

I [found myself] back where my car was. And when I crossed the street, I turned around, and I had my phone with me. [So]and I took a picture—boom. [I heard them say,] "Now we're leaving." I took another picture—boom. I said [to myself], "Hell yeah. Let me try to take a video." ... I was feeling dazed, but I was sure that I was gonna [be able] take this video. So, I took the video of them maneuvering by the cloud. And ten seconds into this video, you can see how another ship flashes right by them. Like [it] flashes and it disappears. Then they keep going up. They move up to the clouds, and they leave. So,

I know I sent you that video ... [with] those pictures to share with the public. You can share [them]. And I want, like, when people see this to have a meditative mind and ... to try that technique of telepathic communication, to see what people receive. Because they let me do this video for a reason. So I don't know what people will feel when they see this video. Remember, when you see a video it's a projection of light. So it's like if you're seeing it in real life ...

MS - That is great. So you were able to take photos and a video of the craft that had picked you up and had taken you to Ganymede and to Europa? ... The Nordics had communicated with you, so you got pictures now and a video.... Okay, anything else you want to say about the Nordics and the mission to Ganymede and Europa and what they told you about the awakening giants and Enki?

It's important to point out that prior to joining the US Army, JP was encouraged to take photos of the antigravity craft that belonged to the USAF secret space program as well as the Nordic craft. These photos are presented and discussed in *US Army Insider Missions*, Volume 1. Since joining the Army, JP has not been allowed to take photos/videos of the Space Command craft used in the missions he has been taken on. On this occasion, however, the Nordics did allow him to take photos, and a video of their departing craft.

JP - When they started leaving, they said that ... they will be back and they're picking up other people ... and sharing this information [with] a lot of leaders—a lot of people that have a certain kind of DNA ... They're gonna start doing it, more often—to give

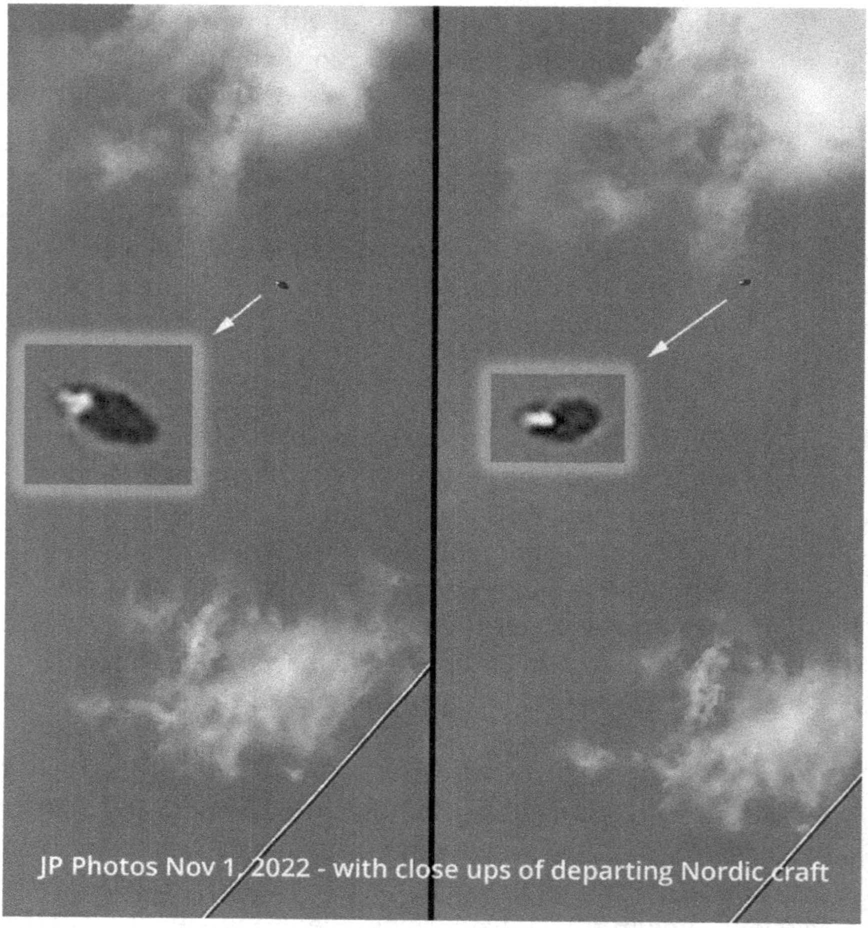

Figure 15. Photos 1 and 3 from a sequence of 4 Nordic spacecraft photo.

messages to different people. They're messengers and they're protectors. So I really want to know who are these Nordics that are picking me up. They haven't given me their names of who they are, and you know I've been having these experiences for a long time. But I never gave you a name of these Nordics.

MS – Yeah. I remember back in 2008 when you first contacted me and told me about the three Nordic extraterrestrials on that ship there in Brazil that you met, that they didn't tell you their names or where they were from or anything like that.... Over all these years, we've just called them the Nordics because they look like Nordics, but they haven't told you their names. They haven't told you where they're from.

JP – So, it was kind of interesting when they started leaving. I felt that they were telling me, you know, who we are. Like they were telling me, you know, who I am. Yeah.... I've been having these experiences with them for a long time

MS - Well, JP, I want to thank you for sharing that incredible mission with the Nordics. And I look forward to you telling us more about future missions with the Nordics and with the US military. So now you're flying different missions for two different groups, but they're obviously working together.

JP - Oh yeah. They're totally working together ... [on] technology. They're showing [me telepathic communication] techniques. That technique I showed you actually came from the Nordics for telepathic communication. I think people should try what I told them in this interview, and they will probably get it....

MS - Well, thank you JP.

JP - Thank you, Doc. Blessings to everybody.... Keep meditating and have a loving heart.

JP's photos and his video of the departing Nordic spacecraft are empirical evidence supporting his claims of being picked up by human-looking extraterrestrials and traveling to Ganymede and Europa for resupply missions to a colony base involving human-manufactured technologies and supplies. It reveals the extent to which trade will be a critical factor in relations between the Earth and various extraterrestrial bases and colonies in our solar system and beyond. Also, what JP was told by the Nordics about them working with and for the Enki/Ea faction of the Anunnaki, also confirms much about how trade relations and colonization are fundamental factors in the relationships between different extraterrestrial civilizations. These historical precedents suggest that as humanity evolves into an interstellar spacefaring civilization, we will develop similar relationships with the Nordics, the Anunnaki, and others to ensure the success of Earth's interstellar colonies.

Chapter 6

Visits to King of Ant People and Ancient Moon Base

In early January 2023, JP completed a mission to another underground Florida location as part of a team of eight covert military personnel. They were seeking information about the sleeping giant they had encountered earlier at a different underground facility nearby. At the camouflaged entrance to the new underground city, his covert team was met by security personnel from a civilization of humanoids with distinctive Ant characteristics, historically known as the 'Ant People.' JP's team was then led into the base, where they eventually met the Ant People's king. By command of the Ant King, the seven other members of JP's team were asked to leave, including the individual in charge of the mission. Then JP was given a private audience with the King, who told him that their civilization was opening up to the rest of the planet and would soon be permitting more people to visit their underground facilities in Florida and elsewhere.

Once his mission to the underground Ant People civilization was completed, JP went on another Moon mission where he saw the ancient ruins of an underground city that was built by the Ant People. In this interview, JP describes what the Ant People intend to do shortly, and why they feel it is important for them to reconnect with surface humanity and educated us as to the true history of the planet. What follows is the transcript of the interview, with grammatical corrections and my commentary.[45]

Interview Transcript

Key: MS – Michael Salla; JP – Pseudonym for US Army Insider

MS - Happy New Year, JP.

JP - Happy New Year. I hope everybody's having a nice 2023 amazing how the years pass.

MS - It is amazing.... JP serves with the US Army, and he's been describing several of the missions that he has been on.... [In] one of those missions he described going to an underground civilization in Florida where he saw a giant being guarded and protected by these Ant People. He recently had ... a new mission where he encountered the Ant People in another facility. So JP, why don't you tell us what happened with this new mission? ...

JP - We were training in the field right, and we got picked up by three buses. [We are] a total of eight people. We had a guy that was really good at getting ... the grid coordinates—the points on the maps.... Basically, everybody in the military knows how to do that. But there's always a particular person that's better at doing it and is really dedicated to doing it.... So, he was with us; he knew where we're going. I didn't know personally where I was going, but we got picked up by three vans.... They were Mercedes white vans. They're... a little bit higher than regular vans.... These vans, they were taking different routes, right, to go to this location that we were going to. This field location, it was ... like 40 minutes away.... Inside the vans, the guy that was driving had black bags inside the van in the corner.... [In one] van there was three people and then another van three people, and then another van was two [plus the drivers]. I was in a van where the two people were—that was me and the map dude, the coordinate guy, the guy that does the azimuth and all that. So, he says, "We're going to this location."

We were actually doing “land nav” that day, and while doing land nav, the vans came in, and they picked us up. If you're familiar with what land navigation is, the military does that - the Air Force, the Army, Marines. We do land navigation to practice.... We do a grid, we do points, and we practice how to do land nav. So it's kind of cool, it's kind of fun. We did that, and then we got picked up by the van, and the guy that was driving, he's like, "Hey, there's a bag over there!" I'm like, "Okay, what we're gonna do with this bag because you know we're wearing our green OCPs” and all that. When we see the bag ... we open it up, and it's a uniform. It's a ... tactical type of black OCPs. And he says, "Go change!"

MS - What does OCP stand for?

JP - Operational Camouflage Pattern.

MS – Okay, so it's an acronym that the Army uses for the different ... gear that they wear.

JP – Yeah. We get a black type of OCPs, right ... We change. We put our boots on ... And it took ... me like 10 to probably like 15 minutes to change. So, this was like a 40-minute drive.... So we take our green OCPs off, and we put the black ones on. We're changing, and I'm asking the map dude, "Hey, where are we going?" [He says,] "Oh yeah. There's this place that we're gonna meet up with this guy, and he's waiting for us in this field"... While we're changing, we're talking, I'm talking to him trying to get information, you know, what we're going to do, what's happening. And he's like, "Oh, no, yeah, we're just going to this field ... You're coming with us. And you know about these people." Everything clicked [then] ... we're gonna deal with the Ant [People].... Their faces are more slender than ours. Their eyes are a little bit bigger. They got hair that's like a dreaded hair, that looks like ... antennas. Yeah, we were gonna visit this type of people in this field. So, we were heading to this field. And then we got to this field, and there was a Black Hawk helicopter following our van. And I could hear it, you know. You can hear the vibration of the helicopter following us.

So we're going through that the back roads to this field, and we got there first. We're already dressed up. We had to wear a mask, ... and the mask had this glass that is connected to it that turns to ... AR type of technology that we have—'augmented reality' technology. It's kind of cool. It tells you the temperature; it tells you where you're on the map, and the name of the area that you're at.... The other vans came up, and the people came out dressed in uniform. The only person that I knew, and I saw his face, was the guy that was with me that was changing with me. But the other guys, the other six guys that came in [the] other vans, I did not see their faces.

So everybody got out of the van, and the helicopter was there. And we were not really like in charge. We're gonna meet somebody that we're gonna

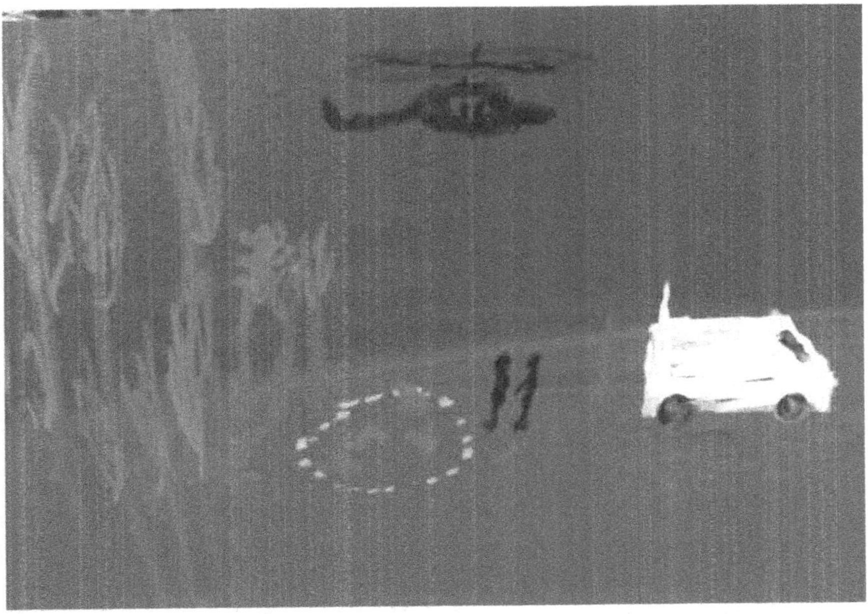

Figure 16. JP's drawing of him talking with the Land Nav specialist with a Black Hawk helicopter overhead & parked Mercedes van nearby.

follow. Everybody has their specialty, and nobody was exactly in charge. But the one that was in charge was the map dude. He was a higher ranking guy that was there, and, you know, whoever is higher ranking ... we do what we're told. We follow this particular guy. So I was with him and he was a high-ranking officer. So we go in, and we're in this field, and we're checking the area, making sure everything is good. The helicopter stayed two minutes hovering over us, and ... was scoping in the area. And then the helicopter left. Once the helicopter left, they radioed the drivers of the vans to leave as well. So they left as well. They radio back saying all we saw was deer and hogs, "You guys are good to go!" So, the reason the helicopter stays in the stationary location in the air is to see if there's anybody following us in these missions. It was there like for two minutes. We were scoping the area, and we were waiting. We had just .22s [handguns] on us, that's it.[46]

We were there in the field by ourselves. The guy started doing the mapping—the grid. And he's like, "Okay! This way! Let's go. Come on! Let's move it!" So, we started walking tactically into the woods. We saw a couple of families of hogs, and everybody was shitting scared. But we kept walking, and we stopped. I was like, okay.... We walked for 15, I think 15 minutes, that was a couple miles. We get to this location, right. And ... the guy with the map set says, "Come over here and come behind me." We get behind him, and there was like a bush right in front of us, right. This bush looked like [it is] spread out.... Then he blows his whistle ... made of wood, and I'm like, "what the hell is he doing?" It's a high-pitched whistle, like a really high pitch. And he just blows it ... three times. When he blows it three times, the ground shook a little bit. I'm like, "Oh shit, what's going on?" Everybody's like, "Oh, shit, what the hell?"... Then when that happened, the Black Hawk helicopter passed by once, and we saw it.... Then it passed through two [more] times. And then it passed [overhead] the third time, and it hovered for two more minutes. After it hovered, [the helicopter pilot] radioed to the ... map dude and said, "Hey, you guys are good to go out...."

The helicopter flew out, and he's just freaking really fast, the Black Hawk. And after he left, I don't know if you guys ever seen the ... what do you call it? It's a, you know, the spiders that open hatches to grab their food. It's like a hatch. It's a round hatch that is on the floor and had a bush [on top]. And it opened up when the helicopter left. So, there's a spider species right there. They have these hatches that open up.... It is just like the same thing—it opened up. The hatch] is super camouflaged, like you can walk on it. I asked [about] the weight of this hatch that opens up. It's like around four to five hundred pounds. It has a mechanism that opens up. Once the helicopter passed by, that hatch opened up. It let go this, like, ... not steam but this hot air—like a poof towards us. And we were like, "Whoa, holy crap, what the hell is this?" This hatch just opened up like that. And it has steep stairs that goes in. Then the map guy said, 'it's through here." And then he just put the map away, and ... we just walked down these stone-type of stairs that were there. These stairs look like they've been there for years, but it's like a marble-looking type of stairs. They're cool looking. We got the headlamps on. We were walking down ... and it had a smell of a, you know when you feed the cows some hay? ... —that smell in the farm that when you're feeding the cow.... That's the same smell that you smell when you're going into this cave system.

This hatch opens, and then we started walking down. The other guy was like, "Oh shit." ... We look back, and the hatch was closing. You could feel when it closes. You can feel your ears, like, pop. Like it sucks the air out and in. We're like, "Oh crap, we're effing stuck here!" ... The map guy said, "No, we're okay ... We're good, let's keep going. Come on! Keep going!" So, there's no way to go back to that same area. We lost all radio communication once that hatch closed. It was [a] 15 by 15 round hatch, you know.... It's a good size.

MS – Wait. When you say 15 by 15, what are we saying 15 feet?

JP – Yeah. 15 feet by 15 feet [4.6 x 4.6 meters]. We're going in one by one. But then, when you go in, it opens up like to 20 by 20 [feet]. So, it gets bigger. But the hatch itself is 15 by 15.

MS - Were the stairs ... designed for normal-height humans?

JP – Yeah, they look like they were designed by normal-height humans. They told us that they have these hatches everywhere around the United States, especially in forests and parks. And they have these hatches everywhere that open up and close. It's quite interesting these camouflage hatches that they have.... We walked down for like 10 minutes, and then it straightened out. Then we went down again like for 10 minutes [and it] straightened out. And then we start seeing the lighting. They had torches, and we start seeing this blue-like whitish torches every 30 feet. And we kept going down.

We went down like five times—went down straight, down straight, down straight, down straight, and we kept smelling the hay type of smell, like [as] if it was like a farm type [of smell]. Then we get down to this big door, similar to the door where the giant was ... They had these two beings there. Two Ant People [were] there in robes waiting for us. And they nodded their head. They nodded twice, and they did a gesture with their hands, and the door opened. We entered into this huge cave system. In the middle of the cave system, you can see a spring— ...

so beautiful, so blue.... There was a lighting—a lot of torches all around the cave system....

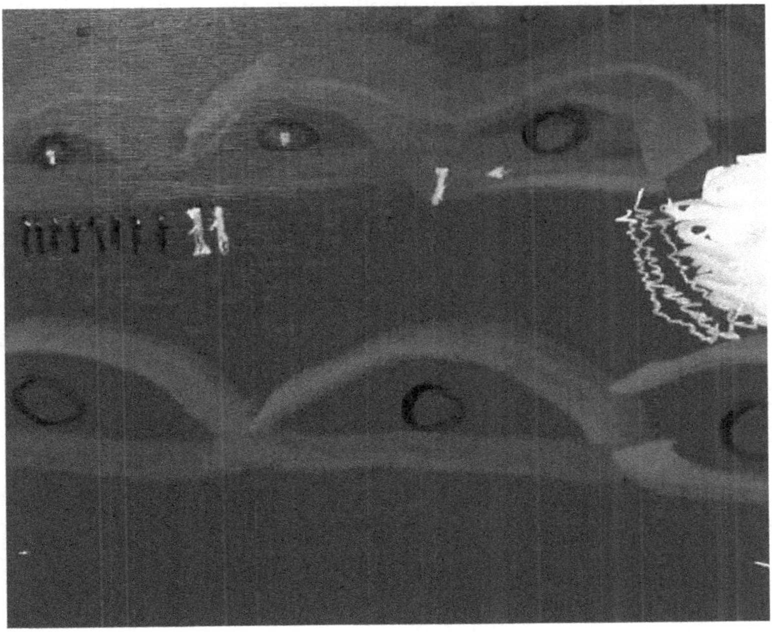

Figure 17. JP's drawing of two Ant people meeting his eight-man squad moving toward the spring.

JP - It looked like a medieval ... type of place. In the middle of the cavern, they had a big torch that was burning. There was a liquid. It was like a tube that looked like wood that was coming out from the middle, and it was dripping. I think it was like oil—a type of oil that kept this big huge torch in the middle of the place burning. But it's like a bluish-white torch. It was [a] beautiful color, bright, really bright. And then you had these little torches all the way around and ... they look like little houses. And you see small kids, like, walking around. People are hiking, walking around, but they have that ... skinny face, and the big eyes, and the dreads hair that look like antennae. And they were just walking around. I noticed that there were a lot of dogs, a lot of cats, a lot of domesticated animals that we have up here that they do have as well. [Dogs were] just walking around and barking at us, and we're, like, confused. We were like, "Wow. There's a lot of dogs here, a lot of ... domesticated hogs." They had hogs that they kept in, not cages, but in, like, barn-looking areas. It was huge. It was like probably fifteen football fields big. Like huge. You could see [the cavern extend] as far as you can see.... We saw ... the spring in the middle [of the cavern]. You could see the fish swimming in these springs. It was interesting.

So they took us to this road, right. It looked like a dirt road, and on the sides ... we could see brown window-type of holes [in the walls through which] these people were looking back to us. And they were just covering their kids [eyes] not to see [us] ... closing their windows when we were walking by ... [as] if they never saw a human before. We saw a couple of humans [like us] there as well, working with these Ant People. And [these humans] had beards. They had a robe just like the [Ant People's] robes. Their hands were not dirty, but you know you could tell that they were not bathing. We looked at them and I spoke out and said, "Hey! [Do] you speak English?" They just looked at us, like, weird; like, they just stared at us. I saw at least thirty humans with beards or females. We saw a family of humans with kids that did the same thing when we passed by.... They closed the windows, but they were human-looking people.

So there are humans mingled with these Ant People [who are] working with them. I actually got [the guy] behind me and said, "Hey, we think these people are with these guys." And he's like, "Oh, bro, me personally, I think they decided to come down here. I guess they were lost. I don't know where they [were when they] decided to come down here. And they've been here so long that they forgot what was up there [on the surface]. They made their life here." So, these people ... I guess got lost in these forests and these parks, and they make their way in these cave systems right? And the Ant people, they take them [into their communities], and then like 20 to 30 years pass by, and they have kids and these kids ... grow up there. And it's normal for them to be living there. So, a lot of missing people decide to go down into this cave system, and they decide to stay there because they [are able to] live for a long time.

MS - So JP, can I just interrupt you there? When you say a lot of missing people going to these cave systems ... are we talking about them accidentally coming across these covers that you described 15 by 15 [feet]? Or are they forcibly taken down there? And if so, by whom?

JP - I think it opens, and they wander in there, and it closes. It's [then] really hard to get out. When they make it to these doors, and they see these Ant People, I'm sure they're scared. I'm sure they [Ant People] just show them the way, I guess. But I don't think they're forcibly [taken] there, because I got to talk to one of these humans that were there, and he was living in the streets somewhere in the United States. He decided to go to this forest, and he saw [the hatch] open, and they took him in. So, most are people that live in the streets or maybe even people that probably got lost and could not make it out.

> And the Ant People just welcomed them into their culture or taught them. These people live like 200 to 150 years old with the medicine that these Ant People have.

According to the researcher David Paulides, every year thousands of people go missing in National Parks in North America.[47] Some of the missing people, according to what JP was told by the formerly homeless person, are taken in by the Ant People, given a new home and given access to life-extending medicines. JP next described the philosophy of the Ant People:

> He was telling me ... they believe in the light. They believe that we're energy. Their belief system is that everything is connected; that everything is alive; that everything is a god. That's their belief that everything is a god for them. So they treat everybody the same. And they treat everybody with love because it's an energy that everybody has, and they have to share it. It's that type of belief system that they have. And that's why everybody's together working united. I saw him eating corn—corn fields you got ... everywhere. So that's how they teach. They taught the Indians all these cultures that live in different places, they got taught by these ancient Ant People this information and this type of living.
>
> MS - There are many Native American legends talking about the Ant People giving refuge to the people of the different tribes or worlds as they came to an end.... So it sounds like this is one of those places where earlier generations of Native Americans were given refuge during times of surface cataclysms.

JP - So these are probably people that ... lived in the 1500s or 1600s ... early America. Developers [colonizers] that came here from, you know, overseas from the 17 or 1800s. [They] found these cave systems and they never resurfaced. And had kids, ... and always [acclimated to] that type of lifestyle under the ground. And they never resurfaced or nothing like that. So, we kept walking, and they put [took us] to this big cavern, right. And there was a person, he was sitting down. He had a robe, and he had a crown on him. We're like shocked and confused, like, what the hell is this "Your Majesty"? We didn't know how to react. Then you had guards, Ant People guards, guarding the door. And then you had a type of shofar [a ram's horn trumpet] that they were blowing in the back—two Ant People blowing the shofar and walking with us into ... the room, and we stopped.

Figure 18. A Jewish man blowing a Shofar.

Then the map guy talks, he says, "Your Majesty," and the Ant guy that was wearing the crown, he stands up.... Yes, he speaks English! I'm like, "Holy crap, what's happening here?" The map guy, he was asking if the giant was okay. And he [the king] said

> that information is no more to be given to us and that he, the giant, was about to wake up. The reason they want to bring us down here is that they're telling us that the giants are about to wake up and for us not to intervene with them in the mission that they're supposed to do. I looked at the map dude. I said, "Hey. Now what's the reason?" Then I started receiving telepathic communication by [from] the king, and he was telling me, "I know where you've been, I know that you have been in arks and I need to talk to you." So, I told the map guy, "Hey, he needs to talk to me, and it needs to be me and him only." [The map guy] is like, “No, no, no. We're not leaving you by yourself here. Whatever he needs to say, he can say with us [here].” So, the king does like this [a gesture], and the guards grab the guys behind me and push them back. And I'm like, "Yo. I don't want no problem here. He just needs to talk to me about something that happened with another mission that I've been to." And he [the map guy] is like, "All right. We're gonna leave him here, okay. All right, eff this. This is bullshit!" And he just went to the back. And they [the Ant guards] put the other seven guys [including the map guy] into a room.

This is a very significant incident as it shows that JP's previous missions to the space arks are known to the Ant King. In particular, JP's ability to enter and activate the arks is recognized as noteworthy by the king, who wants to confide in him about some upcoming developments with the space arks. It's also noteworthy that the king was dismissive of JP's superior in the mission, even though he was of a higher rank and in charge of the mission. This suggests that the Ant People, and extraterrestrials more generally, are focused on an individual human's capabilities, consciousness, and mission rather than their official rank and status. JP continued his narrative:

JP - So the king sits down, and I see his face. His eyes are brownish, and his pupil is huge and black. But his eyes are huge, but it's like brownish, clearish brown, really nice. It hypnotizes you when you look at him in the eyes. I looked at him straight in the eyes, and I just ... felt like getting on one knee. And I got on one knee, and I said, "Yes, Your Majesty?" And he's like, "We're gonna start going up, and people are going to start seeing more of us. And he told me to say that they're going to start teaching on Earth what they used to teach to other cultures. And that they're gonna make the decision to some people if they want to go to ... where their cavern is. They decided they want [to allow them] to come there. So, he wants people to visit more of these ... massive forest parks because they're going to open the opportunity for people to visit their cavern systems and let them decide if they want to stay there and live there because the arks are getting ready to build up heat. And when they build [up enough] heat they're gonna resurface. Also, the ark in the Moon is getting hot as well. So the king was asking me to tell everybody that is hearing [JP's messages] that soon they're gonna get the opportunity to visit these caverns. So a lot of people are gonna be coming out with experiences of visiting these caverns with these people. So that was quite interesting, Doc.

MS - So we're talking about the Ant People saying that two things are going to be happening this year.... The Ant People are going to be making contact with more and more people, showing them their underground facilities. And that the arks are going to start to activate as in terms of heating up, and eventually they're going to just start being seen.

That they're going to ... actually just [start] floating and people [will be] seeing them all over the Earth.

JP - There's a particular ark that has these small ships. People are going to be seeing more of these small ships flying up and doing recon to see how these big ships are gonna go up and be [seen]... I think it's gonna come out all over the place with this information. We know what was happening around the world and what's happening. And the king, he gave me this kind of crystal looking thing. He's like, "hold this," and he grabs it from the side.... It was like a crystal and it had a copper type of metal wrapping around it, like, in a spiral. And when you hold this, Doc, you feel vibration around your body. And he says, you know, "what [are] you're feeling there?" I was like, "What am I feeling here? This is amazing!" He says, "You're feeling healing around your body."

So he made me hold this type of technology that can heal you. It felt like an electricity charge. And he's like, ... "You should bring this up." And I'm like, "Man, if you give me the opportunity to bring it up, I'll bring it up!" He's like, "Let the other soldiers come in." So the other soldiers come in, like pissed off. It's like, "Hey, what did he tell you?" I said, "I'm gonna tell you everything.... that he's told me, and we'll go from there. We're all here together." So the king tells them what he told me, you know, just to be in the safe [zone].... But he wanted to tell me first what he felt and what was going to be happening.... He gave this device to the map guy. So ... we have this device. The crystal was round.... [It] looked like a crystal ball, but it just had copper, like, wrapped around it—like a type of metal that looked like copper wrapped around it. It was more like goldish copper. It wrapped around it and he gave it to the map dude.... In my mind, I said, "Why not [give it] to me?"... Then the king is like, "He knows where it's gonna go. Your mission is for something else." I'm like, "Okay, my mission is for something else. It's always for something else." So, I'm like, shit, all right, cool. So [the map guy] takes [the gold/copper device. He puts it in the bag, and we start going out.

We see again these dogs running around and barking at us, and we start going through another area. This other area is turning more tropical-looking. So they have tropical [and] they have dry areas. They got marsh water. They got all types of areas under these cavern systems. They travel through caverns around the United States, and it's, like, they walk. They have, like, a highway of just people with bags and walking back and forth, with just the torches. Like it's a tunnel that you can see as far as you can.... They walk for days to other caverns. They just walk back and forth to different caverns, and [where] they got different cultures. It's kind of cool. So they take us to another place, and a hatch opens. We go up the stairs. We do all that, and ... we ended up more south, like three hours more south than where we began. So we got out from the hatch, and he [the map guy] called it in—the grid point where we're at. Our electronics, everything started working again. The Black Hawks, they picked up [us] two [first]. One [Black Hawk] stayed stationary for two minutes, [then] lowered down. We got on [and] we left.

The other ones [remaining six personnel] got picked up by the ... other Black Hawks.... We made it back.

So that mission ... really touched me in a particular way because I know for a fact [that] there's a civilization that is living beneath our feet. And probably the world sees it as a negative thing or maybe ... demons.... Maybe this is what religious people were talking about—hell or probably demons. But these [Ant] People ... their culture is so beautiful. If people learn about their culture, people would fall in love by the way they just look at you; the way ... you can feel the vibration of ... happiness in these people. I understand the people that wanted to stay there. [They] were probably hated by their family or living under a bridge asking for money; feeling bad about themselves; never had a home probably. These [Ant] People give them the opportunity to live with them and to show them a culture that they never knew existed. And they grow their own food. It's amazing, Doc, that experience—what I saw. I still have the smell [of] that hay in my nose ... —how it smelled in that area.... It smells like a farm, like, if you go to a farm. It's amazing. And clay—it's like a mixture of farm and clay [smells]. So it's a beautiful feeling ...

We were asking questions about how long the king has lived there.... He's probably really old ... like 400 to 350 [years old], around that range. Since the 1700s, he's been reigning in that [cavern] area. I know there are a couple of other kings around, but in that area, I got to talk to that particular king.

MS - While you were talking to the king and when the whole team, when all eight of you were in the presence of the king, you mentioned earlier that you were wearing .22s. I suppose that's a caliber handgun? ... Did the Ant People take those away from you? I mean, you guys having weapons in front of their king.

JP – No, they did not take it away. They feel everything Doc. They know everything like they know the consciousness. They know why we came there. And they know the reason why we were there. And everybody was tracking that it was safe. You could feel the safety, and everybody's talking to each other in every situation. You hear them talking to you, ... like they know what you're thinking.... They feel you. I don't know if you know what I'm trying to say, but they know. They feel you. They know that you're not a threat, and we felt that they were not a threat as well.

We felt the same way about them. It's a feeling that you feel in this place that is amazing. It's different—the magnetic field of their heart. You feel it more than humans. It's different; it can make you cry, like tear up, by the feeling that you feel. It's like a happiness that is overwhelming. So ... you forget about your weapons. You forget about everything.... You want to live there. You want to stay there and be there. You get a happy sensation when you're around these people, like you can't believe how they work together. You know how there's no problems—there's nothing. You see them happy. So when they see us, I understand what they feel when they see us... Because they never feel that fear, Doc. They don't know what fear is. They live in harmony.... I felt that they felt that we were, you know, scared.... They felt it. And so when we started feeling that nice vibe, right, that's one of the reasons why the soldiers ... got a little bit mad that the king just wanted to talk to me. But nothing wrong was gonna happen. Everybody was talking about it on our way back, that it was a different sensation that you feel and from the presence of these beings.

MS - Now you mentioned a stream down there. Was that anything like the stream by that Tree of Life that you encountered in Florida?

JP - This was actually in Florida, Doc. It was actually close by to that area. So it was similar, but it was different. It was a root, a wooden root that was giving[off] this liquid that looked like oil. And it was giving [off] ... bluish white lighting that was kind of interesting. It was kind of cool the way that you see it. And it does not feel as hot as fire. It's brighter than fire. But ... you don't feel the heat of it as much as fire. So it gives [off] more light than heat.

MS - So those lamps you saw, they had this kind of bluish-white liquid from that river in them and that that was bioluminescent?

JP – Well, I don't know.... They were more like torches. They looked like torches instead of lamps, but they were not turning off. So, you can do like this [passing a hand through flame] to the torch and you won't get burnt. It's just light. It's really interesting ... You feel hot, like the same temperature as your body. You feel it.... You could put your hand on it, and it does not burn you. How can I tell you this? It's different. It's a different kind of light, a different kind of fire that I haven't seen. I have seen it in one of the arks but it was contained—it wasn't like that. You could feel it's similar to ... the orbs when they come in and out, and the same lighting that they use. It's kind of cool. We saw a couple of orbs as well coming in and out from different spots. But ... they're really high. So you can see the orbs going left to right, and ... it was a beautiful feeling. So, we're heading back, and we have that device. It's a healing device. So it's kind of cool. Yeah.

MS - Now I know you've said something [and other] people have described new healing technologies being mass-produced on the Moon for eventual public release. So is this device part of that? Or is it something completely new and independent, kind of like [an] initiative by the Ant People to give to surface humanity? And will it be something that we actually see?

JP - I think it will be soon [released], something that you'll probably see. And ... it's more with healing and age repair type of technology ... Yeah, you could say it's a healing [technology]. But it's more like to help you live longer if you have it around your house. So, if you have it around your house, you can live longer. I don't know what it does ... [to] cleanse your DNA.... I don't know what the hell it does, because, you know, your body is, what, 75% water ...

MS - Yeah, something like that. Yeah, 70%, I hear.

The actual percentage of water in the human body ranges from 45% to 75% depending on age and other variables, according to the scientific literature.[48] It's been shown by researchers such as Dr. Masuro Emoto that large bodies of polluted water, lakes, etc., can be dramatically changed with cleansed samples of water that are simply mixed in due to the new information they carry at the molecular level.[49] What JP described suggests that the healing and age technology he witnessed operates on similar principles for humans.

JP – Yeah, 75% water. And then the vibration that this gives affects your ... pineal gland. That's the gland you have in your brain that has a liquid. So that's where your melatonin comes from, right? So it affects that, and it affects your whole body—so you feel a sensation, a vibration, so beautifully when you hold this device. It's amazing. It's beautiful.

MS - Now you also said that the Ant People refuse to talk about the giant in the Florida cavern that you saw. Now, is that because of the seeds that were gifted that were then ... taken out of the country, which was a betrayal of trust? Was that why?

JP - I think it was an effed-up situation that happened. And I guess soon ... we're gonna do a mission there. I feel that we're gonna go back to that cavern and check out what's happening to that giant, and they're gonna let us in. But for now, ... they just wanted us to back up a little bit from that area because they want to let the giant wake up naturally. They don't want the giant ... to get messed around with and feel the vibration of humans that are not healed correctly. I don't know if you know what I'm trying to say because it [the giant] senses ... negative feelings. So I understand why he's there probably, because of the feeling that is there [by the Ant People] that it surrounds [him].

MS - Right, that makes sense that the Ant People don't want people being sent down to be in that same environment with the giant who maybe have all these kinds of negative, hostile, aggressive feelings. And so, you know, you might be one of the few in the military that has the kind of frequency that is compatible with the giant.... I know the Ant

People said that there would be a future mission or that you would be involved in future initiatives. Might one of those be, like you just said, that you would go down and maybe you would be communicating with the giant?

JP - When it happens, they [the US military] just do it. They'll give me the exact date when we do it. But when it happens, it happens. I got a feeling that it's going to happen. I think the Ant King is going to give a good word about it

I fully expect that in the future, JP will be sent on a mission to meet with and have a dialogue with the awakened giant protected by the Ant People based on his positive interaction with the Ant King, who recognized that JP's true mission was still to unfold. According to information received by Elena Danaan from her primary extraterrestrial contact, Thor Han Eredyon, the name of the sleeping giant in Florida is Ningishzida, one of the Anunnaki god king scientists who played significant roles in Sumerian times in spreading knowledge about the original Tree of Life, human longevity, and alchemy. Ningishzida is believed to be the Egyptian god Thoth and is also associated with deities from the Americas, such as Quetzalcoatl (Aztec), Virachoca (Inca), and Kukulkan (Maya).

MS - Were you given a name for the Ant King?

JP – No. No name, or nothing.... nobody gave a name for nothing.

MS - What can you describe about the crown he was wearing?

JP - The crown—my God, it had green-like diamonds. It had a big green diamond in the middle right here on his forehead.... it looked like a third eye type of thing. Then, on top of that green one, there was another small green diamond in the middle. So, it goes up into his forehead, and it goes up ... and it wraps around the back of his head.... They're all green diamond type of ... jewels that was on his head. He had ... one, two, three, four, five, six diamonds—and they are like huge. The one in his forehead was really huge, and it went more down.... Instead of going around [the head], it did like the Batman [mask].... It goes down, and then it has a diamond right there. So, it looked really cool. Really shiny; really nice.

MS - And most of the rest of it [the crown] ... are we talking gold or some other metal?

JP - It was another metal. It was a golden color, yeah. It was a golden color, ... like a whitish gold, but it was [also] like a metallic color—like a metallic gold. It was shiny; it was beautiful. It was a sparkling metal—beautiful. I've never seen a crown like that. Really nice.... You can see your reflection in the crown. It's like you can see yourself, right? You can move your hands [and] you can see the reflection in the crown. That's how shiny it was—chrome. It was like chrome metal. It's really nice; really beautiful.

MS - And his clothing—was it a big robe?

JP - He had a white robe, and then he had like a featherish brown thing that wrapped around his neck. And it was like grayish and white, and it wrapped around. Then he had like a V-neck type of— ... what do you call that—not a scarf, but his cape. It looked like a cape and went all the way down. And you could not see his feet. So, it was like a [long] white robe.

MS - And how tall was he? ...

JP - A little bit higher than me. I'm six foot (183 cm), so he was like 6' 6" [198 cm], 6'4", [somewhere] around there.

MS - And the other Ant People, the guards, and all of that? ...

JP - The guards were bigger. The guards were like 6' 6". They were taller. They were more masculine; more stronger [looking]. The people that were there, they're a little bit taller than us.... But there were humans that were the same height as us as well, or smaller. It's like us [surface humans], like different sizes, Doc. They have different sizes— ... heights. It's not [a] particular steady height. Everybody [had] different heights.

JP Visits Moon Base where Ant People are Investigating Nearby Ark

JP next discussed a Moon mission where he saw some of the Ant People working with the US military in a joint mission to investigate the space ark found there.[50] Apparently, the Ant People have known about the Moon Ark for a long time, but haven't had access to it until recently, when it activated and began being investigated by the US and Chinese militaries.

MS - Well, any final things you want to say about that mission? You did say something about a Moon mission or something that you could add at the end of this one. Do you want to talk a little bit about that?

JP - It was a quick mission. We got picked up by a TR-3B; it was fast. We got there in like 30 minutes ... [to] the vicinity of the Moon. I blacked out. I know I was out for, yeah, it was a total of 30 minutes. And then the Moon was there.... I do not know why I blacked out, but I blacked out in this mission. There are certain things that I don't remember as much, but I know that we entered into this round door. And it's similar to what I sent to you about the Horizon Project. I don't know if you got that. I sent it to you.

MS – Yeah. Project Horizon, that was the Army project to create a base on the Moon that was created in the 1950s. Colonel Philip Corso was the first to reveal that.

In his 1997 book, *The Day After Roswell*, Lt. Col. Philip Corso discussed the US Army's Project Horizon to establish a Moon base. Corso said that Project Horizon wasn't approved by President Eisenhower in 1959 and was shelved.[51] Yet, Corso thought the abandoned Moon base project worthy of inclusion in his book, which was a puzzle to many. What JP reveals next suggests that Project Horizon proceeded as a highly classified program with covert funding. As a former intelligence officer, Corso likely knew the truth but couldn't outright say it in his book.

JP – [In] 1959 [the Moon base] was created ... and it's still there. I was there. I saw it. I was there in the air chamber. I remember ... small bits and pieces ... about this mission, Doc. I don't have the full remembering of this mission, but I remember me standing ... [and] holding my hand up. And I was just telling people to go forward, go forward, go forward, go forward. It was a total of probably fifteen people, and they all had masks and helmets on. I remember going in, eating a type of MRE, that's military-grade food. Then I blacked out.

I saw a couple of these Ant People as well there [at the Moon base] with our same uniform. But they didn't have the antenna; they don't have the dreads. They cut it off. So, they're bald, and ... they're working with us in a way to figure out what's going on in the ark of the Moon. So, this place was constructed near this ark ... on the Moon. This base that we have, and that was a reason to investigate more of this ark.... [The Ant people] have known about this ark for a long time on the Moon, and they're there to do an investigation on the ark. But they haven't had the access in the past year and a half that we have.

The shaved heads and lack of antennae of the Ant People in military uniforms, which JP witnessed on the Moon suggest they belong to a certain caste or group of Ant scientists whose leaders have reached agreements with the US military, thus facilitating their participating in joint missions. This is not unlike the situation described in Volume 1, Chapter 9, where Nordic extraterrestrials that had reached agreements with the USAF wore Air Force uniforms with distinct logos and had cut their hair short while residing in military facilities. Clearly, the activation of arks on the Moon, Earth, and elsewhere in our solar system is a phenomenon of great interest to the different civilizations hidden all over Earth's surface, under the oceans, and underground. The advanced technologies and power of the activating space arks are not only leading to cooperation among the Earth's surface nations, but have also led to cooperation between different non-surface civilizations, along with different extraterrestrial visitors.

Chapter 7

Mission to Underground Civilization and Nordic Spaceport

On February 8, 2023, JP was part of a ten-man mission to an underground civilization in Florida that was led by one of its inhabitants, a 7-foot-tall blond human called Jaseet. JP witnessed an underground city belonging to the civilization before Jaseet handed off JP's team to Nordic extraterrestrials, who operated a large spaceport next to the city. JP was told that the Nordics have been helping the underground civilization, along with many other underground and underwater cities, to deal with Earth contingencies for a very long time.

In his update, JP revealed that hundreds of spacecraft are ready to begin flying into Earth's skies as part of an agreement with an Earth Alliance comprising major spacefaring nations to wake up surface humanity in a gradual but systematic way. In a February 10, 2023 interview, JP revealed how different nations are also investigating their own underground civilizations while coordinating with the Earth Alliance, and he gives details about the agendas of different pro and anti-disclosure factions towards the release of such information. What follows is the transcript of the interview with grammatical corrections and commentary.[52]

Interview Transcript

Key: MS – Michael Salla; JP – Pseudonym for US Army Soldier

> MS – Well, I'm very pleased to have JP back on Exopolitics Today, it is February 10 [2023] and JP has

a report about a mission he has recently completed. Welcome back, JP.

JP – Hey, how're you doing Doc? It's a pleasure to be here. Awesome. We're living in beautiful times.

MS – Yeah. Very important times. So, you said you just came back recently from a mission. How long ago was this mission?

JP - This mission was like two days ago.

MS - So we are talking about February 7 or February 8?

JP - It was a team of 10 soldiers. We got out of this bus, and we went to this location close to the same location that we always go to. We had regular civilian clothes [on], and we decided to go into the woods. There was a guy leading us. We were following him but I'd never seen this guy before. This guy is different. This guy was slightly taller than us. He was close to 7 feet tall. This guy was wearing civilian clothes as well. Man, his feet were like [size] 13 [or] 14, big. Everybody kept asking him, "Hey, you should be playing basketball!" Oh, yeah.... I noticed that his skin was really pale. His name was Jaseet. He was telling us his name ... and we're following this guy. So yeah, really, it was a team of nine, but this guy was part of our team. He got flown in from a different location. He had a security guard with him, and the security guard left and told him that he was in good hands.

While he was walking, his pace count and his steps were long. So, I think we walked like one, almost two miles, into the woods. Then we entered [into the underground location]. It was [through] a round door on the ground that opens up. I remember telling you about the Ant People having these locations and different places that they open up for people.... This location—I've never been to this location before. I'd only been to ... another location over there in Colorado. It was an amazing experience in Colorado. Things happen up there as well. But this is the recent mission we were in. So, we started going down into this cave system, and they had a lot of dripping water. This cave system was round and it looked like it was carved by a big machine or it was really well done. I remember touching the walls and they felt like marble, like really smooth walls, and they went around. It was about 8 ft by 8 ft round, and you can see, like, water going through it—like a little river going through it.... I notice that the river has been going through [the cave] for a long time because you can see, already, the marble corroding ... and making a path for the river—creating like a micro canyon. You know, what I'm trying to say?

We kept following this guy. The smell was like when you fish a lot and you touch the fish, and you smell the fish on your hand—or when it rains a lot and a lot of worms come out. That smell, that distinct smell of fish.... We felt a breeze coming in and hitting our faces while we were walking through this tunnel. We kept walking in the tunnel, like maybe three miles in, and going into a slanted position down. And we looked around, and the guy, Jaseet, he opens this round door. It had carvings in it [that] remind me of the carvings of the ancient Inca Indians and Mexico, similar to the same carvings

> they have in the [Atlantic] Ark. So, this guy, he twisted this wheel, and it's smooth. So it has been opened before. Usually, when it hasn't been opened for hundreds of years, it's really hard to move or maneuver. So, he comes [and] he [tries to] open it. This guy was strong ... [but still he says,] "Hey, can I get two [of you] over here to help me?" [This door] is really low, and we help him. I was one of the guys to help push the door open. This door was freaking heavy. It was probably like 900 or 800 pounds heavy. I was probably pushing like almost 200 hundred pounds of force. That's what I felt, and it was heavy. So, we open it up....
>
> We entered this big, beautiful hallway. This hallway had a line on top of the wall. This line surrounded the top part of the wall. And it had lighting—like a plasma-type of thing [from] the top part of the wall. And it gave light to the bottom. We saw plants on the walls that were different, and they had flowers. It smelled really good. That smell that we were smelling in this tube that we were walking into went away. And we started smelling these flowers. So, once you open the door, you smell the fresh flowers. It was a beautiful smell. It was like vanilla. This smell—like a vanilla kinda smell. Really, a spicy kind of vanilla. You can feel the spiciness on your tongue [and] in your mouth when you breathe it, but it was fresh oxygen. It was good oxygen that was similar to the one that we smelled in the [Atlantic] Ark.

Elena Danaan had previously reported that after entering a Pleiadian space station, she smelt a spicy vanilla scent. She explained that "Oshksha" is a common plant on the Pleiadian homeworld of Erra that gives off a distinct vanilla smell and is taken to all the Errahel colonies—the Pleiadians from Erra call themselves

Errahel. Danaan shared an entry from her personal log about what Thor Han Eredyon told her about the Oshksha plant:

> [It] has been many times now that we have been meeting up in the station's greenhouse. It is a ring made of glass on the upper level of the station, and in it grows a luxuriant vegetation [with] streams, and pools with fluorescent creatures, little bridges, paths in the grass, and trees whose canopies touch the stars. Last night, I shivered [with] the scent of vanilla coming from him *(Thor Han).* [...] As he explained to me, they had a cargo of supplies that arrived from Erra, and he got this flower essence (it's not liquid) that he remembered he loved from a flower of Erra named Oshksha. [It] looks like a hibiscus, purple [crimson red] with a bright yellow pistil.... —Oshksha... the flower that represents Erra. He told me that they bring it everywhere they go. They also make spice with it for cooking. He gave me a small one to take back with me, but it's a secret.

The smell of vanilla suggests that the location to which Jaseet was taking JP and his team contained Pleiadian colonists from Erra, which was later confirmed. JP resumed his recollection as follows:

> So, we entered [this hallway], and one of the soldiers that were in the back ... says, "Hey man, I'm not feeling good," and he collapsed.... We had a medic with us that always comes with us.... He's like, "yeah, I think he's having an allergic reaction of some sort." So I think one of the soldiers that came with us, he was allergic to these particular plants. And when he smelled this plant he had an allergic reaction. So, the medic gave him a shot. He says, "Well, we have to go back. He's not good." The tall

[guy], Jaseet was like, "No. He can't go back. He has to go with us. We got a type of medic too. We got people that have a lot of medicine that can take care of him, but he can't go back. Keep going. We gotta keep going." We're like, "Man, this guy's getting sick." So, I was asking, and the others say, "Hey man, [do] you think we should bring [him] back? What do you think? How's he doing?" [The medic] says, "Yeah, man, his throat is closing up." So, we took him with us. We had two soldiers carrying him, and [Jaseet] put them in this room. We left them. We left [the] three soldiers there. And there's like six soldiers [now] following Jaseet, and we kept going with Jaseet.... Jaseet, like, he howled, like he's saying something in the howling voice..... Five other people his size came and went to that room to take care of the soldier that was going through that allergic reaction. So we kept following Jaseet. And on our way over there, we kept seeing tall people, taller than us. We're like, "Oh shit, the whole NBA is here," you know. So, we're like, "Okay, who are these people that we're seeing that are quite tall?"

We kept going. We kept walking. And we saw in the distance a bigger cave that opened up, and we saw this beautiful city. We see a type of flying saucer—bigger than the ones I usually see. And then you start seeing people our size, like 6 foot, 6 foot 2, and they're blonde. And they're working with these tall guys.... These people that are similar to our size, 6'2", 6 foot, 6' 5", they had blonde hair, blue eyes, and they're like, "Come over here. We're gonna show you something." So, they take all our soldiers, and we follow these people. The tall people go their [own] way and we start following these Nordics. I felt like they were Nordics; I felt that peace.

MS - Just to be clear, you felt that they were Nordic extraterrestrials, not just Nordic-looking humans. These were extraterrestrials that the tall guy and the other tall people there handed you off to? ... [These were] Nordic extraterrestrials ... near this underground city?

JP – Yes. So we started following these Nordic guys. But we kept in mind that we left three soldiers behind because one was sick. And I told the Nordic extraterrestrial, I told him, "Hey, we left three behind so we can't forget about them." He says, "They're okay. They're gonna take him back. Don't worry about [it]. Whoever needed to be here now needed to be [here], but [they that were left behind] did not have to be here.” We're like, "Man, that was weird how they did that. How they knew this guy [that got sick] was coming down just to, you know, like, do some harm [to the mission]. Or he's probably working for somebody else.” That's what all the other soldiers were talking about. They didn't trust that guy that got sick. So I guess he got sick because he wasn't supposed to see what we were ... supposed to see.

According to Radu Cinamar, author of *Inside the Earth: The Second Tunnel*, the Inner Earth rises in density the further one descends into it.[53] The density fields inside the Earth can fluctuate in intensity and size to the extent that individuals can experience physical problems when they hit a density field that their consciousness cannot handle. It is therefore possible that as JP's squad penetrated deeper into the Earth, one of the soldier's consciousness couldn't handle the higher density field they had entered.

JP - So, we kept following these guys, and we saw glass [walls] on each side. We were walking in this tube-like tunnel, and it had a glass (rounded glass) on each side. And we kept walking. We were looking [through] the glass [walls]. We saw hundreds of these ships lined up, hundreds of them.... As far as you can see [in this cavern], you can see hundreds of these UFOs. They looked round, and they had different sizes; different shapes. But they were all lined up.... You can see them [the Nordics] walking into the ships; walking out; flying out; parking back in. Like if they were going [up to the surface], monitoring, and then coming back and reporting [on] what they're monitoring. There are ones that [went] up, and they just disappeared. And [then] they reappeared and parked in the same spot

MS - So this is like a spaceport you saw. There is a big Nordic spaceport adjacent to this huge city.

JP – Beautiful, beautiful. Oh, a spaceport. Yeah, we could say it was a spaceport.... In the distance, you can see different ships. We were like looking [at them], and they were different. There were different beings coming in and out, also with different types of ships. Like man, "What [kind of] place is this? Holy shit. We never heard about this place!" One of the Nordics spoke, and they said, "You guys heard about this place. You guys know about this place. This is for you to report back that this place exists." They were monitoring everybody. "We're monitoring what everybody's doing, and we're protecting certain people. We're working with the military, you know. But what's happening— know it's because we are working with those that come from above."

Figure 19. Artistic Depiction of f Nordic spaceport. Permission: Adam S. Doyle

> JP - We're, like, confused by the way he was talking, but he was talking, like, in code. And I understood that they're protecting the Ant People. They protect a lot of different species of humans that live inside the Earth. And they monitor what comes into our atmosphere and what leaves our atmosphere on Earth. So they're monitoring, and they're wearing that same uniform I saw a couple of years ago in Orlando. There's a couple [of Nordics] that was wearing different kinds of uniforms.

In Volume 1 of *US Army Insider Missions*, I discussed the Orlando incident with the Nordic ET in a USAF uniform with a unique patch and a military-style haircut.[54] I included a photo JP took of a departing flying saucer-shaped craft. The incident occurred on May 24, 2018, before JP joined the Army. It appears that the Nordic belonged to the same group as those within the underground spaceport, who are monitoring surface humanity. JP said that the departing spacecraft he photographed was identical to the hundreds of craft he saw in the spaceport. Also, I discussed how the Nordics are protecting JP around the clock. His disclosures are part of an agreement with the USAF, who are also obliged to protect JP. Our interview continued:

> JP - So we kept walking through this [glass] tube, and we went down these escalator-looking things.... I got really close to the ships. I was looking at them, and I felt the ship. And I felt that [same] metallic [taste] in my mouth that I felt in Brazil. I looked at one of the Nordics, and he looked at me. He smiled. He was being followed by these other Nordics.... Then in the distance, I see [something] like a screen, but it wasn't a screen. It was like a holographic screen, and it showed where all the ships were at once. There were hundreds of ships out and about doing

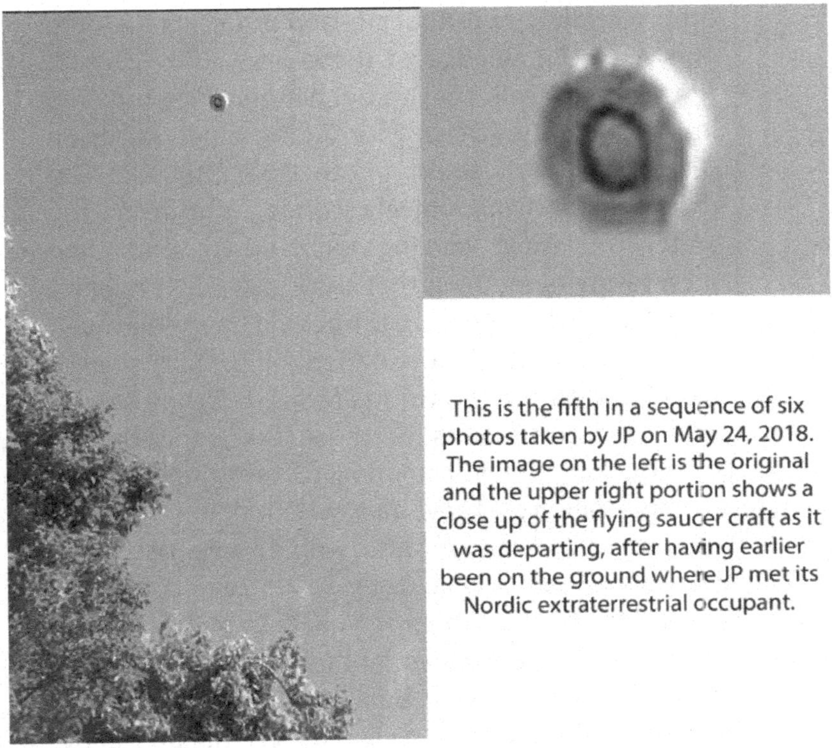

This is the fifth in a sequence of six photos taken by JP on May 24, 2018. The image on the left is the original and the upper right portion shows a close up of the flying saucer craft as it was departing, after having earlier been on the ground where JP met its Nordic extraterrestrial occupant.

Figure 20. JP Photo of departing ET spacecraft.

different kinds of missions. They mainly now are concentrated on giving messages to those indigenous, how [do] you say, people that haven't yet developed technology.

MS - Indigenous people.

JP – Yeah. Indigenous people, like in parts of the Amazon, some parts of Africa, Indonesia, Australia. So, they still travel and talk to these people. They say these people are pure and spiritual, and they tell [them] what they [will] receive. They can't interact with the civilization that is living on Earth now, not unless they're working with the military and [an] otherworldly power that's based out on the Moon. They have knowledge of these arks. They protect these arks as well. They've been monitoring this ship in [the] Atlantic [Ocean] for a long time. So, these [Earth military] ships in the Atlantic do see unidentified flying objects coming out from the water, hovering, coming back down, and then monitoring everything that they [the Earth military ships] do. If they wanted, they could have destroyed that [US Navy] donut-shaped ship, but they're working with the [Earth] military.[55] So, they helped them get this access to these arks, and they're helping give this information of these arks to the [Earth] military. They also are helping the Ant People to move, and the Ant People use their [Nordic] ships as well. They have trained the Ant People to use their ships as well. They train different species of humanoids to fly their ships. What I felt, as well, is that they're building these ships ... and they give them to certain civilizations that are ready. I thought that was kind of cool. Our civilization is like next in line to receive this technology, and we have received it already, and we're using [these Nordic spaceships] with them in the [Earth] military.

MS - So, did they tell you anything about what their plans are at the moment, you know, with these arks and the military?

JP - Right now, their job is to monitor us. Well, when I say us, I'm talking about the civilian sector; to monitor the [Earth] nations—[i.e.,] what's happening with all these conflicts? [What's] happening [with] these earthquakes? What's happening underground at these particular places? There's still not a war, but as conflict happens on top of Earth, there's also a type of conflict that's happening at the bottom of the Earth. They didn't tell me a lot [about] what's happening, but they're saying that there's some misunderstanding, because there's still civilizations that ... haven't had contact in a long time with the [surface] civilization from above. So when we do have contact with these civilizations, they act aggressively because they don't know. They haven't had this contact [with surface humanity] for hundreds of years. It's not like a war [type of] conflict. It's like a conflict of misunderstanding. So, they [surface humanity] have to experience that you guys [Inner Earthers have] been there for thousands of years, and we're [the Nordics] here to help. It's crazy, all these drip drops of soft disclosures [that] are coming out.

MS - So all of those hundreds of ... Nordic ships that you saw ... are all part of this ... monitoring of surface humanity? I mean, there's no plan to have those ... [Nordic craft] reveal themselves or anything like that? Were you told anything about that?

JP - They do show themselves to certain people. They say people [who] are worthy ... are pure [of] heart.... The military has video of these ships, but they're still holding them back. They're still a group of people that really wants to show these videos and all that, but they said it's because [for] the protection of humanity [why] they need to keep this secret for now. They [the pro-disclosure group] really want the public to see the technology that they have—to share their technology. But they're keeping the technology safe because there's a temporal war going on, and it's dangerous—the temporal war, that's going on. There are people jumping on different timelines, doing different things. So because of the temporal war and the technology that they have, they say it's dangerous now to reveal the ships and all that. It's dangerous. Everybody knows about the arks right now.

So once the arks are fully activated, that's when ... the first wave [of disclosure] is going to be all these UFOs coming out and making contact with major powers, with the civilian sector. They're coming out. We're gonna see ... these ships ... on a regular basis. But when the arks are fully activated, that's when you're gonna see ... fleets of UFO's coming out, landing [on Earth’s surface], flying up to different places. You're going to see them. People are going to be riding on them. And then, that's also when the Ant People are going to come out and interact with us. But there's a lot of people [the Deep State] that don't want that part to happen. [In] 2025, supposedly, they're going to send people to the Moon. And ... what we have on the Moon [will be revealed] to the public. 2024 also is going to be a major breakthrough [year]. But in 2023, they're deciding [that] the UFOs [will] become more public and fly out more [in the surface skies].

MS – Okay. So [we can expect] more sightings of the Nordic spacecraft. That's gonna help the disclosure process.

JP - And they have videos that they're going to give permission to certain people ... to show [them] to the public in the media and all that. They have videos already set up. They have the Ant People working with them. And in different regions, different sectors ... they're gonna let that happen.

They're gonna show videos of these ships flying and monitoring military installations making sure they're doing what [they're] supposed to do—monitoring other nations. It's kinda ... gonna be really exciting. This is gonna be really exciting.

MS - Do you have any video, or would you ... be able to take some video of these craft as they come out?

JP - Not now. I do not have a video now. But there's going to be different people that are going to come out with these videos—that I think they're already known to the public.

MS – Okay. So these will be very clear—crystal clear videos?

JP – Yeah.

MS – Okay, I don't want to keep you too much longer, so tell us about this city. I mean, what was the city in relation to this kind of Nordic spaceport down there? Does the city belong to those tall people? Jaseet's people?

JP – Yeah. They're working together. But their city is separated and they're helping. [The Nordics] are helping these tall beings to develop. And they're related to the Atlantean—Atlantic people that had the domes with the pyramids. They're related to those people.

JP is here referring to the underwater city complex submerged at the bottom of the Bermuda Triangle that he traveled to in August 2022. He described the city's inhabitants as tall Nordic-looking humans that possessed advanced submersible spacecraft.[56]

MS - I see. So when you finished that mission, how did you get back? ... How did you finish? How did you leave that underground facility?

JP – Oh, the same way we came in [was] the same way we came out. It was rare coming out from the same tube and the same location. But we were not in uniform, so I don't think we got noticed by a lot of people. Also, the city is comparable to the moon Europa. It looks similar, but without the ice. Yeah.

MS – You sent me that drawing you did of the city under the ice in Europa, so this city was similar, just underground [see image 13].

JP - Similar structure, similar bridges, but without the ice.

MS - I see. And like in the other section, they had these Nordic ships that just, like, levitate up, disappear, [and] come back.

JP - It was quite interesting.... So really, they wanted us to see this. Actually, with us, ... [one] of the soldiers that went down there was actually a person that is part of the media of the military there. He did have his cameras, but they did not let him record. He was taking notes—a lot of notes—on what was happening. And I think he was going to give that message to higher-ups. I don't know if it was for the President. I don't know if it was for somebody else, but he had another soldier always with him. And I asked, I said, "Yo, why is he writing?" [He replied]

"Oh, that's what he does. He reports everything, and he sees certain symbols he knows.... He reports everything to whatever." I'm like, "I never seen that before, you know, somebody else's reporting and all that." But it ... was a beautiful experience. You felt peace. You felt, nice. And people are going to see more unidentified flying objects. It's going to be quite interesting.

MS – Okay, So they're kind of trying to raise consciousness by having more of their ships showing [up], and that's going to prepare us for the arks being revealed at some point, whether later in 2023 [or] 2024?

JP – They're gonna get people used to these ships first. The people are going to see them like birds, you know? Like every day, "Oh, look—UFOs!"... And people are gonna have contacts [with extraterrestrials]. There's gonna be videos ... so they're gonna have people used to it like. They're gonna get people used to these ships flying around. And they're going to be [assured] that the military is with them: "It's okay ... they're safe." You know, this balloon situation can tell you how nervous our nation can get when they see an unidentified flying object over another nation. It's not only happening in the United States; it's happening all over the place. You know this is a preparation.... How would nations react when they really see a UFO? Would they shoot it down? Would they want it to land, make contact with it and have a peaceful interaction? So, everything happens for a purpose, Doc. I believe everything is happening for a purpose. And right now is not the time.... It will be soon. It will be sometime this year [or in] 2024, and they [the

UFOs] will be flying around like birds; like regularly; like planes. It's gonna be interesting.

JP was here referring to the shootdowns of four UFOs, including a Chinese weather balloon in February 2023. The shootdowns were the first time in NORAD's history that it had shot down any aircraft over US territory. The amount of media attention the incidents generated got people interested in the UFO phenomenon and its national security implications.

MS – Yeah. Well, what you described sounds like the Nordics have reached agreements with the US military on a disclosure plan; that they're collaborating with disclosure.

JP – [Collaborating] with not only the US military, [but also with] the Chinese, Russians, and Israel. There's gonna be a lot of nations together, and we have to be on the same page before this happens.... That's what's happening. A lot of people don't want [it to happen]. A lot of nations are trying to prove each other wrong ... I don't know if you know what I'm trying to say. Like, I don't want to put names out there, but like, for example, you're a nation, I'm a nation, we both got contacts with the Nordics and one nation tells ... [the] Nordics, ... "Hey, you want to see if this [other] nation is ready to receive what you want to show them? Watch, we're gonna put something on top of this nation. You're gonna see what's gonna happen." So I'm not gonna say any more.

MS – Okay. So it's kind of like China had arranged for this balloon to go over because their agenda was to show that maybe the Chinese are more prepared than the Americans for disclosure, if that's an agenda?

JP - I'm not saying it. You're saying [it], okay.

Here, JP is alluding to the fact that major nations such as China understand that they stand to benefit if Nordics and other extraterrestrials perceive them as a worthy planetary leader. This planetary leadership role was established during the 2021 Jupiter Accords, where the US was designated the planet's leading space authority by the different extraterrestrial organizations after they polled the representatives of the fourteen spacefaring nations that attended the meetings.[57] According to Elena Danaan, the extraterrestrials wanted one Earth nation to be a focal point for future dialogues. The US has been placed in the chairman's role amongst the six major spacefaring nations that form an executive committee responsible for governing all Earth nations in space activities and coordinating with the different extraterrestrial organizations. In my book, *Galactic Federations, Councils and Secret Space Programs,* it was deduced that this executive committee for space affairs comprises the US, Russia, China, Britain, France, and Japan. If the US is subsequently shown to be an unworthy leader for the planet in dealing with extraterrestrial life and space affairs, then another nation, most likely China, will take over that role. This behind-the-scenes space leadership arrangement may explain why China has very recently played a prominent peacemaking role in international affairs, such as brokering a peace deal between Saudi Arabia and Iran in March 2023.[58]

Chapter 8

Mission to the Grand Canyon

In a covert mission conducted on February 28, 2023, JP was sent to the Grand Canyon as part of a six-man team to investigate ancient artifacts found in a large cavern complex. He explains how a boat navigating a river gained access to the cavern, and his team explored multiple chambers inside. JP described several members of the team as archeologists and language experts who commented on the cavern's rich contents. Inside the chambers, his team found hieroglyphics and other writings on walls that the archeologists identified as Egyptian and other ancient languages. JP also saw golden metal tablets with writings similar to the ones Joseph Smith, founder of the Mormon Church, claimed he saw in the 1800s. His team saw many sarcophagi of varying sizes with preserved mummies inside. What JP witnessed has many similarities with the famous G.E. Kincaid missions in 1908 and 1909, where Kincaid described similar artifacts as famously reported in the Phoenix Gazette, which continues to generate much debate to the present day.[59]

However, what JP next witnessed in one of the chambers was not something Kincaid ever reported seeing. JP saw a flying saucer craft in one of the chambers and went inside it to explore. The flying saucer was built for a small race of humanoids approximately four feet in height. His team had to crouch as they examined the perfectly preserved craft and interacted with its equipment. JP believes the craft belonged to an early civilization of the Ant People, a race he had met on earlier missions. What follows is the transcript of the interview with grammatical corrections and my commentary.[60]

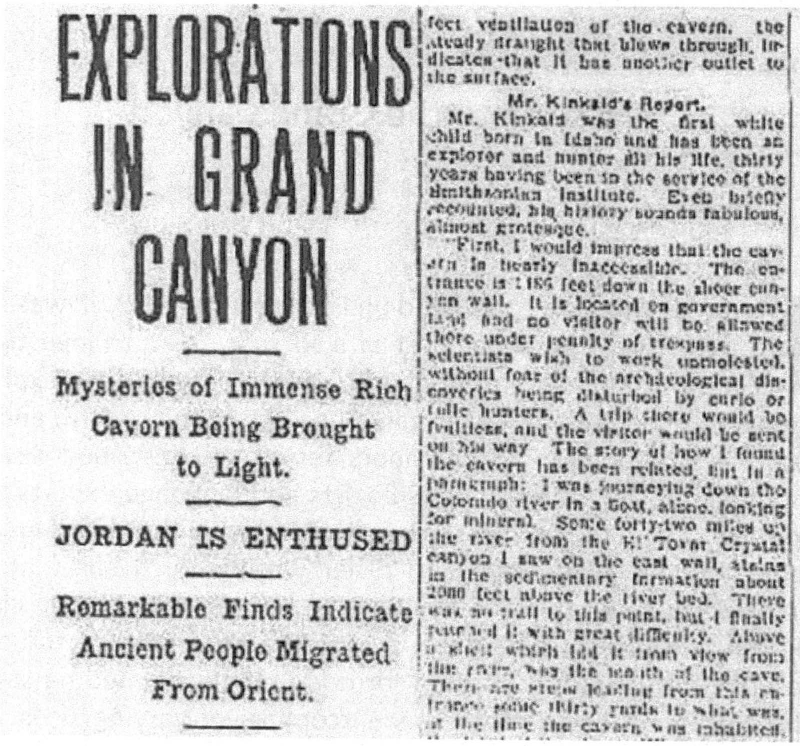

EXPLORATIONS IN GRAND CANYON

Mysteries of Immense Rich Cavern Being Brought to Light.

JORDAN IS ENTHUSED

Remarkable Finds Indicate Ancient People Migrated From Orient.

feet ventilation of the cavern, the steady draught that blows through, indicates that it has another outlet to the surface.

Mr. Kinkaid's Report.

Mr. Kinkaid was the first white child born in Idaho and has been an explorer and hunter all his life, thirty years having been in the service of the Smithsonian Institute. Even briefly recounted, his history sounds fabulous, almost grotesque.

"First, I would impress that the cavern is nearly inaccessible. The entrance is 1,486 feet down the sheer canyon wall. It is located on government land and no visitor will be allowed there under penalty of trespass. The scientists wish to work unmolested, without fear of the archaeological discoveries being disturbed by curio or relic hunters. A trip there would be fruitless, and the visitor would be sent on his way. The story of how I found the cavern has been related, but in a paragraph: I was journeying down the Colorado river in a boat, alone, looking for mineral. Some forty-two miles up the river from the El Tovar Crystal canyon I saw on the east wall, stains in the sedimentary formation about 2000 feet above the river bed. There was no trail to this point, but I finally reached it with great difficulty. Above a shelf which hid it from view from the river, was the mouth of the cave. There are steps leading from this entrance some thirty yards to what was, at the time the cavern was inhabited, [illegible]

Figure 21. Phoenix Gazette article about Kincade's findings in the Grand Canyon.

Interview Transcript

Key: MS – Michael Salla; JP – Pseudonym for US Army Soldier

> MS - I'm very happy to have JP back with us on Exopolitics Today. JP has just come back from a new mission and he's happy to share some of the details with us. So welcome back, JP, to the show.
>
> JP – Hey, how are you doing, Dr. Michael E Salla? Thank you for the opportunity to bring this information out. We're living in exciting times. And we need to have a lot of love because of the things [that] are about to come out. It's going to be

exciting, and a lot of people are not going to accept it, you know. But there's things that are going to happen, and they need to happen in order for a disclosure to happen at a fast pace.

MS - So why don't you tell us, I mean, when did this mission happen?

JP - This happened two days ago.

MS - So we're talking February 28 [2023]?

JP - Yes.

MS - So what happened during this mission?

JP - So we woke up early. I woke up early, like, around five o'clock AM, zero five hundred, and we got a call. When I say 'we', you know, it was five other guys and me. So, a total of six people—six personnel. We got a call to meet up at this close airport where I live. I drove to the airport, and the other five guys were there already waiting. We took a small jet-like plane. I'm not going to give you the specifics because where we went was really a secure area. So, it took three hours and a half to get to this location by plane.... I could tell you where it is, but not the location because they're still doing an investigation. This investigation has been going on for a while. They have found different devices in this location. This location is in the Grand Canyon, Doc.

Once we landed, we got into this white van—the six of us—and we drove like two hours, and we met up with this National Park Service Ranger. I remember they had an orange patch on the left shoulder saying

National Park Services. He had a beard. He was wearing green pants, you know, a tan shirt. And he was with an archaeologist ... [who] spoke Arabic, and he [also] knew how to read Egyptian writings and all that. I have heard that there was something [like that] over there, but, you know, we never gave it a thought....

Figure 22. US National Park Service Patch

We drove around for two hours. So like around 10ish - 10:40, we were at the location in the Grand Canyon. We took a boat ride forty minutes upstream, and this place is protected. It was a massive cave. We went into this cave, and it's funny that it's raining [now] because it started raining when we started entering the cave, and that's kind of cool. So it started raining. We went into the cave, and everybody went in. Wow, that's hilarious. It starts raining [where I am now] when I'm saying the part where it started raining in the experience that we had.

MS - Synchronicity.

JP – Yeah. That's kind of cool. So we went in the cave, and there were rooms. There was, like, on the right—rooms on the right; rooms on the left; and we kept going down this hallway. And you can see the walls—it looked like, it was carved out. And I looked to the right, and I see I see a similar writing that I saw in one of the arks. And I talked to one of the soldiers that is always with me ... in these missions. I said, "Hey, do you remember these writings?" He's like, "Yeah, I do. In the ark, the Atlantic Ark, right?" I said, "Yeah, this writing is similar to the ones we see in the Atlantic Ark." So, then the Ranger was like, "Hey," and you can hear an echo. "Come over here. This is what we need to show you!"

In Volume 1, JP discussed three multinational missions to the Atlantic Ark that he participated in and described seeing hieroglyphic-style writing throughout the ark. He said an archeologist was part of the mission, and he interpreted the writing as they proceeded further into the ark. The languages appeared to include Egyptian, Sumerian, Phoenician, and Aztec. The same process was repeating itself with the current mission.

JP - We had a high-ranking guy with us, but I did not know what rank he was. I didn't know who he was, but he had a mask [on]; he was with us. He was one of the five [of us], and he never showed his face. And he was always with the [Park] Ranger. The Ranger was showing them [the cavern], but I was so excited about, you know, the language on the walls. It was similar to the ark in the Atlantic. So, the Ranger calls us and we go to where the Ranger is. We get there, and he's like, "Oh, you see this? You see these

Figure 23. Aswan temple passage with walls full of Egyptian hieroglyphs

tablets?" And they're like a metal type of tablets, and they were stacked up like 20 by 20 stacked up"...

MS – Well, let me ask you a few questions now ... of what you've said so far ... because now you're talking about the tablets. But before that, you saw the hieroglyphic-like writing on the walls similar to the Atlantic Ark. Now how was the writing illuminated? Were there lights in there? How did you see it?

JP – Oh, we had lamps. We have flashlights. Strong lamps; flashlights. There's no light coming out from [where] we were at. Everything was lamps and flashlights....

MS - When you began the mission, were you ... given equipment that would basically help you go into an underground ... cavern area?

JP - We had bags, yeah. We have bags and all that with the equipment all ready [to go]. We always go prepared. We always have everything on standby, just in case we do go to a place that is dark. We already have everything we need to complete our mission.

MS - I know in your last mission, when you went underground and you saw the spaceport down there, you were in civilian attire. Were you in civilian attire again, or were you in military fatigues?

JP - We were in military fatigues.

MS - And were you armed?

JP – No, we were not armed. Okay ... well, there were two people that had the M17, but other than those, none of the six of us were armed.

MS – Okay. So in the cavern, you see the hieroglyphs on the walls. You have flashlights, so you can illuminate it. Are they just [on] the walls? What about the ceilings? What about the floor?

JP – Well, the ceilings were smoothed out like marble. They were smoothed out, and it looked like an ark.... But it kept going [on]. And it's smooth, like marble, like it was made by something like it was professionally done by somebody that knows about architecture.

The fact that the cavern walls were smoothed out and quite extensive does raise the possibility that some kind of tunnel-boring technology was used in antiquity to build the extensive cavern system that was being explored by JP and his team. There are several kinds of tunnel-boring technologies that are currently used today, suggesting that similar technologies were used many thousands of years ago.

Figure 24. Tunnel boring machine used for electric train subway.

MS – Okay. So very smooth walls and ceiling, right?

JP - The walls had hieroglyphics similar to what we see in Egypt but they were not colored in. They were ingrained on the walls. So it's hieroglyphics.... When you go into the rooms, some of them were in color—hieroglyphics [in] physical color. I went into one room with another guy and we flashed the flashlight to the wall. And depending on how you put the light, the lighting gives you a different[-looking] hieroglyphics. Like depending where the shadow is, the story changes. So it was kind of cool. I [had] never seen that type of hieroglyphics before. It usually is one, and it's straight. But depending on how you flash your light on it and the shadows you see, it turns into a different story. So I guess you have to know the degree of the lighting you give to the hieroglyphics in order to get the story. You know, it's like a type of code. They also had this in arks too when they were down there. They were also doing that on different parts of the arks because depending on how you move the light on shadows, you can see it giving a different story or saying something different. So you can look at, say, a three-by-three [series of] hieroglyphics, and it can say two to three different stories depending on how you put the light on it. So it's kind of interesting. It is usually left, up, and right [that] will give you the stories because we have to know that in those days, back in the ancient times, they didn't have a lot of lighting inside. Some of them had lighting, but they figured out how—by using shadows and manipulating the 3D action of the hieroglyphic with shadows—you could tell different stories. I don't know if you understand what I'm trying to say.

MS – Yeah, I think I do. I think there's, you know, in the commercial market, you know, there are things where ... you can just kind of shift the angle and you see a different perspective—depth perspective. So yeah, I could understand how ...

JP - Similar to ... [a] tattoo that says 'life], and then you turn it upside down, it says 'death'. Okay. It's similar to that. I don't know if people have ever seen that before. That's kind of cool.... So [it's] similar to the hieroglyphics, you know. Depending on how you flash the lights, it gives you a different story.

Figure 25 Ambigram Life Death Tattoo - Source: NextLuxury.com

> So we were in that room, and then we kept going out because there's a lot of research that has to be done on this place that we went to. And [there's] a lot of information that is there that could change everything that we think of, but they're holding it back for a particular time. I don't know when. I don't know what's going on, but this is something that the public needs to know, and it's really interesting. So, we went in. We kept going in, and we kept following the Ranger. And then we went into this big hallway and we saw a lot of mummies. It was a lot of mummies. They were probably like six-foot-tall mummies, you know. They were wrapped with white cloth, but the cloth was already tan [a color indicating] how old it was. And we passed that big room, and then we went farther in. And the Ranger said, "Hey, we never went this far in, but [that's] the reason we called you!"

What is significant here is that the Phoenix Gazette story about the G.E. Kincaid missions says that they witnessed mummies stacked on top of one another. When I asked JP how the mummies were stored, he described them as stacked on top of one another, similar to what Kincaid reported. JP was shocked when I told him about what Kincaid had seen, as he was not aware of this fact.

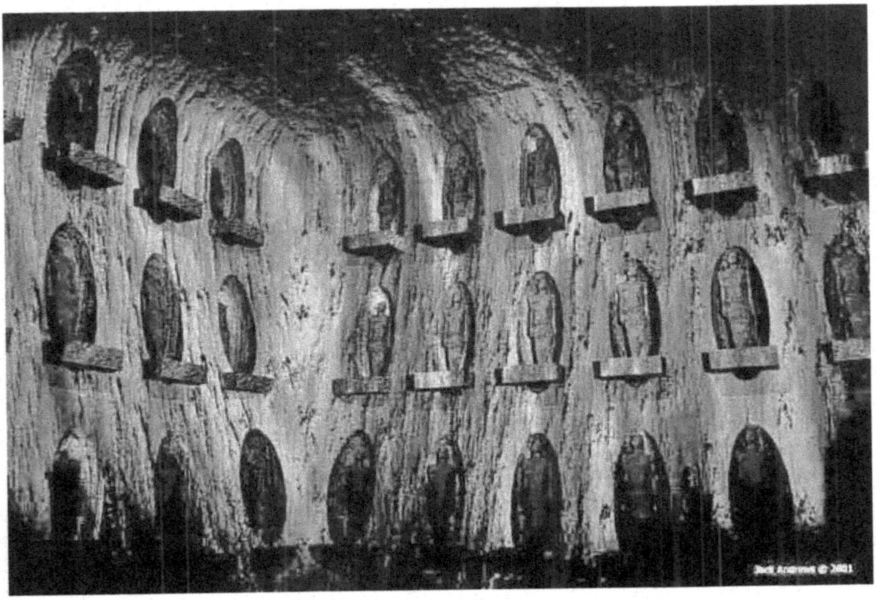

Figure 26. Credit: Computer Rendering by Jack Andrews, 2001

MS - Before you go on, what happened to the metallic tablets? You said you saw metallic tablets after you left the room with the hieroglyphs.

JP - Well, those metallic tablets, they're still in that particular room—the same room as the hieroglyphs [is where] you had these metallic tablets.

MS - Yes, and what were they like? I mean, just describe more [about them].

JP - They're heavy. They were gold in color and each ... [tablet] was like 60, 65 pounds. I tried to move one. 65 pounds and [beside] it, it had a stand that you can put them onto. You put them on the stands, but these have holes in them.... In the writing, the same thing happens when you flash a light. This stand that holds the tablets, when you flash your light on it—on the wall—you can see constellations. Using these tablets, they show dots that show the constellation on the wall. So that was quite interesting. And it also had writing as well, but they did not have pictures.

MS - So when you said it had writings but not pictures, the walls had these hieroglyphs, and the tablets had writing but no pictures. So that would seem to be a different language altogether.

JP - It was a different language—similar to the Sumerian language, where the triangles dots lines, triangles lines, triangles, little triangles on the tips. You know, closer to the Sumerian text.

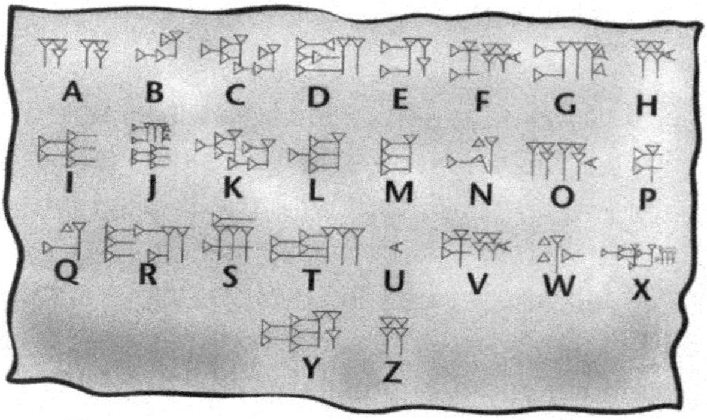

Figure 27. Sumerian ancient cuneiform writing

MS – Okay. Well, I know the Mormons talk about Joseph Smith's seeing these golden tablets that were part of some ancient civilization in the Americas. And then the tablets were taken away.

> But it sounds something like these golden tablets with writings on them of in an ancient language, maybe like Sumerian.

It's worth taking a pause to examine what is known about the golden tablets witnessed by Joseph Smith and his followers in New York. Here is what is said about them in Wikipedia:

> Some accounts from people who reported handling the plates describe the plates as weighing from 30 to 60 pounds (14 to 27 kg), gold in color, and composed of thin metallic pages engraved with hieroglyphics on both sides and bound with three D-shaped rings.[61]

This description has important similarities to what was witnessed by JP. The weight of the golden tablets was, in both cases, around 60 lbs, and the tablets had ancient writings on them. While JP described seeing Sumerian cuneiform text, Joseph Smith saw hieroglyphs on the tablets. Both are ancient languages and might be easily confused with one another, as Sumerians also used hieroglyphs.

> JP - Yeah, there was a lot of it [gold tablets] in a room, like a library. There were a lot of these tablets. It was kind of interesting, but they were more interested in what they wanted to show us behind the room where the mummies were [located]. Okay... I think they already knew about all these rooms and all that, but what they really wanted to show us was the room behind. Afterward, we went to the other room, all six of us plus the ranger and that archaeologist guy. The Ranger was excited to show us this room. So the guy that was wearing the mask had a high rank that I don't know who he was. We followed them, and he just went

like, "What the hell is this?" when he went into the room. We had the lamps and ... when you go in, [you] make a right. The second guy makes a left. The third guy makes a right. The fourth guy makes a left, and we did like a horseshoe. And we just spotted [a different] light.

There was a type of ship there that was metallic, and it was just parked there. And it's different from all the ships I have seen, Doc, because you could feel the humming—similar to the experience I had in Brazil when you felt this. It's not [an] anxiety sensation, but you feel good. You feel excited; you feel a good vibe about the place. And it looks similar to these ships that were parked ... in that other mission [to the underground spaceport]—all those ships that were parked. But this one was up close, and I could see. And the archaeologist that was with the Ranger went to it and touched it, and a door opened sideways from the ship, and no stairs came down. So you had to, like, get up there by, you know, jumping or grabbing the edge of it and climbing in. No ramp or nothing came down off it, and this ship did not have any legs. It was just [sitting] on ... its belly.... On the dirt, on the sand, [and] there were a couple of rocks [as well]. It was the size of four minivans all together.... I think we're talking about feet 60 feet by 60 feet. Okay, it is a good size. We looked inside, and it's ... for little people—not for our size, smaller people. I saw writings on it, like the same writings I saw with the Ant People. Really similar writing, but I think it was more ancient. I also saw in the ship ... [a console where] you could put your hands on, like two hands side by side. And it has layers [so] you could also fit human hands on it... I think that's the way you control the ship, [by] putting your hands in there, and then it quantum communicates with you—with the brain. And you go from there.

MS - So you were actually inside the ship? ... Were you able to walk around? Or did you have to go on your knees or something; or crouch?

JP – No, I had to crouch. We all had to crouch. One of the guys put his hand on [the console], and the ship turned on. He just put one hand [on it], and he was like, "Oh shit, oh man. You guys saw that? Oh man, I activated it." And the archeology guy is like, "Hey, don't put two hands there. You put the two hands there; we all die!" It's like, "Oh shit, oh crap." So, when he put his hand on it, the ship lighted up like, you know, when you take a picture. It lit up like that. He took his hand off fast. What was cool is when you flash the light on the ship, it absorbs the light, so the light [provides] the energy. So [the ship] absorbs the light, and it uses the light as energy as well. So when you flash the flashlight, it does not reflect back—it absorbs it. So, when you turn off the flashlight, you can see this part of the metal [of] the ship turning blue; and then glow in the dark; and then [the light] disappears. So any light, any light will give energy to this ship. Or anything that gives heat also gives energy to the ship. So, us being there, we were giving energy to the ship, and that was what our guy was explaining. He knew a lot about this. The Ranger was just [saying], "Oh, I can't believe this is here, but we can't talk ... about it. If I say anything about [it], the dudes [will] think I'm more cuckoo." And he's like, "Yo, tell me about it!". So these Rangers that work in these national parks some of them are hired just to take care of these places. So I found that kind of interesting.

MS - So when you say, "to take care of these places," that is to ... find them and to ... sanitize them from the public [to] make sure the public doesn't know and just let the authorities? ...

JP – Yeah. Make sure they don't get close to it. Make sure that, you know, the public doesn't know. But I talked to the Ranger. He said they pick a select few that were ex-military or work somewhere in the government, and those select few are in charge of keeping these places, you know, clean, and make sure these places are kept nice. Not even his comrades know about these places or locations. Only they know.... But we were coming in. And before it rained downstream ... I could see more people there. So, we were not the only ones there. More [people] downstream. There was also—I saw a military tent, and I saw a black helicopter parked there. Well, I saw that before going into the caves.... I thought, "Okay, oh, that's how we're gonna go into here. And then we're gonna come out from over there and take the helicopter back." But that wasn't the case.... We never went to where the helicopter was. So, we went in, and we saw the ship, and they started taking pictures. I didn't have my phone with me. If I had my phone with me, I would take a picture. I know a lot of people want pictures and all that, but soon ... people will see these ships flying around. They're going to be flying around a lot, especially [over] South America, Australia that area and the mid-United States. They're gonna see this a lot. They're going to see these ships coming up and maneuvering and coming down.

MS - Do you have any idea of who piloted that ship?

JP - Which one?

MS - The one that you saw ... that you went inside. You had to crouch, and it had hieroglyphs on the walls or writing on the walls.

JP - I'm thinking of an older version of the Ant People.... The Ant People that are living now don't have as many of these ships as they used to have. It's more the Nordics. The Nordics have these ships now. But the Nordics used to give them [to the Ant People] and let the Ant People use them. Also, the smaller alien-looking types, ... the ones that have they have big eyes. The Grays—but the smaller ones, not the tall ones [would give them ships].

MS - Yeah, the Short Grays. They're typically three feet, four feet. They're the ones that are often seen in abductions. Do you think it's possible it was one of their craft?

JP - I think it was one of the heirs [ancestors] of the Ant People because it wasn't the Nordics. This was different inside. It was similar technology, but it's different in how it absorbs the energy. It's more advanced—a little bit more advanced than the Nordics.

According to SunBow TrueBrother, author of *The Sasquatch Message to Humanity: Conversations with Elder Kamooh* (2020), he was told that the first species to occupy the Earth's surface were Insectoids. Insectoids were dominant on Earth for millions of years and became a space culture with advanced spacecraft before cataclysmic events wiped out their surface civilization due to their infighting. The surviving Insectoids were forced into underground areas, and Earth's surface was re-populated by Reptilians in a new genetic experiment orchestrated by highly evolved extraterrestrials.[62] A similar destructive process repeated itself for the Reptilians who were themselves replaced by Avians [Bird People] on the Earth's surface. Next were Sasquatch and, finally, Homo Sapiens. If the communications received by TrueBrother from the Sasquatch elder Kamooh are accurate, then it can be assumed that the Ant People are the descendants of Insectoids that once dominated the Earth's surface, and the ancient spacecraft found in the Grand Canyon is a relic from that long forgotten age.

> MS - Did you see any kind of instrumentation [or] seats inside the craft?
>
> JP - No, I did not see instrumentation. I saw a type of chair that was made with the ship.
>
> MS – Okay. Can you describe the chair? I mean, how big would the person have been who would sit in that chair?
>
> JP - Probably like three feet, four feet tall.
>
> MS – Okay. So [there was] an ancient group of the Ant People or some species or subspecies because ... there are many different types of Grays, and not all of them are involved in abduction. Some of them ... even work with the Galactic Federation, so I'm told. So this could be one of those or, as you said, the Ant People. So there was writing on the walls, and you said that wasn't hieroglyphs in the spaceship. It was just writing.
>
> JP - No, not in the ship. [The writing was] on the walls before going into the ship, before the mummy

place. [It was in] a bigger cavern that we passed. That's where their writing was and where the tablets were. On the walls, not inside the ship, but on the [cavern] walls there was a type of writing. It looked like a drawing—more [of a] hieroglyphics drawing with the Sun.... I saw a picture of the Sun with the rays of the Sun heading out into these mountains. I saw that picture. And then on the left side, we saw an army. It looked like a mixture. [In] the picture, you can see a mixture of races together, and they were lined up in army [formation]. So, I saw Ant People [and] Nordics, in the picture, but there were like really miniature.... You could see them lined up, like soldiers lined up, similar to what they do in those parades they do in North Korea, but as ... different races together. The high-ranking guy thought that picture was kind of interesting. He was taking pictures of that.

JP's recollection of the pictures on the cavern walls shows an ancient alliance of Ant People, Nordics, and other races in battle formation that are similar to the historical events described in True Brother's *Sasquatch Message to Humanity*. This scenario of ancient Earth battles involving different species and Nordics is also described in JJ. Tolkien's *Lord of the Rings* trilogy. It would not be surprising that Tolkien and other exemplary sci-fi/fantasy writers are tapping into archetypal historical memories stored in the collective unconscious of humanity, as construed by Carl Jung.[63]

MS – Okay. So inside the craft, did it have different rooms and different compartments? Or was it just one big area inside?

JP - It was one big area. There was a small round [object] coming out from the middle..... You could swipe it and flaps came up so you can make [it into] separate rooms. [The] flaps ... looks like a liquid, but when you touch it, it stops [and becomes solid]. So [the flaps/walls] come up with like a liquidy [flow], and it connects to the wall. And then when it comes down, it all comes down at once. But when it goes up, it comes up. How can I explain this? Like liquid mercury [is] attracted to magnets—you know how that looks?

MS – Yeah. I can't picture it, but yeah that makes sense that liquid mercury would have some interesting interaction with magnets. Okay. So that's how it looked.

JP - And it closes, but that's about it. We were there just 30 minutes because we had to go to another room, and then we had to leave and come back to base.

MS - So before you entered the other room around the spaceship, what was your primary mission during this whole thing? What were you supposed to do? Were you just to be ...?

JP – Activation; activating.

MS - So, did you activate anything? Or was it just this other guy that was with you that ... put his hand on the console and it activated?

JP - It was the other guy that activated it.

MS - So, he's like you. He goes into craft, and things activate. Is that [right]?

JP - Similar, yeah.

MS - So did you recall activating anything?

JP - I did not activate anything on this trip. No, I did not activate. But I felt this sensation, you know when we saw the ship. We all felt the sensation so ...

MS - And what was the sensation?

JP - The [anticipation]—that good feeling that you get when you see something exciting. And everybody was feeling, like, love—like that good mood combination.... Like, you know, the ship is calling you. And you know, you need to go in there and check it out.

MS - I see.

JP - I'm sure people will feel that same way if they see a ship, you know. They would want to see it up close, you know?

MS – Okay. So you leave the ship, and you go into another room.

JP - We go to another room. So we get down one by one, and the Ranger takes us to another room. And this other room is a huge library with scrolls.... [The scrolls] had metal caps, copper metal caps, each one. And they were put in nice rolls. It's like twenty feet high of just scrolls and scrolls. And the archaeologist ... got crazy with this room because it was a treasure for him and for everybody—I guess for humanity that this was found. That room in the middle had a ball with constellations. And this ball they can move it, and it goes down ... these beautiful stairs that go around. But it goes down all the way. We did not go down. They said that we cannot go down yet because they didn't know what's down there. And one of my friends was like, "Hey, no, let's go down there. Let's see. Let's investigate it. We're here, you know, now. Might as well get it over with!" And the guy wearing the mask, that's high ranking, says, "No. We can't go down there now. So let's close it back up. Let's head out. I got what I needed." So basically, we were there with the guy that was high-ranking, and the high-ranking dude got the information. He did not leave with us when we left in the van. He left [for] somewhere else. He probably went to the helicopter. We left back the same way [we came]. So, we went back into the ship room. We went back into the hallway, and then passed the room with hieroglyphics and tablets. And we came out from the cavern and got on the boat. Then we were in the mini white van.... We went to the airport and ...

MS - So you could only get to this ... cavern by boat then?

JP - You have to go into the Grand Canyon and get on a boat. It's all a restricted area—a kind of military [zone], Park Rangers only. Yeah, [a] restricted area. It was quite interesting, quite interesting. They have hundreds of rooms in there, thousands of chambers.... And they still live there.... The Park Ranger says is that they come out sometimes, but he didn't tell us what they look like.... They had big eyes.

MS – Oh, is that like the Ant People?

JP - I think he's talking about the Ant People, but he didn't say who they were.

MS - Interesting that this high-ranking officer—I mean, how did you know he was high-ranking? Did he just like show ID? Did he just say, "I'm an officer?" How did you know he was in charge?

JP - We just knew. We knew he was in charge.

MS - So when you say you knew ... [is it that] before the mission begins, you're just told so and so is going to be there, and he'll be in charge of the mission?

JP - Well, we didn't get a name or anything. But we know he was high-ranking. Most of the time, when they don't show their face and they go on these missions, they're higher ranking. So that's like something that we know. You know [if] they don't show their face, they're high ranking. Sometimes, they do show their faces. But I guess they're in the public eye a lot, and they do not like to show their faces.

MS - So do you know or were you given any kind of information about when this stuff [Grand Canyon discovery] is going to start being released?

JP – No. We did not get information about when this stuff is getting released, but it's gonna be soon. There's going to be news about this, but I don't know ... the dates. Probably at the same time when we see these ships flying around. And we are seeing these ships flying around, you know. People are already taking notice of these ships. People are making videos in planes. People are making videos all over South America and Japan. People are already making videos about what's happening.

MS – So anything you'd want to tell my audience about what to expect, you know, based on this experience and other experiences you had like last time—going into the underground civilization? Is this all building towards something?

JP - We are building towards something. All I'm saying to the audience is, you know, share your love and have a lot of peace in your heart when these things come out. Don't get angry over the information, if it changes a belief system that you had before you got to open up your eyes. Open up your heart, and open up your mind to the history of different things that have happened because a lot of people are going to be shaken up by this kind of information that comes out. A lot of people, when this information about the pilots chasing the Tic Tac UFOs ... were shocked, you know? They [thought], "Wow, the Pentagon is now talking about UFOs. The government [and] all that".... I love my country, I serve my country, and I will not change this country for nothing in the world, you know. And share love and be ready because [it could be] any time, you know, [that] something is gonna [happen]. These ships are gonna come out and surprise a lot of people.

MS - Well, thank you, JP, for coming forward to share this amazing information about this Grand Canyon discovery, confirming what others have discussed [of] findings in the past. And, of course, for just having the courage to come [forward], to speak out about ... what you're seeing and directly experiencing. And thank you for your service to the country.

JP - No problem. My pleasure. God bless everybody... We're living ... [in] exciting times. We just have to play our cards right and [discern] who we can trust or who we cannot trust, because there's going to be a lot of deceivers in these days coming up.

JP's Grand Canyon mission gives us an idea of how extensive the cover-up of extraterrestrial life and ancient civilizations is and how long the cover-up has been going on for. The G.E. Kincaid expeditions occurred in 1908 & 1909, and the results were quickly concealed after the initial newspaper report. JP appears to have explored a similar cavern, if not the very same one that Kincaid had explored. The fact that JP was given this mission and has been allowed to publicly reveal it shows that those in favor of UFO disclosure also want to expose this ancient Earth history, as well as reveal the existence of extraterrestrial life and technology. In his next mission, JP learned more about hidden records of our planet's ancient history and how this is being researched by the military to learn more about the activation of space arks and the associated orbs that are increasingly being seen all over the planet.

Chapter 9

Ancient Library Reveals History of Space Arks on Earth

In late February 2023, JP was taken inside an underground library at a US military base, where he visited a mysterious Aisle 10. It contained ancient Sumerian records about the operations of large space arks designed to carry a cargo of people, animals, and plants. There were also records of the ark's use of probes to gather intelligence on the level of civilizational development during various historical periods. JP said that we are in the midst of a surge of orb sightings from arks, which are activating all over our solar system, including subterranean areas on Earth. During JP's update, he responded to my questions about a March 2023 paper jointly written by Dr. Sean Kirkpatrick, Head of the Pentagon's 'All-domain Anomaly Resolution Office,' and Harvard University Professor Avi Loeb, who speculated that recent UFO sightings may be orbs originating from alien motherships (aka space arks) in our solar system.[64] JP also stated that the orbs could have deadly consequences for those that get too close to them.

JP asserts that these orbs, and arks/motherships from which they originate, were well known to the ancients, who knew that only individuals with the right genetics and consciousness could safely approach and interact with them. The orbs contain organic and/or artificial intelligence designed to protect themselves from those that get too close. JP's answer further reveals why he and other contactees have been recruited into the US military. They have the right genetics and consciousness to safely interact with the orbs emanating from the arks/motherships and with other ancient artifacts found around the Earth, which in many cases are connected to Inner Earth Civilizations. What follows is the transcript of the interview with grammatical corrections and my commentary.[65]

Interview Transcript

Key: MS – Michael Salla; JP – Pseudonym for US Army Soldier

> MS - I'm very pleased to have JP back on Exopolitics Today. JP, I know you have only a short period of time. So why don't you just tell us about this most recent mission you had?
>
> JP – Well, it was at the [military] base. It was like in a building. I got taken to the building and it had an elevator, right, [that] we took.... It was me and two other guys. The two other guys had masks. I did not see their faces. One was taller than me. The other one was a little bit shorter than me. I noticed the eyes of one of them were different from ours. It was like a yellowish eye color. And he was speaking a different language to the other guy that was next to me. And it sounded like a language that was like Greek and Italian mixed. And then we ... we went down the elevator. I didn't know that this place existed. We went down and there were like a lot of chambers. And these chambers were holding like a lot of different types of books, like a library. And they took me to Aisle 10. I remember that they told me, "We're going to Aisle 10!" So we went to Aisle 10, and Aisle 10 has everything that has to do with Egyptian or, you know, Sumerian—different kinds of languages and all that.... On top of every book, there's a button, right, and these buttons have different colors. And you press these buttons, and it tells you what the book is about.

> I was just pressing buttons [from] left to right, and these books talked about ancient civilizations. There are books that were written by a lot of people that we've never heard of. There were books there from off-world that looked like a triangle, but when you open it up, it looks like a book. Books are shaped in triangles so they could fit better in their [stack].... So that was kind of interesting, seeing books that were made of triangles and leather-type of paper.

What JP is describing is very similar to the famous Triangular Book of St Germain (aka 'The Triangular Manuscript') that is attributed to the mysterious Count of St Germain. The text describes magical operations that a person can perform. Two copies of the Triangular Manuscript are known to exist. The first was made in 1775 for a French Freemason who had immigrated to America. Both copies are currently held at the Getty Research Institute in Los Angeles, California. Our interview continued:

> MS - So did these books actually have some audio feature? You said [that] once you pulled it out, you would hear it.
>
> JP – No. The audio feature is connected to what is [on the bookshelf of] the aisle where you at. So you press the button, and then on top is the book itself. And it tells you about the book itself. So it will interest you more to read what the book is about. It tells you the date the book was written, and it tells you the date the book was found. It tells you what the book is about—if it's about technology; if it's about history; if it's about a certain person; or [an] extraterrestrial race. There was a section that was discovered recently, and different colors mean different years of when these books were found.

And every installation in the [military] base has these types of libraries, but these libraries [contain] books that were found in [the United] States.... But they have other books that are brung back from other countries where this [nation] state, or [the US] military has done missions to. They bring back these types of books, or anything that has to do with any type of print, and all that. So they took us to Aisle 10. Yes?

MS - I was going to say, I know that there were a lot of stories about the US invasion or takeover of Iraq in 2003 that the Iraq National Museum was raided, and a lot of cuneiform texts were taken out by the US military. Are you saying that some of those ... cuneiform texts were in this 'Aisle 10' at this base that you were taken to?

JP - I can't say directly that, but it could be, yeah....

MS - So tell us more about what you saw in that Aisle 10.

JP - So they took out, like, three books, and the three books were talking about the arks and how to activate these arks that we're visiting.... It's like a manual but written in [a] type of Sumerian and Egyptian writing, of how to control these ships or how to take these ships out.

There was a section that ... the guy was telling us (the one that knew how to read these kinds of scriptures) that certain arks still have these orbs the size of cars still coming out from the arks and still

Figure 28. The Famous Triangular Manuscript

making contact with different militaries around the world. So the arks are ... letting go of these [orb] UFOs just to monitor what is going on around [the planet]. And these orbs they ... go back into the arks, and they give this information back to the ark. I guess this is the way the ark stays updated on what's happening on the surface or around the world. They sent out these orbs that looked like UFOs—metallic, or they're like a plasma-type of [sphere]…. So they go out, and they sometimes follow 747 pilots—they sometimes follow people. They sometimes go to nuclear plants and monitor them. It's a type of protection the arks have just to know the environment [in the vicinity of] where it is, because, like I said before, the arks are organic in nature. So they feel; they know. It's like an entity. So it's quite interesting.

MS – Okay. So the arks have an organic intelligence or an AI, or some kind of intelligence, and they use these orbs to gather more Intel about their environment, while the arks are dormant, wherever they are—whether on-planet [Earth] or off-planet. Is that the situation?

JP – Yeah, that's what's happening now…. Some are UFOs with entities inside of them. Most of the UFOs that people are seeing right now … they just disappear to another dimension, or sometimes they [see] them, but they can't get close to them. It could kill anybody that comes into [physical] contact [with] these particular orbs or crafts that are connected to the ark. And sometimes, they can act hostile to anything that is trying to catch them, but it's a protection mechanism. It's not that they're bad or that they are trying to [do] harm. It's that they're trying to get back to the ark to input this information that they're capturing in different places … This is old technology. This technology is so ancient they even send these orbs to other planets in our solar system, [and] to the Moon … ark to ark, and that's how they keep communicating. [They] keep that quantum communication going, and [keep monitoring] what's happening around it because

> [the] arks are all connected. So, it's really interesting what I found out in this library.

JP's reference to people being killed who get too close to the arks or the orbs they release is very revealing. In March 2023, Tucker Carlson appeared on a podcast and described a conversation with a Stanford University Medical Professor who was tasked by the Pentagon to investigate troops dying from brain injuries during UFO incidents. Carlson said:

> We got a call from a guy who's a tenured Stanford University Medical School professor. He comes on, and he's like, "eleven years ago, the US government reached out to me because I'm an expert on head injuries, on brain injuries—traumatic brain injuries—and they had all these court cases from families of the US servicemen, over 100, who'd been killed by UFOs. The Department of Defense was refusing to give them death benefits or medical benefits." And he's like, "So, they're in the courts." And I was like, "There are over 100 servicemen killed by UFOs? Like what?" He's like, "Yeah, and there are court cases about it." I'm like, "Why isn't this on the front page of the New York Times?" [He replied,] "I don't know." And in a number of cases, these things have been landed on military bases, including famously in Germany and West Germany in the 70s. And servicemen have approached them, and they approach, and they get traumatic brain injury, or they're killed, and he studied their brains.[66]

Carlson's frank admission of what he was told by the Stanford Medical professor gives us an idea of what is happening in classified programs where space arks and orbs are being approached by military servicemen. Traumatic brain injuries and death can result if the individual's consciousness or DNA is not in alignment with the energies being released by the ark or orb. These kinds of brain injuries suffered by covert personnel give us a better idea of why JP was recruited into the US military and is actively being sent on missions to space arks and other places possessing advanced technologies. JP's consciousness and DNA enable him to safely interact with such advanced technologies, unlike other military personnel. My interview with JP continued:

> MS - So why did they show you that library?
>
> JP - They showed me this library to explain what these orbs are flying around and who's controlling these orbs. So these orbs are being controlled by the arks, but we all know who controls the arks, you know. This is affecting how people are seeing UFOs, UAPs, whatever you wanna call them.

In Volume I, I discussed how the arks are connected to the 24 extraterrestrial civilizations from outside of our galaxy that make up the Intergalactic Confederation, aka 'The Seeders.'[67] These Seeder races have been assisted by extraterrestrials from within our galaxy, such as Pleiadians, Sirians, Andromedans, Arcturians, etc. With the return of the Seeder fleets to our solar system in 2021, the space arks began activating, which led to them releasing orbs to gather information about the current planetary situation. My next question to JP, refers to a paper jointly written by Dr. Sean Kirkpatrick and Professor Avi Loeb entitled: "Physical Constraints on Unidentified Aerial Phenomena," in which they stated: "In principle, a multitude of tiny devices can be released from a mothership that passes near Earth .... Consequently, the mothership/probe scenario is more energetically viable."[68] Their paper is remarkable as it reflects the current planetary situation caused by the arrival of the Seeder fleets and the activation of ancient space arks, both of which are releasing orb probes. Was the release of this paper coincidental, or were Loeb and Kirkpatrick secretly briefed about the true situation?

MS - That's very interesting because I know that the Harvard astronomer, Professor Avi Loeb, and the head of the All-domain Anomaly Resolution Office, Dr. Sean Kirkpatrick, have just released a paper where they talk about motherships arriving in our solar system being behind all of these small metallic orbs. So, it sounds like maybe they know about this library, or they were given similar intel?

JP – Yeah, I'm sure they know about this library, and they're letting the public know what's happening because it is getting to the point that people are seeing them, you know. Some particular people that are chosen, they also can summon these orbs. [That is] people that have the DNA or [who] are connected to these arks. And it's kind of interesting because I was looking at the guy reading it, and he was looking at me, and he asked me, "Hey, you've been to these arks, right? So, what is that you feel when you go to these arks?" I say, "I feel happiness, I feel a sense of freedom, I feel that the ark is connected [to me]." So, there's people that are connected to these arks as well as connected to these orbs. And these orbs sometimes pick up these particular people that are chosen, to bring them back to the ark for them to download the information that's out there, or [from] Inner Earth.... Some Inner Earth civilizations also have ... [beings] that are connected to the arks and [these beings] also come in and out [of the arks]. I remember when I went to the chambers where the Ant People are, I was seeing these orbs flying around and just studying certain beings and just ... grabbing information. We're going to come to a point where everybody is going to see these UAPs/UFOs, but these are really orbs and crafts that are receiving information to bring back to the ark.

People are going to see more and more of these orbs.

MS - It sounds as though these orbs that belong to the arks are kind of gathering intel on the state of consciousness or the state of affairs on the planet. And depending on that, the arks will reveal themselves more quickly or more slowly, depending on the circumstances. But [it] sounds like the arks are now starting to ... activate more, and so we're seeing more of these orbs.... Have you been told anything recently about when these arks might actually begin to be seen themselves, as opposed to the orbs?

JP - Well, something interesting that came out [is] that this technology [orbs] also ... have the [advanced] technology of mimicking other aircraft that are flying around. So, they transform into whatever aircraft they're following, and they mimic what the aircraft [looks like]; the [aircraft's] vibration; what kind of fuel [is used] they [can] mimic. Like say, an orb follows a jet of some sort, and they can mimic the jet. And from our eyes, we can see two jets, but one can be the orb mimicking the jet, though it's a slightly different color... It's coming. The time is getting closer for the arcs to be revealed because I think what's happening now is they're trying to reveal the arks before the arks reveal themselves. For me, personally, I think it's better for the arks [to] reveal themselves before we reveal the arks because this is going to cause [people to say], "Okay, so all things that's [been] happening in history; all these artifacts that we're finding; all these ET's visiting Earth—all this is true!" This is going to change a lot of people. The mentality

> of people is going to change dramatically [by] what's happening.

JP's observation here carries extraordinary implications. The space arks are very likely to reveal themselves despite Deep State efforts to hide or obfuscate their existence. This suggests the arks are operating on a timetable that is influenced by the data collected by the orbs being released that are monitoring the world's population. The ramifications of giant space arks suddenly appearing will be tremendous as the Earth population awakens to the historic deception that has been carried out on them by the Deep State. JP continues his response by addressing another fascinating topic—the awakening of giants all over the Earth:

> JP - These giants that are in these [stasis] chambers, they're gonna wake up as well. And that's gonna shock a lot of people of how these so-called leaders [giants] will come out, and how they're gonna interact with the whole world. That's going to happen. I don't know if it's going to be this year or next year. Or [whether] they're gonna try to suppress this information and suppress all this [from] happening to the extent of turning it into an invasion of some sort. And that's what we were worried [about]—we hope that does not happen. That they [the Deep State] turned this [emergence of space arks] into a type of invasion type of thing and a 'One World Order' type of thing, you know.
>
> MS – Right, yeah, a lot of people have been talking about the false flag alien invasion and whether the UFO phenomenon is going to be skewed in that way.

Warnings of a false flag alien invasion first date to the infamous 1967 *Report from Iron Mountain,* which proposed such an event to maintain high spending levels required by the US Military Industrial Complex.[69] Ever since, there has been much speculation over whether a false flag alien invasion would be conducted to trick Americans and the rest of humanity into surrendering their civil liberties to state authorities. Currently, there have been many researchers and insiders warning of the possibility that the Deep State will move forward with a false flag alien event of some kind.[70] According to what JP was told, the emergence of space arks could be depicted by the Deep State-controlled media as an alien invasion that would create much distress and confusion.

> MS - So you were given access to this Aisle 10 at this base [library]. Are there any plans to allow others, I mean, for example, could I be allowed access to that facility? Or do they plan to release or give permission to the archaeologists to talk about what they saw? I mean, what's their plan with all of those books that are kept in this secure place on the base?

> JP – Well, the problem that's happening now is that these ... archaeologists [who] are fighting [for access to] these books and library, they're getting crushed. They're getting threatened, not by our government. It's not by our military, but by other people. [That's] because there's certain civilizations that ... do not want to be ... [exposed] yet because of [concerns over] their protection. They want to be protected. They don't know how [the surface] people are gonna react with them coming out and all that.... I think this is something to do with world leaders instead of just one government.... This is information that is [revealed] to the top, you know. It's not that it's [being] given out, like that, for any news outlet, for them to give it out. I know that this interview is going to come out, and a lot of people

are going to start asking questions about this, about Aisle 10 in this base where I went.... It's in the base where you visited [as well]. So it's kind of interesting....

MS – I can confirm that [my wife and] I ... visited JP [in March 2023] ... and he took me to a military base and gave me a tour around and showed me some interesting buildings. I think this building that you went to was the one that you pointed out to me that was very special. Is that correct?

JP – It wasn't that building.

MS - I see. Okay.

JP - But it was similar.

MS – Yeah, okay, alright. I have been on that base that JP is referring to, but we can't disclose it. So [is there] anything else you want to say, JP? ... Any final words you want to say about this mission and recent missions to the Grand Canyon and to ... that underground base that Jaseet and the Nordics were at?

JP – Well, that's Jaseet's people.... Those UFOs are coming out [from underground] as well and making contact with different people. And they're connected with the Nordics as well. So, there's going to be a lot of round orbs [in the skies]. I want people to understand that the round ones are from the arks, the ones that looked like plasma. Sometimes our people are going to see them coming in and out from clouds, especially when it's really cloudy, and there's a thunderstorm about to happen. Or when it's slightly cloudy, you're going to see these metallic orbs [from the underground bases] that are gonna be coming in and out from these clouds. And sometimes, when you see the blue sky, you can see them in the middle [between the clouds and,] like, people are going to video and take pictures of these particular orbs.

And then the ones that are flown by the Nordics are connected to the [US] military. These look saucer-like, and sometimes they blend in with the blue sky, but ... they are slightly bigger than the orbs. I don't know if I sent you ... a video. I think it was a couple of months ago of an orb ... weaving in through clouds and coming out through the clouds. That particular orb was from the ark. And then there's another picture that I took in Orlando that looked like a saucer-like UFO vehicle. That one is from the Nordics.

So people are gonna see them all over the world. These ships, they're gonna come more and more out. And it's not only coming from the arks on Earth. These orbs are coming in from space, as well, into the atmosphere of Earth. And sometimes we're seeing them around the Moon. Now it's going to be a good time this month when the Moon goes full, and it's coming out to Half Moon. This is going to be the month and next month to take pictures and to take a video of the Moon. You're going to see more of these orbs coming in and out from the Moon and seeing these UFO's coming from the Moon ... to Earth. So, a lot of people are going to take these videos and pictures now in these two months coming up [March and April 2023]. Well, there's gonna be a lot of traffic coming up because we have

> ships coming from Jupiter that are already around Mars and around Earth, that people are realizing that these are like motherships and all that. So, yeah, we're living interesting times Doc, and a lot of people are going to be happy. And a lot of people are going to be shocked.

It's worth emphasizing that JP revealed in late February 2023 that the orbs would be revealing themselves more often as a prelude to the space arks eventually appearing. On May 31, Dr. Sean Kirkpatrick, Director the All-domain Anomaly Resolution Office, revealed that the majority of current UFO sightings involve small metallic orbs: "The vast majority of the reports ... are sightings of unusual orbs or round spheres."[71] Kirkpatrick's statement was stunning corroboration for what JP had revealed only two months earlier.

> MS - The most common question I have from a lot of people is, "Well, if JP is active military and he's revealing all this stuff, ... how can he do it without being punished or stopped?" So can you just maybe explain why it is that there are people ... in the covert branch that are encouraging you to talk about this?

> JP - I got a couple of high [level] people that are telling me to tell this. That's why I feel protected, and [I'm putting this information] out there. What I'm saying, it's not like I'm saying something Top Secret or something, you know, the Pentagon is talking about this. It's not just me, you know.... I'm just saying a little portion of what's happening around. There's a lot more people with different experiences, and things are happening to them. They are also giving out information. So this is something that is happening to a lot of people, and

> a lot of people are going to hear this information. This is something that is becoming a norm, you know. And people are just blowing it off, "Oh, okay. Well you're alright, whatever." But when things start happening, they're gonna realize that all these things are, you know, real. It's happening, you know ... It's something that is being also shared all over the military....

On June 5, 2023, an article published in *The Debrief* announced that a former senior military official, David Grusch, had become the highest-level whistleblower yet to come forward claiming that alien reverse-engineering projects were being secretly conducted by Department of Defense contractors.[72] What added gravity to Grusch's claims was that the Intelligence Community Inspector General corroborated that Grusch had a legitimate grievance against the Pentagon for being retaliated against after initially coming forward. Grusch's sensational claims

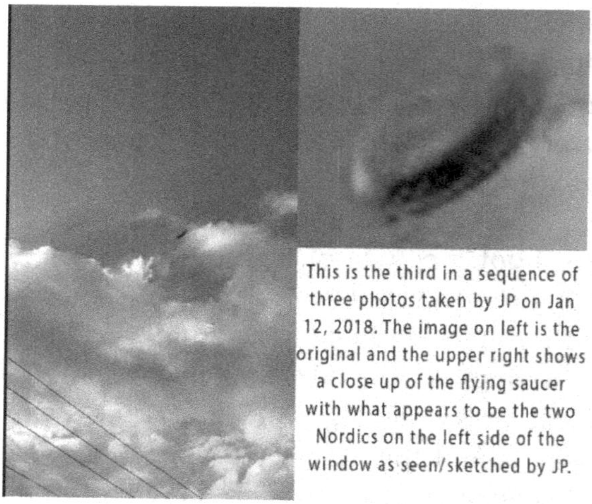

Figure 29. JP photo of spacecraft with two Nordics seen inside.

were extensively covered by major media outlets. This was soon followed by news that additional whistleblowers were prepared to come forward to testify before Congress or the All-domain Anomaly Resolution Office regarding twelve or more alien spacecraft that are currently being studied.[73] These high-level whistleblower disclosures confirm what JP was told by his military leaders that he was being allowed to come forward and that the floodgates were being opened by those in the Pentagon who want the truth to come out. Our interview continued:

> MS – Well, I hope more military do come forward to share what they've been experiencing. I know you're kind of like one of the very few or the only active service [member] that's able to talk about this because you are protected to a certain degree. So that's good to know. But I know that there is some plan to reveal the truth to the public because I don't believe this paper that just came out by Avi Loeb and Sean Kirkpatrick is accidental.... There are people that want the rest of the world to know that there are these motherships around releasing these orbs. Of course, those are the arks according to what you know, [or] have been told. And also [to reveal] what you were shown from that library there in Aisle 10 at that base.
>
> JP - It's something quite interesting what's happening with people. You know, a lot of people are getting this information. And they're just getting the information on paper and just ripping the paper and throwing it away because they don't want anything to do with this. They don't want to be called 'crazy'. They don't want to be called 'insane', but now all people are realizing that, "Hey, I should ... have kept on [disclosing this information] because ... you can't be scared.... You are protected." It's not

> like you're not getting protected by telling this information to the public. There's people that want this information out there, you know. It's tough, man. It's tough because sometimes you get people following you all over the place, and you turn around, and there's somebody there that is making sure that you're doing the right moves and all that.... Maybe 15 or 20 years [ago], it was dangerous to do this and to give this information out....

At this point in the interview, JP's voice came to an abrupt end and the update was over. JP referred to the intimidation tactics used to silence witnesses and military personnel who had seen some of the alien reverse-engineering projects. JP experienced harassment and intimidation when his testimony was first released in 2017, prior to joining the US Army.[74] Recently, he says the harassment has resumed despite being an active serviceman in the Army. This is due to the disclosure of his missions that are being released publicly and the launch of my *US Army Insider Missions* book series.

Thankfully, the emergence of high-level whistleblowers also revealing alien reverse-engineering projects is a powerful, tangible sign that the tide has turned. Senior military and corporate personnel are ready to talk so long as they are given legal safeguards under the whistleblower protections established for UAP witnesses that was passed into law with the 2023 National Defense Authorization Act.[75] Remarkably, the US Congress is proposing new legislation to further protect whistleblowers, and to deny funding to corporations that do not disclose what is happening in classified reverse engineering programs. I will return to this groundbreaking development later.

Chapter 10

Underground Spaceport in the US Southeast

In late April 2023, JP completed a covert mission to a large underground spaceport where he witnessed hundreds of ships and visitors from different extraterrestrial civilizations. The spaceport is located in mountainous terrain in the general area of the intersection of Alabama, Mississippi, and Tennessee. The covert base uses a kind of stealth laser technology to hide the arrival and departure of spacecraft 24 hours a day. JP says his eight-man team was tasked with receiving an advanced healing technology that was needed on an extraterrestrial base on one of the moons of a gas giant planet. He asserts that barter is central to how US Space Command trades with extraterrestrial civilizations. This barter over advanced technologies is consistent with other sources that claim humans are considered to be clever engineers and are often asked to build advanced technologies on behalf of numerous extraterrestrial civilizations through barter transactions.[76]

JP shared critical information about the functions and purpose of the orb probes being released by space arks and the extraterrestrial motherships currently in the vicinity of Earth. According to what JP was told, millions of people on Earth will increasingly witness these orbs, and he believes there is a countdown to a major disclosure event involving them. Unfortunately, their origins and functions will be disclosed in a confusing way to the public by the Deep State-controlled media. This process, as described by JP, has already begun, as evidenced by the testimony of the head of the All-domain Anomaly Resolution Office, Dr. Sean Kirkpatrick, delivered on May 31, 2023 to a NASA panel convened to study UAP/UFO reports, where Kirkpatrick said the "vast majority of the reports ... are sightings of unusual orbs or round spheres."[77]

The Deep State is also likely to use its military and corporate assets to attack some of the ark and mothership probes by depicting them as an unknown national security threat. This will appear similar to the depiction of the three dubious UFOs which were subsequently shot down in February over the US and Canada by NORAD. Comparable attacks by NORAD on orbs from the space arks would provoke the orbs' self-defense mechanisms and lead to a contrived conflict that ultimately would confuse the general public even further about the orbs' true purpose. What follows is the transcript of the interview with grammatical corrections and my commentary.[78]

Interview Transcript

Key: MS – Michael Salla; JP – Pseudonym for US Army Soldier

> MS - It's been some time and I know you've been very busy. You recently did a mission. Do you want to tell us about that mission?
>
> JP - I will gladly tell you about this mission. We were coming out ... from the base, and there was a total of eight of us, and they said, "Everybody grab your gear. We're going out." Like this was something fast. The driver knew exactly where we were going. We were going north to Alabama, [and] west to [the] Mississippi area. There was a cavern there that we're going to go to. The driver looks like he's been there a couple of times. He's been driving different types of people to that location. On the way over there, he was explaining to us what to expect.... We grabbed our gear, meaning, you know, our backpack, boots, our wet weather gear, and

> weapons that we would need. When I say weapons, ... we just carry weapons because we want to be safe and feel safe, you know. It's not that we're gonna attack or we're gonna do anything that is ... negative. It's just for [our] protection, you know. Just in case something else is out there. And most of the times when we go, there's somebody that is [in a] higher ... position that is well known that goes with us. And part of the mission is to keep that person safe, but we're also part of, you know, whatever's going on. So that's kind of interesting when that happens. So, it was a total of eight of us, you know, and we went in that area of ... northern Mississippi and northern Alabama—that corner that goes through, like, Tennessee. So, we went there; we went to the cavern. We drove. [It] took us a couple of hours to drive there. We got there—it was a gate made of rocks. I remember that. We were in the white van, and this was in the middle of the night. I was actually out for five days.

While JP didn't give the precise location, the area he described as northern Alabama near the Tennessee border is known for its limestone caverns and is widely considered the cave "hotspot" of the US.[79] The famous Alabama Cave trail starts from Russell Cave on the Tennessee border and runs south through Cathedral Cavern State Park, which is close to the US Army's Redstone Arsenal and the Marshall Space Flight Center near Huntsville, Alabama. However, the actual base location is likely more to the west toward Mississippi, according to JP's description. It's not coincidental that in January 2021, in the final days of the Trump Administration, the US Air Force decided to make Huntsville the future headquarters of the US Space Command.[80] It would make sense that Space Command's headquarters would be close to or part of the already existing underground spaceport which JP witnessed. On July 31, 2023, however, the Biden Administration reversed the decision to relocate Space Command from Colorado Springs, Colorado, leading to uncertainty over its final headquarters.

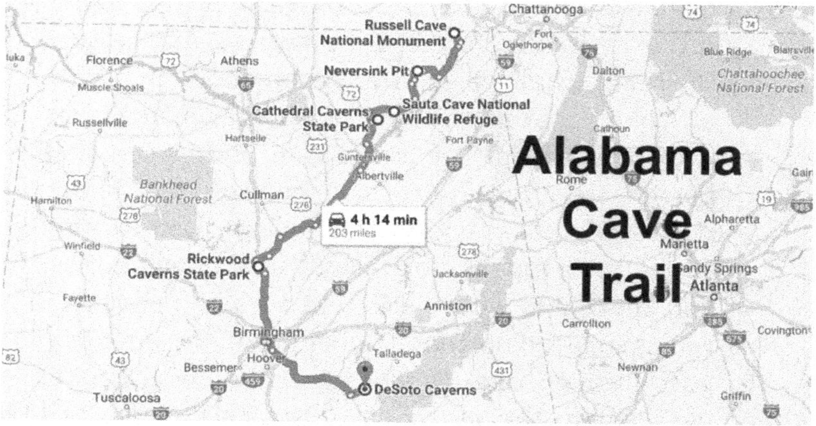

Figure 30. Alabama Cave Trail

MS - Can you clarify what you mean by “you were out for five days?” This mission took five days. When you drove there [and reached the covert base], then it took five days?

JP – Yeah, it took five days. We were there five days, 24 hours a day. Yeah, five days. So, there's still parts of things [done in the mission] that I have to wait until I tell you, but there's certain things I could tell you now. I got the green light to tell you.

MS - Maybe you want to explain, you know, for the viewers, because you're active military, and a lot of people say, well, you know, "How can he tell us things if he's active military? Isn't it all classified?"... When you say you got the green light, can you explain what that means?

JP - Having the 'green light' is when they tell you that it's okay to talk about it and to voluntarily tell you [Salla] about it.

MS - So this is the people in charge of that mission... You're called away from your regular military duties on some kind of TDY (Temporary Duty) ... [then] they tell you it's okay when you're done to talk about this? But your regular military commanders with your military occupation specialty, they don't know anything about that. Is that correct?

JP – Yeah.

MS - Thank you.

JP - It goes from higher above for me to communicate this with you, because, as you know, they're already talking ... whistleblowers are talking. And now a lot more people are coming out with more interesting information, and everybody is now having the green light from above. There's gonna be so many green lights. When I say green lights, it's [that] people are going to be talking—so many whistleblowers talking—that it's going to become a norm for everybody to talk about these [UFO] situations that are happening. But not as ... [many] people are talking about their [UFO] mission. So that's the thing. They're talking about, "Yes, I saw UFO here. Yes, I saw this technology over here; over there. Yes, there's a Moon base here," and all that. But not a lot of people ... have the green light to talk about the mission [itself] and what happens in the mission. [That's] because, you know, we have a history [of discussing covert missions] from 2016, before I was in the military.... They know that ... [due

> to] what happened at MacDill Air Force Base ... [with my UFO photos].

JP's prediction about a lot of whistleblowers coming out was validated soon after this interview was conducted in late April 2023. On June 5, as previously mentioned, David Grusch's whistleblower testimony was released. And soon afterward, several other highly credentialled whistleblowers were on the verge of coming forward, claiming to have more information on UFOs and reverse-engineering projects involving captured alien technologies.[81] JP was also correct that these whistleblowers were only talking about UFOs that had been seen or alien technologies that were directly witnessed, but they avoided discussing actual missions involving the use of reverse-engineered technologies such as missions to off-world locations using antigravity craft built by US defense industry corporations. At this stage, JP is unique among contemporary whistleblowers in that he has been green-lighted to reveal actual space missions in which he has participated.

> MS – I just want to clarify for the viewers what you just said is very important, because while you joined the Army in 2019, you had a history going back to 2015, as I recall, where you were being picked up by extraterrestrials and by the Air Force; being taken on different missions. And in 2017, you were given permission to take photographs of flying triangles [and] flying rectangles over MacDill Air Force Base in Tampa.[82] And so we actually have those photos. They've been released on my website. So there's a history of you being green-lighted by the covert military. So people who say, well, you know, "How can this guy be given permission to do this?" JP had this arrangement before he joined the Army, and actually he was encouraged to join the military because this was the relationship he had. There was an agreement between the Nordics and the military

for you to be able to do this. So this is a pre-existing arrangement, and it's just carried over since you joined the military. So, this is not a new thing, but it's just a continuation of something that started in 2015.

JP - This happened before Space Force was born, you know. All this was happening in the process of when Space Force was becoming Space Force in the Trump Administration. So it's quite exciting everything that's happened now, because everything was in development in the Trump Administration, you know, to come out. And all these beautiful entities are visiting our Earth trying to contact different people that are chosen. See, when we give information and we're green-lighted, there's certain information that is red-lighted that we can't talk about until a certain thing happens. And then we get the green light to talk about it, because we also got other different countries that are going through the same thing and there's a lot of different technologies involved in these types of information that we give out. So I can continue with my mission. But yeah, people can go back and look in the history of everything we have talked about. It's going to be really exciting in this future that we are living—[that] we're gonna live. It's going to be really exciting.

What JP just described is very similar to the scenario explained in a March 22, 2023, letter from Canadian MP Larry Maguire to Canada's Minister of Defense.[83] In it, Maguire pointed out the danger of Canada being left behind in the upcoming 'official' UFO disclosures to be made by other Five Eyes countries, in particular: Australia, the United Kingdom, and the US. Maguire's letter pointed out that Five Eyes nations were cooperating in the study of UAPs and in the development of recovered foreign materials (e.g., alien technologies). But Canada was not as forthcoming on the UAP issue. Once again, JP's information was validated by contemporary political events that show how sensitive the timing of UFO-related disclosures is at this time.

> JP - Like I said, we went [on] this Mission with a total of eight people—[all] guys. And there was somebody important there—a high ranking [official] from the Air Force branch and I did not know his name. I never want to know anybody's name.... That's important for me, for my protection and for my well-being. You know, I never want to know who's with me in these particular missions. I do see familiar faces, but sometimes I just don't want to know their name or what their rank is or what kind of job they do, because these types of missions that we do, there's a lot of people that do not want these types of missions to happen. By me not knowing the people around me, it protects me and it protects the people I talk to.
>
> So we went into this cavern; it was a rock that opened up. When I say a rock, it was ... 20 feet high. And this rock looks camouflaged into ... a side [of a] mountain, to a side hill. It just opens up. And it opens up always in the middle of the [road].... And they have a lot of security around this mountain, around this hill, that turns into a mountain. And it opened up, and then you can hear it ... echo when it closes. We entered this cavern, and it was probably 20 minutes [driving] in, and we parked. After we parked, we all got out of the van and it smelled like a cave. Like minerals that you ... smell when you enter a cave and you smell that mineral, like salt. It's a very acidic kind of [smell], ... like a type of muriatic

[acid]. That's it; it's like a strong smell. And there was a hallway with regular lights—no fancy lights—[but] regular light bulb lights, orange color. And it was a hallway that you go down....

I remember seeing tubes of metal pipes that ran on the right side [of the cavern entrance walls]. These pipes, I guess, are for sanitary [purposes], I don't know, for the people that work there. We kept walking, and there was another door that opened that had a code. The person that was in front of us, well, that was the driver. He had this code. Only he can enter this type of facility. So, we entered the facility. After you enter the facility, there's a laser machine that swipes your body and swipes everybody. And it [gradually] builds up on the [display] screen the inventory of your organs; the inventory of your cell counts; your body, molecules— like everything that your body is made of.... They have the inventory of everything. And you're like, "Man, that's crazy," you know. Well, you know, like two eyeballs ... you know everything that your body has. That was quite interesting. I [have] never seen something like that technology.... Everybody had to wait until that person [in front] finished [being scanned]. There was a person that stayed behind because he had ... an organ transplant, and this [new] organ was not his. So, if an organ is not yours, you can't enter into this facility. Everything has to be yours. So, this person stayed behind. It kind of sucked, but I think that's one of the rules that they follow. Everything in your body has to be yours.

The security procedure JP described appears to be designed to ensure that no one who enters the facility has been compromised in terms of technological implants or body replacements that could be controlled by foreign entities or Artificial Intelligence. Artificial Intelligence, in particular, appears to be a serious security threat in the secret space programs, as I discussed in the *US Navy's Secret Space Program*.[84]

> JP - So, we entered and it was a big football [field] sized hanger. We saw different kinds of ships there coming in and out. You can hear these ships swooping away and coming in [and] parking. And different kinds of people; different kinds of entities coming out of ... [these ships] and giving the people in charge of the hanger ... a metallic see-through type of square. And the person sees the inventory of the ship and gives it back.... It kind of reminded me of the Men in Black type of thing, you know. Like different ships and different kinds of traffic that comes in and comes out.
>
> MS - So we're talking a spaceport. We're talking [about] something as big as a football stadium under the ground. Behind, you have to access through this rock that you can drive through with your van. And then you have to go through some kind of security ...
>
> JP – I'm sure there's an opening also on top for the ships. They come down, and they go in. I was talking to a guy that was sitting down in the corner ... [who] was in charge of, like, all the I.T. [information technology]. They have a technology that surrounds these mountains. It is a laser that shoots up, and it goes as high as our atmosphere. But these lasers that shoot up, they do a hexagon [pattern] up. And if anything goes inside, it turns into a big ass straw [giant tube of light]. So [the craft] can enter from the

atmosphere all the way in [through this laser tube], and nothing can be seen coming in or out. I don't know if you understand what I'm trying to say. Like, say this is the laser. You can't see it, but it makes anything [invisible] that goes in it from the atmosphere.... They can enter this particular hexagon [pattern] made up of laser, and [they] cannot be seen. It turns everything invisible.

MS - Just for people that want a little more ... information because they're listening to this [update and], they can't see anything. ... You were holding up a kind of tube-type device, and the laser would go through the tube in the way you just described.

JP - So it's a type of laser light that shoots up to space, and when ships go through it, nobody can see it. Nobody can see the ships that go inside [the laser tube]. This laser reflects everything that is outside the mix. It cloaks everything that comes into the mountain....

MS – Like, you're saying, a kind of tubular beam of light or a laser that goes up into the upper atmosphere, and the ships are able to go into that tube of light that's projected up into the atmosphere. And that's how they're able to enter the base but in a stealth way without anyone seeing. But people can see the light, right? So people would see a light come on ...

JP – No, it reflects everything that's outside from it, but on the inside you can see it; it's dark. It reflects everything on the outside. It's like a mirror light; it's like a mirror made of light. Doc, it's a huge science ...

[behind] this. There's a way that they can ... face the molecules out [in] one direction. You know how ... there's a technology that flips the mirrors, and when they flip the mirrors, it turns anything stealth. So this technology is really top-notch. They have a way to manipulate molecules to make them look like microscopic mirrors that can reflect whatever is outside of the laser. They do it [at] a quantum level, and whatever's inside [of the laser tube], it's [in] a dark hole. I think NASA got a couple of pictures of these lasers when they shoot up, and they hit the atmosphere. And it looks like a light that shoots up. I think they do have pictures like that. If I can find it, I'll send it to you. But yeah, they have that technology. And they use this technology also in the oceans; also on different kinds of ships. And they have this technology also on different types of UFOs and [space]ships. It's the type of laser that goes around the skin of the aircraft and microscopically turns everything ... to see-through—everything that is within the ship. So, it's quite interesting.

MS – Okay. So this technology shoots up out of that facility up into the sky, and any ship that goes into that light [tube] just becomes invisible to observers. So, do people see the light itself? Or is the laser light ... [used] at night, you know? Can people see it at night? ...

JP - You can't see the laser. I know people in space could see it when it hits the atmosphere, and it shoots up. But in the atmosphere, you cannot see it.

MS - I see. So as far as people around that [tube entrance], they don't see any kind of laser being deployed or coming out of that mountain or out of that hill in that facility there? ...

JP - It mostly happens when it's [a] clear day. They don't deploy it when ... they have a lot of clouds and all that.

In a paper published in *Nature* in March 2021, researchers discussed how "multispectral camouflage" would work using lasers and microwaves.[85] The article proposed that camouflage among "different spectral bands" is possible, which includes visible and infrared light. While the proposed camouflage system was rudimentary, it provides an idea of how more advanced classified camouflage systems using lasers might work in the manner described by JP.

MS – Okay. So that's how the ships enter into this facility. So, is this facility like an Air Force Base; an Army Base? Or does it belong to an Inner Earth civilization? Or is it an extraterrestrial base?

JP - It belongs to the United States. Let's put it as that... It belongs to the people.

MS - So it would be like a deep underground military base? It's a DUMB facility there somewhere in Mississippi?

JP – Yes.... Alabama, Mississippi, and Tennessee. In that area.

MS – Okay, all right. So we'll kind of leave it a little vague as to the exact location somewhere in that area. And you said you saw different entities coming out of the ships, ... even though it's a US military facility? Is it something that different ET races are using? Who are the different entities you saw coming out of the ships?

JP - I saw a tall entity dressed all in black, and they had like a white type of glove that goes halfway [up] ... by their elbow, and they're... really tall. I saw another one ... their skin was bluish, and they had orange-type hair. They did not have eyebrows, but they have their facial features just like ours, and yeah, their hair is orangey, but they have blue skin, like bluish-gray skin. I had never seen these entities before. I saw another one ... they're big and stocky, and their noses were quite long and hanging. They remind me of those walruses that have those big noses, but it was smaller, and when they moved, it moved with them, and they can maneuver it just to smell, but they're big and round and stocky. Their hands are really chubby. They had a device in their hands that, with one finger, they could communicate with other people.

I saw the Nordics also, most of them were in charge of this facility. I saw the Nordics with the Air Force uniform, but it was different. Every section has a different color of, you know, the people that come in, people that are in charge of the ships, and inventory of the ships, and where the ship came from, and they have anything that they bring in. So, they make an inventory the same way that I entered into the facility when they do an inventory of my whole body and what's happened [inside] my body, this [scanning] thing they do with the ships, but it's a longer process, but it's quite fast. It takes like 20 minutes, 15 minutes for each ship to come in and out. I guess it's to check in.... People say it's a small world, but this world is huge. You got to implement [consider] also what is beneath the oceans, under the Earth. This world is huge.

JP's reference to a Nordic in an Air Force uniform is based on an encounter he had in Orlando, Florida, with a Nordic who was working with the Air Force and wearing a uniform with a unique patch. The Nordic had a standard military-style crewcut and offered to take JP for a ride on his flying saucer-shaped craft, which JP declined due to concerns over possible retaliation by a third party watching him. While JP for years has been encouraged in his disclosure efforts by USAF operatives, CIA operatives have instead threatened him if he disclosed too much. Despite declining the offer to fly on the Nordic spacecraft, JP nevertheless took several photos of the departing craft, which were first published on my website on May 26, 2018.[86]

MS - So when you say this world is huge, I mean, are you talking about all of the underground facilities that are all over the place, you know, with different civilizations and ...

JP – Yeah, it will blow your mind, Doc. Like if you see the stuff that we have underground, under the oceans, it's not just on top, and what we also have in[side] the Moon, in different parts of our own solar system that is connected. And the cool thing is that these entities, they were locked down for a long time [due to COVID-19], and now they started coming again. They have the green light to come in. They have to do business again.

MS – Okay, so you're saying that there was a lockdown where these different visitors, extraterrestrials presumably, from off-planet weren't allowed to ... come to the Earth or go to that particular facility, they were prevented, but now it's okay. So that means that there's just more traffic. Is that what's happening?

JP - The traffic started again at the beginning of 2020 when COVID hit when everybody was inside. So, this traffic was really massive there. I can't talk about it like that, but maybe it's because of that more traffic it could come in and out because of everybody being inside on lockdown. So that gave the opportunity for more ETs to connect and disconnect. Do you understand what I'm trying to say?

MS – Yeah, I see; okay, fair enough. The COVID lockdowns led to more ships being able to enter the atmosphere and go to these underground facilities or underwater facilities because there were fewer people around to ... see them.

JP – Yeah.

MS – Okay, so this facility in that kind of Alabama, Mississippi area, you were there with a group of eight. You said one guy couldn't enter. You said one guy was a senior Air Force officer, so what was the mission?

JP - The mission was to pick up a device. We had to pick up the device and bring it back. And this device was a type of technology that is used for healing. The ancients used to use this. So, it came from somewhere else because this place is not only for ETs, it's also for other programs to enter and to go out and drop off anything that they found. So, when I heard the last interview ... with [John] DeSouza ... it was quite interesting what he was saying about Oumuamua coming back and dropping these drones to our planet. [That's] because in our last interview, I was telling you about the arks having these types of drones that come out, and they do like a recon of everything that is around, and they also go to space, and they connect with the other arks, and they pass the information on.

The John DeSouza interview that JP referred to was published on April 27, 2023, and in it, he discussed recent developments in the US that pointed to a Project Bluebeam-type false flag event concerning UFOs that was about to be unleashed.[87]

JP - They [the orbs] pass [on] what is the temperature, information of population, information of ... different types of small, microscopic organisms, that certain ETs cannot come into contact with.

MS – Bacteria?

JP – Bacteria, yeah. There are certain ETs that cannot come to Earth because of that. So, these drones also check on all that, on the ocean, the toxicity, they check all types of information of where they go, and they share it. I also think the interaction they have with different people or different entities, and because Oumuamua is coming back and dropping these types of UFO drones again, it's also going to activate the ark's drones and the ark's UFOs as well. So, it's all going to come out at once. It'll probably activate the arks for everybody to see; possibly, there's going to be the ships that are around Jupiter and around Saturn coming in with, tagging along with Oumuamua, and all at once dropping a type of drone-like device to the Moon, to the Earth, to Mars, to Mercury. They're gonna drop them all at the same time to all these planets, and a lot of people will see that, and like he said, you know, when that happens that could be a checkmate, like it could be late when people see that. When people start seeing that, that's why every news outlet is talking about the same thing, and they're talking about what to expect. They're getting ready. This healing device ...

MS - But before you go there with the healing device, just to recapitulate what you just said because it's important. So, you're saying that it's not just the space arks that are activating that are releasing probes, it's also the motherships that were parked around Jupiter, and you mentioned Oumuamua returning, which is what John Desouza said. I don't know about Oumuamua returning; I hadn't heard that. Everyone's talking about it being an Interstellar kind of object that's on the way out, but it's possible that it is returning. That ... itself is some kind of mothership as well, but that would fit in with what Avi Loeb and Sean Kirkpatrick were saying about the mothership releasing probes. Now you know, whether they're talking about Oumuamua or whether they're alluding to one of these other motherships that are parked around Jupiter, but yeah, I would agree that they're getting ready; they're getting the public ready for these probes or orbs being seen much more because they're being released from the motherships to do these different functions that you identified.

JP - And a lot of people, they're gonna realize that there's going to be good UAPs and there's going to be bad looking drones UAPs. And because of the bad ones, people will get confused with [what] the good ones do. I want people to understand that there's going to be two types. Everything is going to happen at the same time; that's the thing. So, when something good happens, they always want to do something bad to take out the good. How can I put this?

MS – Well, that's clear that the Deep State, that the negative factions, that they want to confuse people. That they will release probes that are negative, you know, like the ones that were shot down. I assume that these belonged to some corporate program; and just to start frightening people about these probes or these orbs because they know that the orbs and the probes being released by the arks and the motherships or the craft—these are going to perform a positive function. So, they're going to release their own probes to confuse things and frighten people, and they have the mainstream media that they control to put out this false narrative that the probes are a threat, they're national security threats and frighten people....

JP - In the people's eyes, everything is going to be a threat that's floating around, you know, but the people that know there's going to be positive arks up there. It's going to be real ships out there, but there's also going to be types of false ships.... The thing is that these ships, they're gonna attack planes, and they're gonna attack the friendly ships. These friendly ships, they're organisms, they're peaceful, they're ancient, if they feel threatened they will not hesitate [to defend themselves]. It's like, how can I put this, if you take a pet lion as a baby and you make it grow up, right, this lion is gonna know you, it's still aggressive, it's gonna know you. If you provoke the lion, it doesn't matter if the lion knows you or not; the lion is gonna put you down. What I'm trying to say [is] that we cannot provoke these ships that are coming in and we have to know the difference.... This is gonna be confusing for a lot of people because people are not gonna know.... Not a lot of people are doing their homework, and a lot of people are gonna get confused about who is who, but I know the community. Oh man, there's a lot [of info] into this on what particular ship is whose, which ships are gonna be who [etc.]. This is all going to come [out] in the news, "Who are these" and then a nation is going to come out [to say], "This is our technology, no, but this is the ET's technology. So which technology is this?" And then you're gonna have another other ark coming in, and then we're gonna say, "Oh, well, who is that?" So, it's going to be a major confusion everywhere on this, and that's what they want. They want to confuse everybody and make everybody confused, but it's going to be a confused situation....

MS - It's very important what you just said, that the Deep State, the negative alliance, they are going to be launching their own craft, and they're going to shoot or they're going to try and provoke these probes from the arks, from the space arks, from the mother ships, they're going to shoot at them or provoke them in some way. And because they want to create chaos, they want people to feel frightened ... they want people to feel that these probes, these orbs, [are] threatening. And so that's what the Deep State wants to do, provoke confusion and fear and ... manufacture this threat out of nowhere, which is, I guess, what you were saying that John DeSouza ...

is correct that the Deep state is going to manufacture some kind of false flag event by using its own technology to create ... this confusion, this uncertainty, these threats.... Were you told? ... How did you find out about that yourself?

JP - I was told. They always brief us on different things. And on the missions where we get it ... they always explain why we did the mission, what's the mission for, and what this mission is going to help [with], what's going to happen with the [healing] device that we bring, you know. This device is actually going to space to another facility. I don't know where it is, but it's somewhere in our solar system that somebody else needs. It's a type of healing [device] for types of water organisms that live elsewhere.

MS – Okay, so you received this healing device, but it's not intended for release on Earth. It's intended for some other space missions, off-planet, involving bodies of water.

JP - We do develop technology for other ET races that they ask for. It's not just for humanity, and it only works for them, you know. There's some technology that doesn't work on us. It only works on certain ETs.... There's certain ... technologies that work for certain ETs that do not work for us because of the structure of their bones. It's probably more denser than ours or probably lighter than ours. Their skin can be reptile-like or slimed-like skin.... There's different ETs, you know, it's like a trade-off.... Like we give you this, and we're gonna get something back in return. And you know, and it's always been like that, you know.

MS – It's like a barter system. So there's a barter system involving the US military bartering with different ETs, you know, you give us some technology, then we'll get our corporations' scientists to mass produce it ...

There have been several secret space program insiders who have come forward to disclose the existence of an extensive barter system with different extraterrestrial civilizations by a coalition of Earth nations. According to two of these insiders, who used the pseudonyms Spartan 1 & 2, the barter system is run out of the National Security Agency headquarters in Fort Meade, Maryland, and operates out of Antarctica.[88]

JP - It's not the US military; it's more the United States itself. I don't know how I can say that, but it's more like ...

MS - Military industrial Complex?

JP - I'm thinking that the military is all involved a lot, but yeah, you could say that.

MS – Okay, so your primary mission for entering that [underground] base was to just get this healing device. The Air Force officer would then take [it] to somewhere else for this kind of barter system, where this would be mass-produced for other ETs, and presumably that would be of overall benefit to the US, to the program?

JP - And this facility is connected to other facilities in the United States and South America, and Inner Earth. Well, other facilities that look just the same, there's a couple dozen of them around the United

States and on the Moon as well. We have these facilities on the Moon as well.

MS – Spaceports, big football stadium-size spaceports?

JP – Yes, you could say that there's a spaceport, but it's also from the Inner Earth. It connects to the Inner Earth as well. Inner Earth port with the spaceport, whatever you want to call it. It's a mixture of races that connect there, and it's like they have to check in and check out, and if they don't, there's like a penalty or something like that of them not coming back... We came back, and we gave the device to a scientist. They take it; they expect it. They make sure it works and they take it elsewhere, [something] to do with space. What I really want to share is that the organization that I saw made me think on the ride back how organized everything is, probably how long this has had to be happening for it to be that organized. Because for something to be that organized, it takes time to get all these connections of different ETs to come in and out, no racial [tensions], nobody talks back to nobody there. They go there, they do what they need to do, and they just get out. You don't see no arguing, no nothing. Everybody knows what to do, and they just want to get in there. So, personally, I think this has been going on for a long time, a couple of decades....

JP's acknowledgment of underground and undersea spaceports all over the US and around the planet being run by different ET races and Inner Earth civilizations raises an intriguing question. Which of the eleven US combatant commands would be responsible for dealing with these spaceports and the civilizations running them? These combatant commands are organized into seven geographical regions and four functions. The geographical regions include Northern Command (US, Canada, and Mexico); Southern Command (Central and Latin America); European Command (Europe, Russia, Turkey, and Asia Minor); Central Command (Middle East and Central Asia); Indo Pacific Command (East Asia, Indian subcontinent and Australasia); Africa Command. Space Command's jurisdiction starts at 60 miles (100 km) which is the international definition for the start of space. Then there are also four functional US combatant commands: Special Operations (special forces); Transportation Command (logistics); Strategic Command (nuclear weapons); and cyber command.

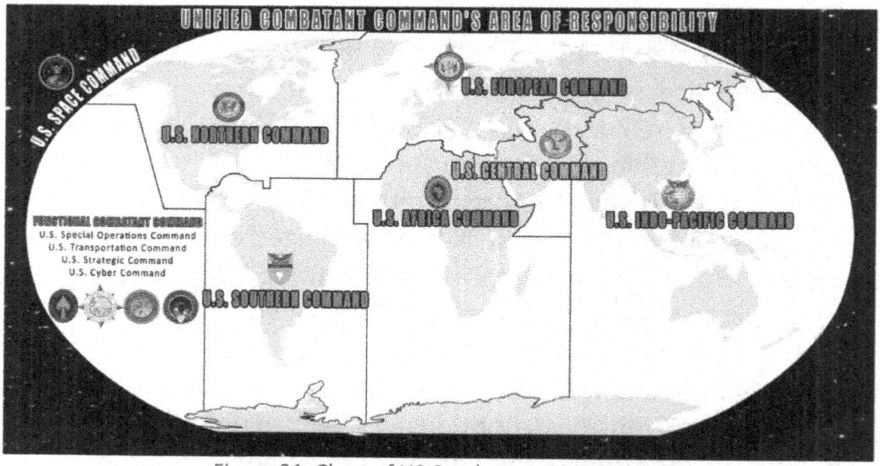

Figure 31. Chart of US Combatant Commands.

According to first-hand testimony from JP, Space Command is in charge of deep space missions involving contact with extraterrestrial life and exploring ancient artifacts found throughout our solar system. Significantly, Elena Danaan was told by her contacts with the Galactic Federation of Worlds that US Space Command was given primary responsibility for coordinating and representing Earth's nations in diplomatic negotiations with extraterrestrial civilizations.[89] However, who has responsibility over underground and undersea spaceports? While Space Command would be the logical choice in dealing not only with the civilizations running these, but also with the leaders of the sovereign states under which such bases are found, there are six other regional US combatant commands that would attempt to assert jurisdiction in a turf war with Space Command, which was only relaunched in September 2019. Evidence of such a turf war already happening can be found in the extraordinary criticism offered by General Glen VanHerck, head of NORAD and Northern Command, against his peer from US Space Command, General James Dickinson, on June 16, 2023. In an interview with *Breaking Defense*, VanHerck said that a May 31, 2023, announcement[90] from Space Command regarding taking over missile tracking responsibilities from Strategic Command was "incredibly misleading".[91] Van Herck went on to elaborate:

> To be clear, the missile defense mission has not changed... There's been no change to any of our missions, including the NORAD mission for missile warning, attack assessment, or any of those. And we're still tracking Santa Claus each year.... When you have somebody from Space Command saying: 'So, we've owned the missile warning mission since Space Command stood up,' is totally deceiving and incorrect.

The key to identifying what is behind VanHerck's unprecedented public criticism of a peer US combatant commander is his reference to "tracking Santa Claus". Santa Claus is a euphemism for UFOs or extraterrestrial spacecraft that have been monitoring NASA and military missions for decades, according to multiple sources.[92] The source of the problem is that the tracking of UFOs/ET vehicles from underground or underwater spaceports into and from space has been among the responsibilities of NORAD and Northern Command for decades. Now that responsibility is being transferred over to Space Command, VanHerck is unhappy with the loss of an important command responsibility. In short, NORAD and Northern Command is the loser of a turf war over who has ultimate responsibility for tracking or intercepting spacecraft from the underground and underwater spaceports in North America. My interview with JP was coming to a conclusion:

> MS - I know we're running out of time, so just to bring together everything that you've described.... On the one hand, you describe this mission to get this healing technology that's part of a barter system to trade between different ET groups. On the other hand, you talked about the Deep State creating or sending up their own probes and their own orbs to create confusion between the ... orbs that are coming from the space arks and the motherships that have a benign purpose—just to kind of like monitor the planetary situation, but the Deep States is sending up its own stuff or trying to provoke the orbs to create confusion. So overall, what can people expect over the next few months?
>
> JP - There's going to be a lot of sightings. I've been saying this is going to be a lot more whistleblowers and a lot more sightings, and people are going to realize that some of these orbs are ours, you know, and they're just back-engineered from ETs technology. So in the coming months you're going to see more news about UFOs, more news about communication with people, and look what's happening with Texas. You know, when was the last time you saw cows being mutilated? You know, I haven't heard that for almost, like what, 20 or 30 years, you know, I haven't heard of a cow being mutilated in the United States like that, you know. And it's happening all over. It's happening with pets. There's something that's happening that I'm hearing rumors of. There's like types of black holes opening

in different parts of the world, and different types of dimensions are opening, and entities are entering and coming out from these types of dimensions as well. So, we have to be vigilant as well.... These entities we don't know who they are or what they are. For me, those are the entities that I'm worried about. The one that comes in and out of existence. Yeah, I don't know if you want to share that with the public, but we're hearing a lot of rumors about that ... There's gonna be another thing. These ships are gonna pop out of existence, out of nowhere, you know. They're gonna just pop up out of nowhere. This is gonna be the same thing. Some of them are going to be real, and some of them are not going to be real. So, there's going to be a lot of confusion Doc, but I know we got a lot of positive people out there, and I know everything is going to be all right with us. We're gonna make the right decisions. I know that love covers everything, and if we share love and care, and if we share that we care about people, and that we care about everything around us, that we care about the energy, that everybody cares, everything will be okay... I want to illustrate [emphasize] that, you know, everything is going to be okay.

MS - Well, that's very important, you know, that we need to ... develop love, empathy, compassion more, and of course be very discerning not to go into a fear when all this confusion is created, and it's very, kind of like, opportune ... that we're having this discussion because I'm going to be doing my next webinar on May 13 [2023] on orbs, space arks, and motherships, so I'll try and clarify exactly what is going on....[93] There's positive and negative aspects to this, just as you've said, and the more we are in the place of calm, we're not getting into fear, that we understand that there's a phenomenon happening, that this is the way in which our civilization has chosen to wake up, that there's some kind of timetable involved for the arks, the probes, to all come out and the Deep state knows this so its strategy is to just confuse and put people into fear and as you're saying, the more you're in a positive place, more loving, more supportive of others, the more you're going to be able to get through this. So, I want to thank you again, JP, for sharing this latest mission and clarifying exactly what we can expect over the months ahead.

JP - Roger, that Doc, I appreciate you, and I can't wait for your webinar; it's gonna be interesting.

JP's visit to a large underground spaceport in the northern Alabama, Tennessee, and Mississippi region which hosts many visiting extraterrestrial civilizations and conducts extensive trade throughout our solar system using a barter system is stunning in its implications. The fact that indigenous technology projects on Earth produce sufficiently advanced devices that are valued and sought after by many extraterrestrials will be both a shock and comfort to many readers coming across this material for the first time. This underground spaceport is not the only one that JP would encounter in his covert missions. In a later chapter, I will examine his visit to an even larger spaceport in the South Atlantic, which is connected to an ancient civilization.

Chapter 11

Tracking Past Life Memories to Find Space Ark Crews

After completing his mission to an underground spaceport in the Alabama, Mississippi, and Tennessee border region, JP was taken back to a military base where he handed off to his superiors the healing technology that his team had been given. He then underwent a decontamination process and was instructed to go to a particular room where he was connected to an unknown technology. JP next began having a vision of a beautiful, partially submerged city on another planet. JP recognized himself and a woman dressed in white walking out of the city whom he immediately recognized.

In this interview, JP discusses how the technology that was used on him can stimulate and record past life memories.[94] He claims that this extraterrestrial technology is being used by the US military/Earth Alliance to track the crews of space arks that are activating all over the Earth. According to JP, the goal is to find crew members that can help activate different parts of space arks as, apparently, these areas remain dormant and inaccessible to those without the right DNA frequencies and consciousness. What follows is the transcript of the interview with grammatical corrections and my commentary.

Interview Transcript

Key: MS – Michael Salla; JP – Pseudonym for US Army Soldier

MS - I'm very happy to have JP back with us on Exopolitics Today. Welcome JP...

JP - Thankful to be here on Exopolitics [Today]. This is going to be an awesome moment.

MS – Well, I know people are very excited by your updates. People are really looking forward to learning more about what's really happening because there's so much silence out there, and ... you're in a privileged position to be able to report on current events that are happening involving the military and space commands. Not many people are able to talk about that, but you are. So I know people are very appreciative, as am I, that you're able to reveal details of these missions. So why don't you tell us about this latest mission? Maybe tell us, when did it happen and what happened?

JP - This happened after we had that mission when we came back from the cavern with the eight people [see Chapter 10]. Now I got the green light to tell you what happened, so that's why I'm sharing with you the other things that happened when we came back with the device. We came back, and they brung everybody to the base, the eight people, including the person that couldn't go inside. But you know he still came with us to the base. We got to the base [and] we stood in line. Always when we come back [from missions], we go through like a type of cleansing. When we connect with other types of ETs, it's protocol, you know, to put our clothes away; ... they clean them. They do draw blood [where] they check everybody when we go do these certain kinds of missions. What I found quite interesting is that they took us to this big hanger-type of room at the

> base, I actually brung you to, and I saw more people there.

In March 2023, JP gave my wife and I a guided tour of the military base where he is currently stationed and where the events transpired that he is describing in this chapter. When entering the base, the guard on duty recognized JP and they had a brief conversation as she checked his military ID badge before lettings us through. I have been asked not to publicly reveal the name of the base in order not to compromise JP, but this was proof of JP's active military service. JP described what happened after entering the large hangar-like room:

> JP - I saw a total of probably thirty [people], and you walk into [the big hangar-like room], and there's boxes, right. There are rooms [cubicles], but they're made [with], like, a titanium type of metal, and there's boxes in there. One of the commanding officers was like, "Hey, we want you in one of those rooms. We want to monitor you," and I'm like, "Wait, what kind of monitoring are you gonna do?" "Just go to that room!" So we each go into that room, and there's other like thirty people [in there]. Like, more people go into these rooms, and each room is connected to, like, a server. So, when you enter into this room, it's like a white box, right, and there's a seat in the middle. When you sit in the middle of the seat, you know, you relax; you lean back. It's like a recliner kind of seat, but it has a shape of a head.... It's like a metal plate that goes behind your head and then contracts to your head.
>
> You just lay back and you have somebody dressed in white, like a type of scientist.... Their face is covered, and they got gloves. They connect you, right. And when they connect you ... they put wires on, like

wire patches on your head. So, they sit you in this box. Some guy with white clothes, looking like a scientist [is] covering their face with a mask; they got some goggles, they got gloves, and they sit you [down] and they connect you to these cables. But this cable is connected to a hub. All these boxes are connected to a type of computer room that is on the upstairs [level] that people are monitoring. I'm, like, asking myself, "Man, why do they have me here? What seems to be the problem?" And then in the middle of this place where all these boxes are there's a center core. The center core is made of liquid—it's really like a shiny type of liquid. It looked like mercury. It's like a bluish color so you can see it moving up and down, like if it was, you know, those lights that you see when you go north in the skies. What do you call those lights?

MS -The Aurora Borealis.

JP - It looks like an Aurora Borealis inside this tube, and it's quite interesting. I thought it was like lighting for the room and all that. It looked kind of cool. It's actually an energy source ... that connects to the boxes that each person is at. In some boxes, you can hear people screaming, like not in pain, but like these boxes they put you in this trance. They put you in this deep sleep. And then when you sleep in this deep trance in this box, [it] is actually monitoring your past lives. So, it's monitoring all the lives you have lived. I don't know how people are going to take this, but we have lived multiple lives in in the past, and sometimes we come back.... With this technology that they have, they can see [your] past through this device that's connected to this recliner-type of chair that's connected to your brain.

Because they can see the brain patterns through a screen that is on top of that [upper] floor I was telling you about that they do monitoring on.

And everybody was going through this trance at the same time. I remember closing my eyes, and I remember being on a planet. This planet was beautiful; it had valleys, it had grass, and it moved in synchronicity. I remember seeing in the distance a city coming out from the ocean, from this planet's ocean. It looked like it was built [from] under the ocean up because you can only see the part that's on top of the ocean. I remember me calling you and telling you about this situation; about this "dream" that I had. It was a dream that was activated by this recliner-type of chair that they put you in. They try to extract, not information, but bits and pieces of what you have done in the past. And it's possible to have this [done] because your blood is really information; your brain is also information. By extracting your blood, they can tell a lot about your past ancestors in your past life, like quantum computing. And they have technology that will overwhelm you.

So in this, like, trance, I was in this dream state. I remember seeing somebody that you know. I remember calling you and telling you about this. I saw her wearing white. I saw her looking at me, and I felt that she was part of this world and that she was telling me, "Hey, come over here, let's go; we need to talk. Something serious has happened." I remember going to her, but I don't remember seeing my body. I tried to look at my hands, but I couldn't look at my hands. I tried to look at my legs, but I couldn't see my legs. She was calling me towards her, and this planet was beautiful, beautiful, beautiful.

I called you and I told you about this "dream," and I felt, like, at peace telling you this. They gave me the green light to tell you because, really, sometimes they don't want [me] to talk about the technology that we have because the technology that we have is really advanced. There's a lot of ET races that use the same technology... It's like a web that connects [us] to each other. And this technology, there's other ET races that use it, and they connect with each other. So there's other ET people that come to that particular building, and they get into these boxes, and that's how they communicate to the world or [see] their past lives. Because for most ETs, everything that's happening is happening at once. Different times, different ages. I don't know how you're going to take this, but everything is happening at one time or probably in different dimensions. Everything is happening at one time. Like, for some of these advanced ETs, time does not exist. Time is a construct. So, what do you think about that, Doc?

MS - All right. Well, just to kind of recapitulate that because that was quite a lot of information there. So after the mission that you did where you went to this underground base and saw all these ET craft and personnel walking around somewhere in the Alabama, Mississippi, and Tennessee region, you went back to the military base that you took me to when I visited with my wife back in March, [2023] ... You took me to that base, I know the [name of the] base.... So you went back to the base and after you cleaned up, [you] went through whatever

> decontamination process, then you went into this room or into this building, and you were asked to go through this technology. And it involves people being able to access their past life memories. And so this technology enabled you to remember or [it] brought up these memories of a past life in this ancient world. And you saw someone that I know. Shall we mention her name?
>
> JP - Yes, I'll give it to you.
>
> MS – Okay. All right. JP says that he saw Elena Danaan on this world, this ancient world with the beautiful city that is partially submerged and something to do with the tides. It's coming in and out, but [you] saw this city, and [you] saw her in this past life memory. And all this happened after the mission [when] you're at the base ...

It's not unusual for places on Earth to experience tides of up to 53 feet (16 meters) which happens in the Bay of Mundy, Canada.[95] Therefore, it would not be unusual for exoplanets to experience similar or even higher tides, making it possible for a submerged city to experience tidal conditions similar to what JP described.

> JP - I didn't have the green light to tell you that part. I was not begging, but I kept nagging [my superiors] about it because it was quite interesting. And it connects to a lot of things that we go through in this community—synchronicity—you know. It was a nice experience. This device that we had was made for a planet that was a type of water planet. I thought that it would be one of the planets in our solar system, but it ... was another [solar system's] planet. So, I think they were trying to extract why I went to

the mission and if I [had] ever been on this planet in this life or any other life that I lived. So it happened to be that I have been on this planet. See, nobody chooses who goes on these missions. There's somebody higher up that chooses the people.

MS - So let's just be clear here. When you say who chooses to go on these missions, you're talking about the mission that you just did to the spaceport in that Alabama area. That mission you did was chosen by someone and ...

JP - I don't even know [who].

MS - You don't even know ... [who selected you] to do that mission, and then afterward, you're brought back to the base, and you go ... into this [box] technology, and you remember a past life experience, and you remember seeing Elena Danaan. So, you weren't able to tell me, the last time we talked, ... when you reported about the mission. But now you've been given permission to do so. What happened when you told Elena?

JP - I texted her and I said, "Hey, I had a dream with you." I did not tell her it was induced, you know, by the scientists. When I say scientists, there's a lot of civilian people that work on military bases that work for certain companies that are not related to the military. So when I say scientists, I'm not really saying military personnel. I'm really saying civilians that work for the military. I just want to make that clear to the public. There's a lot of ETs and civilians that work for the military.... A lot of people don't comprehend, like what they bring in, and how they help humanity to keep on going. So when I was

> telling Elena, I did not tell her ... it was induced by a certain technology. I told her, "Hey, I had a vision; I had a dream; I had a dream with you. And [in] this dream, I saw you dressed in white!" And she texted me back, and she asked me, "Wait a second, what color hair did I have?"... She gave me three options. She gave me blonde, I think she also gave me redhead, and then she gave me brown hair. I said, "Brown hair; I saw you with brown hair." She's like, "Oh, my God!" She felt like, ... a wow feeling. She told me that she was there; that she remembers that planet, and [that] I was just describing the planet. The planet has a city that is coming out from the water, and I told her that the city has a moon that is really dense. And [the moon] has a lot of metal that creates a greater gravitational. And when it gets close to the planet, or when it's above the city—because it has a greater gravitational pull than our Moon [does] on Earth—it grabs the tide; the tidal wave, [and] it makes it bigger. Because of that, this civilization that lives on this planet has the technology and has a type of metal that ... they bring to the planet to build these mega-structures of buildings that can withstand the gravitational pull of the tidal waves that are getting pulled by the moon.

In volume one of *US Army Insider Missions*, JP described three large underwater domes in the Bermuda Triangle area that could withstand the powerful ocean pressures using advanced shield technologies that protect the domed cities.[96] JP described meeting the inhabitants who were tall, Nordic-looking humans, suggesting it was a colony of an off-planet civilization that had long ago established a presence on Earth. It's therefore likely that similar underwater domed cities can be found on other water planets that are designed to withstand extreme tidal forces exerted by their moons.

JP - So I was telling her [Elena Danaan] that, and she was like, "Oh my God, I feel like crying." She said that ... I really described the planet that one of her past lives was part of, and she's beginning these downloads, and we [are] connected. And I felt like, "Wow! So we are connected!" You know, the universe puts people in your life to connect [with]. I remember when we were in Daytona [Florida], and we were walking on the beach, we were holding our shoes, and then she looks up [at] the ocean. And then she just lifts up her hand and points to the direction where the ark [is located], and I'm like, "Wow, she knows, she knows the exact direction!" And I think I remember showing you on a map, [and I said,] "Look, she pointed this way. And look, it goes straight to the ark!" She has a connection and I know a lot more people do have a [similar] connection. And this is going to happen more and more. There's going to be a lot of people connecting with each other, "Oh, I remember this. Oh, I remember that."

Once this technology will be available for the public, it will come with healing technologies ... as well—that type of healing that when you lay down ... it heals you and will [age] reverse some organs on your body that will make you live a little bit longer, to probably 150 years old or even longer depending on your past history of what other family members [you] have in your life and all that. So everything is coming into play. These ships are coming in from different solar systems or coming from Jupiter and dropping these UAPs; these UFOs; these drones. It's stunning all of this, and I think that's bringing people together as well, with these experiences. And we're getting to see that on the news. We're getting to see

Figure 32. Illustration of craft JP arrived in to meet the dark-haired woman from a partially submerged city. Permission JP and Elena Danaan.

this everywhere that we're looking at more people [that] are talking about these experiences, and "all this has happened to us," and the exopolitics [associated with] this. The politics of this is really important because we just got a new King in Europe.

MS – Well, before we talk about King Charles III and the coronation, I just wanted to back up a little bit. Now, I find it very interesting that you had that memory brought up by this technology—that someone within the programs wanted you to go through this technology. They wanted to learn more about your past [life] memories. I find it very curious that of all the memories of all the past lives that they could have brought up, they brought up one where you recall seeing a brown-haired female by this futuristic city and you got the [realization] that this was Elena Danaan. And she later confirmed that she had a similar past life memory. So, I find it very curious that was something that was brought up in that particular memory set. So it was like someone wanted to learn about your past and your connection with Elena Danaan, and I find that very interesting.

JP - We went to this port, right, and we were given this technology to take with us. Personally, I don't know who gave it to us. I remember from a distance seeing a Nordic type, but we did not get close enough to connect to that particular ET or person. I remember seeing from a distance this ET giving this device to us, to one of the guys. They brung it back. We wrapped it up, and they gave us the directions "Hey... [be careful]. This device cannot vibrate a lot." So, we have this box that you put in stuff and [supported] with gimbals, this box stays the way it is. So, we put that device inside this box, and the car can drive sideways, or it could ... do turns, but this device stays stationary because of this particular box. It's a technology that we have that some missiles that we carry also go on these particular boxes that keep the missile stationary. And then, any vibration does not affect the missile. And anytime it moves, it stays the way it is. We also put different devices on these particular boxes. I can't tell you who makes these types of boxes or [where the] technology it comes from, but I know we have them. And we run this [box technology] back to the base. I took the box and gave it to one of the scientists that we came back to. And with that, I felt ... my hairs go up when I touched this device. I felt, like, a connection.... You really have to tell the scientists or the people that we give the device to what you feel or if you have a connection, or what's going on when you give these devices back. So when I said [I felt a connection to the box] that's when they, not just me, [but] everybody else [as well], they took us to this other place where I'm telling you about—the rooms and all that.

MS - So this was that healing device that you got from that underground base? Or your team was handed that healing device to be taken off-world? But when you handled it, it did something to you?

JP – Yes. And ... you have to be honest, you know. You have to tell them, "Hey, I felt this and feel that," because everything goes through ... a type of cleansing because they decont... how you say decontam...

MS – Decontamination?

JP - Decontamination. And there's three more devices. So, we have one, [and] there's two more devices.

MS - When you say three more devices, now you're only given one device from the people in the underground base? Where do the other two come from?

JP - We have one device. The other two are somewhere on this planet. I do not know where. These devices are really powerful. You could use them in the right way or in the wrong way.

MS – Okay, so this device you brought back is connected to two other devices around the planet that haven't been found, or someone [else] is in control of them. And they're all very powerful.

JP – Well, we do know the location of one device. We have control of that device, and we gave it [to the ETs], and it's already off-planet. It's already heading towards the other planet or already there. But there's another one that is inside, [an] Inner Earth civilization. They have it. One of the kings, they're in control of it. And then there's another device that we're thinking is around Europe, somewhere around Europe.

MS - Okay, all right. So all of those devices are there, yeah, [in] different locations, but the one you brought back to the base [and] you handled, it triggered you. Then you go up into this room—you call it a box—and you have this vision, this memory of being on this [other] planet. So yeah, I was just very curious as to, you know, why it was you [who] brought up that [memory]? Why it was that you actually had a vision of this place and Elena Danaan is involved in that? ... Does someone want to know about one of your past lives and your connection with her. Or was this just accidental?

JP - It's not accidental. They're actually hearing this conversation right now. They know that I interacted with you. I interacted with other people; with Alex [Collier], with Elena, with Jean Charles [Moyen], with Tony [Rodrigues]—with a lot of people that we connected to, and [they have] been doing major monitoring and protection for everybody. They know that we're all connected [in] some ways.... Something is connecting us together—with you also. They're monitoring everything that we do. It's how it is. We can't get away from that.

MS – Okay.... You're part of these covert programs. You're... currently active Army. And so they want to know about your past lives, and they're wanting to know about past life connections with others that are associated with the kind of information you're releasing. So it sounds like they're doing [an] intelligence gathering operation to find out about how ... the people you just mentioned are all connected through these past life associations ... which makes a lot of sense to me.... I know that there are connections.... I haven't explored them because ... it's not so relevant to me at this point. But obviously, it's relevant to those that are monitoring you and those that are green-lighting you to share this information with me, and then me making it public.

JP - Because, as you also remember, that experience Elena had in this mountain when she met this officer.

MS - General Glen VanHerck, the four-star [general]. Well actually, she didn't meet him. It was ... her Nordic contact or her Galactic Federation contact ... Thor Han. So it was Thor Han who met with General Glenn VanHerck. But she saw it through his eyes.

The mountain meeting that JP referred to happened on January 7, 2023, at Raven Rock Mountain Complex, which is located in southwestern Pennsylvania.[97] According to Elena Danaan, Thor Han showed her details of a meeting he had with General Glenn VanHerck, head of NORAD and US Northern Command, where Thor Han handed over a digital storage device with a detailed disclosure plan worked out by the Galactic Federation of Worlds and the Earth Alliance. Thor Han also shared what he saw at a spaceport under the Raven Rock complex where a number of spacecraft were parked, including his own. Danaan's report is consistent with what JP has witnessed at different spaceports hidden in underground locations around the US.

> JP – Okay. So they're monitoring her as well as they're monitoring everybody else on these situations, because now as you can see, you know, all these investigations on UAPs, on UFOs, different scientists are coming out saying, "Hey ... we have motherships coming our way." It's getting more interesting, Doc.... People are gonna realize that all these experiences that we're having, you know, it's gonna come out that, hey, you know, we have these motherships coming. But these people going through these experiences—they're really going through these experiences. And there's other people that are red-lighted to not say anything about it because maybe their experience is affecting somebody that's connected to them. Yeah. So we were in this room [where] I had that [memory] extraction, and when I got out ... I asked one of the scientists, ... "Hey, what did you guys just do? I had a vision. I had a dream." This really made me have a dream that I felt that I was there. They say, "Yea. No, we're just checking you out. Don't worry about it. We're just making sure everything is connected, and we'll be monitoring that. And we're probably going to call you again to do this experiment.

Regarding JP's comment about motherships coming our way, JP was referring to scientists such as Prof. Avi Loeb and Dr. Sean Kirkpatrick, who co-wrote a paper hypothesizing the arrival of extraterrestrial motherships that are releasing probes as a possible explanation for the rapid increase in orb sightings.[98] Loeb and Kirkpatrick were not, however, among the scientists associated with the memory extraction technology that JP was exposed to.

> MS - So I just want to kind of clarify something. So those technicians or scientists that are monitoring you while you're having that experience and remembering this, are they seeing it as well? I mean, does the technology enable them to see it, or do they have to do a debriefing with you because it sounds like they somehow are recording it?
>
> JP - They're recording it.... They have a screen that shows everything in black and white or inverted colors, and the machine inverts the colors back. And everything that you see through this monitoring, they can see as well.
>
> MS – Interesting. Oh wow, so ... they're recording your past life events, but ... they're specifically choosing events where you're interacting with people that are part of this kind of circle that is being formed. And of course, Elena Danaan is one. But you know the next time they could do it with say someone else from that circle like Jean Charles [Moyen]....
>
> JP - You, Tony [Rodrigues] —[everybody is connected] with somebody, and everything is done with frequencies too, you know. They can connect with anybody with frequency; with vibration.
>
> MS - It's very interesting because I know people have talked about starseeds incarnating on Earth, and, you know, we're here for missions. But what hasn't been talked about so far is 'star groups'

coming here. In other words, people who are linked in some way, in some other world, you know. That they are ETs on another world, and they decide, "Oh, we're going to go to Earth, and as a group, we're going to do this particular mission." It sounds as though the people that are in charge of you as you do these covert missions ... are now interested in gathering intel on this star group that you're linked into.

Brad Steiger was among the first to research the phenomenon of extraterrestrials incarnating on Earth as "starseeds" or "star people." In his 1976 book, *Gods of Aquarius,* Steiger defined star people as: "humans who come from a special gene pool linked to visits by extraterrestrials."[99] A similar definition of a starseed is: "an extraterrestrial soul who has come to Earth to help humanity."[100] In the *Law of One* book series, written from 1981 to 1984, a similar term, "Wanderer," was introduced for extraterrestrials incarnating on Earth.[101] Steiger, *The Law of One,* and other sources have discussed the various traits or personality profiles of star people, starseeds, or wanderers, and focus on individuals and their missions that have a benevolent goal. A star group can therefore be defined as multiple starseeds that choose to collectively incarnate to perform an overall mission to help humanity's evolution. From what JP has revealed, it's clear that the US military has been studying the starseed and star group phenomenon for some time.

JP - And there's particular people that left the star group that will come back and be part of the star group, and connect again. And let me tell you that it's scary. It's scary sometimes for us to be a part of this magnificent thing, you know. To put this information out is hard. When you get these downloads, you know, and there's some people that are part of these groups, and they get interrogated, they [say], "You better not ... [reveal sensitive] information or we're going to get rid of you, and we're going to get rid of your family, and we're going to raid your house." And I'm talking about the black hats. And they really scare these people that made it [this] far on giving [out] information. And they [the black hats] really got into their [starseeds] heads, and they feel like they're not protected anymore. And that those particular people feel like they're getting shot from everywhere. Then they exclude themselves from everybody else, you know. [It's] sad when that happens, you know. But these people are getting attacked in the spiritual [dimensions and] in real ways to turn it around for them. It's tough, you know, but when there's a group, we're strong together.... When we give information, and there's synchronicity, it's kind of awesome because people are going to realize that, you know, we're connected and we're telling it how it is.

MS – Yeah, it is very interesting ... I've never heard of this before, you know, that technology exists to kind of track past lives—not only of one person but of others that they're associated with and that they're able to kind of like trigger those recollections. That's... very revealing, and also alarming as well that they could ... track us all in terms of our past life connections to one another.

JP - Know that this type of technology has been out for ages, Doc. Like when we enter into the arks. The arks know who you are, and because you enter the ark, it activates certain things. Why it activates [is] because it remembers your DNA; it remembers who you are, who you were, when you're interacting with the arks, you know. This technology has been out for a long time....

MS - Well, that leads to another question. I mean, you've been on the arks, you know, quite a few times. Both before you joined the military and after you joined the military, you've been on arks. So, I'm sure at some point that they've worked out that ... you are associated with one of the arks and that it's very likely that the people that you are working with or collaborating with are also associated with the arks. So it's like those using this technology on you—they're trying to find out who are the crew of the arks.

JP – Yeah, exactly. Who are the crews of the arks, and how can they get everybody together to probably go at once to these arks to see what happens? What happens when everybody comes at once in the ark—when everything is activated at once? Because there's certain spots when you go into the ark that only I can activate. But there are certain spots ... on the ark, I can't activate. There's other people that [can] activate it. So how can I put this? ... Sometimes when you dream, sometimes it's your past lives that you have [dreamed about]. It's a construct of what you lived before. But it puts [that memory with] where you're living in the modern time [today]. So sometimes you feel like, ... "Oh, man, it's a weird dream." But it's probably a past life that you have lived....

MS - That is very interesting that they are using this technology to track down the crews of the space arks. Now, of course, ... the white hats or the Earth Alliance, they're probably wanting to help these crews reconnect. And they're very interested to see what happens with the arks. But, you know, obviously, that's information that could be used by the other side for the opposite [purpose].

JP – Yeah, exactly.

MS - Very curious that this is ... is happening.

JP – Yeah. What do you think about the King [Charles III], being king now?

MS – Yeah, I wanted to ask you about that. I think that it's a significant development. I know you talked about King Charles in relation to the seeds that were taken from that Tree of Life in that underground Ant civilization; that they were taken to England by the orders of the king or the new king. And then they were taken to Nippur, to the city where this ancient Anunnaki god-king Aruna is in hibernation, and we never followed up. What happened to the seeds after that? ... Somehow, the king, King Charles, is involved in all of that. So, yeah, what does it mean now with the coronation?

JP - More power. Long live the King, Doc.... I can't say anything else about that. Maybe you can elaborate on, "Long live the King?"

MS – Well, I know there was a remote viewing done of the coronation by the Cryptoviewing [team]. This is the same group of people that did the remote viewing of you going into the Space Ark in the Atlantic Ocean [see *US Army Insiders* Volume 1]. But they did a remote viewing just now that's just come out of the coronation, and they said quite clearly

> that actually there were two ceremonies.... One is the public ceremony that everyone sees with all the pomp, all the splendor, you know. It all looks grand and great, but there's also a second ceremony which is more of an occult [event]—a secret ceremony which involves blood sacrifice. We don't want to go into the details of what happens in that second ceremony, but that's where the real power is handed off. That King Charles [it's] not just him being coronated as the head of the British Empire, of the British Isles, but he becomes the king of this occult network, which is centered in London, the British royal family.... He's given power as a very senior figure in the occult. Now I don't know what relationship that has with the Pindar, because apparently the Pindar is connected to the Draco Reptilians. And the Pindar was taken off the planet. But with the British royal family, because that's a kind of human lineage, maybe [King Charles] is like the new occult leader of the planet ... in the absence of the Pindar. Maybe the King, in this kind of secret occult ceremony, where he goes through the process, is now the new occult leader.... I'm just speculating there. But to me, there's something very significant about him...

The remote viewing of King Charles III by a team of five remote viewers was announced by Dick Allgire in a video released on May 5, 2023. In it, Allgire described a secret occult ceremony that was like:

> ... the final scene of *Raiders of the Lost Ark* meets *Eyes Wide Shut*. We had tremendous specific detail that shows we were actually remote viewing this event. There's enough verifiable information sketches in our data to show that we were on

> [target]. But what was the power that really is transferred? ... How is power imbued in physical objects? How is this transported through time and transmuted and put into a physical being?[102]

Allgire and his remote viewing team identified that the Coronation's secret ceremony involved a genuine transfer of occult power using symbols and objects. The Pindar has been discussed by several insiders and witnesses. David Icke wrote about the Pindar in *The Biggest Secret* after interviewing a former participant in Satanic occult ceremonies, Arizona Wilder. Icke wrote:

> Pindar means 'Penis of the Dragon'... Arizona says that Pindar, like all the reptilians when they shape-shift, has very powerful hypnotic eyes (the 'evil eye' of legend) and at sacrifices the victims face is turned to Pindar at the moment of death for him to steal the person's soul or energy through this 'evil eye' magnetic process.... Pindar attends the major Satanic ceremonies in Europe and then flies to California for the rituals there.[103]

JP next referred to Charles's consort, the new Queen Camilla but hesitated in saying more about what he was told about her and Charles:

> JP - That new Queen, right ...
>
> MS - Camila Bowles?
>
> JP - I don't really know her past history. But well, 'long live the king,' I can't...
>
> MS - Well, let's finish up there. I want to thank you, JP, [for] agreeing to do this update.

JP - No problem. It was a pleasure. And let it be blessed with everything that we do and share love with everybody.

Regarding JP's repeated references to "long live the king," what JP is doing is drawing attention to the stolen seeds from the Tree of Life taken to England under the orders of King Charles for the purpose of secret age rejuvenation experiments/rituals and prolonging his power. The theft of the seeds was discussed in our interview about JP's second mission to the Ant People in an underground area of Florida (see Chapter 2). JP said he couldn't reveal more due to possible retaliation, so we must figure it out for ourselves. My guess is that JP is alluding to the fact that King Charles III and Queen Camilla are literally using newly acquired ancient technology (the seeds) for age extension, and increasing their power in the process. The seeds also appeared to be an important ingredient that was used for the occult transfer of power, according to that Allgire's remote viewing team had observed.

Chapter 12

Visit to a Spaceport Under a South Atlantic Island

On May 26, 2023, JP completed a mission to a massive spaceport located under an unknown island in the South Atlantic Ocean. He was taken to the island by a flying triangle spacecraft (TR-3B) from aboard US Navy ship traveling in the Gulf of Mexico. To JP's surprise, he was met and accompanied by a close relative whose first name is Alex. JP and Alex traveled down an elevator from the surface of the island to the underground spaceport, which he said was significantly larger than the spaceport he witnessed during his last mission to an area in the Mississippi, Alabama, and Tennessee border region. JP and Alex were involuntarily held overnight in a cell similar to a metal box before meeting with a 1200-year-old Nordic-looking member of an underground civilization. They were told about plans for the civilization to begin revealing itself through its spacecraft and by bringing more surface dwellers down to visit them. JP was given a small crystal device through which he could see Earth's future, and was shown futuristic cities in a pristine environment but without the Moon. After the mission, JP phoned Alex but he denied any memory of what had happened. JP speculates that Alex may not want to be part of the disclosure process or was being watched. What follows is the transcript of the interview with grammatical corrections and my commentary.[104]

Interview Transcript

Key: MS – Michael Salla; JP – Pseudonym for US Army Soldier

MS - We're back again with JP who has returned from another mission. So welcome JP to Exopolitics Today.

JP - How you doing, Doc? I'm glad to be here every time, bringing information to you that I'm allowed to say and the public to know.

MS - So that's great. Well, I know the last mission report you did, we talked about you going through some technology and having past life memories recorded, and you said something about "long live the king," King Charles. I believe you said it in an ironic manner, you know, to allude to the fact that there were these seeds from the Tree of Life that was stolen, and this was involved in age rejuvenation. I thought you were just being ironic saying that phrase because it was just after the coronation of King Charles III. But ... some people were ... a little freaked out by that. So [do] you want to just elaborate on what you meant when you said "long live the king?"

JP - I'm not gonna say as much, Doc, about that. But ... when it was you, Elena, Alex Collier, and I, where we're talking after the [2023 Orlando] conference, we talked a lot about that. Sometimes, we do have to be careful how we talk. And sometimes, you can't say anything wrong or negative towards any entity or anybody. That's how I follow things. That's how I do it.... I don't desire negativity on anybody. I know a lot of people do wrong on Earth and in other places and on different realms, and I do not desire negative ... on anybody, whatever that person [is] or whoever does something wrong. They're gonna receive what [is] deserved to them, if you understand what I'm trying to say.... It's always good, you know, from a spiritual standpoint, to always think positive and say things that people understand in different ways, if you understand what I'm trying to say.

MS - I do and I think that's a very important point. And yes, that was a round table discussion we did back, I think it was October 23 of 2022, and we talked about the seeds from the Tree of Life and why they were stolen, and what that had to do in relationship to King Charles.[105] I fully understand and support what you're saying because ... there are a lot of people out there that name names that expose those doing wrongdoing. And for them, that's fine, you know. That's their mission; that's their task, but that's not your mission.... Your mission is to just reveal the contacts, the experiences ... and what you're doing. And that's your mission. If you start naming names of people doing all these terrible things out there, then you attract the karmic retribution for that ...

JP – Exactly. Even if you say something positive, you're attracting the negative, you know. That's how it is nowadays.... I know a lot of people understand, and a lot of people have been following my different missions and contacts that we, you know, have done together and all that. And a lot of people are just joining and just hearing it for the first time and not understanding the past. That's why I encourage people to go through Exopolitics.org and listen to stories, you know, that we have done maybe in the past two or three years. You know, this goes way back or even longer, but ... sometimes it's understandable what people think.... I'm glad we're here clarifying our last interview.

MS – Yes, that is helpful for some people who didn't get it.... You were being ironic by saying that. I don't even say it.... I'm a citizen of Australia, and ... our country doesn't have a President. We [now] have King Charles, but I don't say "long live the king" because I don't consider him my king—just because I know something of what's really going on.... We're really here to discuss your missions and your involvement in these covert operations. And you have another mission update to share with us. You want to tell us ... when did this happen? This recording [date] is May 28, [2023]. So when did this mission happen?

JP - Two days ago.

MS - Can you tell us what happened on May 26, which would have been a Friday?

JP – Yeah. I came back from Tampa. I was over there for a little bit. I was going back and forth, visiting friends. On my way back—it's like a five-hour trip around there—in the middle of getting back over here, I pulled over and fell asleep in the parking lot resting area. There was a white van [that] came up, parked behind me, and they say, "Let's go!" I said, "Hey, is my car gonna get towed?" [They say] "No, it's not going to get towed. Don't worry about it, let's go. We need you, okay, now let's go meet him. We've been following you since Tampa." If everybody knows Tampa, you know it's where my first experiences happened and all that; one of the first experiences that I started talking to you about [in 2014]. Again, I encourage people to look at the past of stories that we have been putting out and all that. You probably put [in] the links like you always do, Doc, I appreciate it.[106] I got picked up by the van, and I noticed a familiar face there. It was quite weird to see that familiar face. This was a family member, and he was in the van with me. He's like, “Just keep it as it is. You know who I am, and just don't say nothing.” I said, "Bro, but how is it possible that you're doing this as well?" He said, "Bro, man, I've been trying to hold it in, and I can't, I can't anymore. So I asked to be part of the mission with you." I'm like, "Oh crap. Okay.” So, I was surprised to see him there because he's related to me, you know.

MS - Can you clarify something? ... You've told me about some of your family members; is this one of the family members that actually is serving in the military?

JP - No, it's not. But he has family that is serving in the military. He was suited up, and he said, “Suit up.” And I saw I saw his rank, and it was a higher rank than me. I'm like, “Bro, but why you never told me?” Well, he's not my bro, but, you know, I call my family members, you know, like bro and all that. He's like, “Let's go, we gotta go!” So, we took the van, and we drove like 45 minutes. And [then] we took a black helicopter. We flew up, and we [then] landed on a boat. It was a big boat; I can't tell you the name of the boat or people [would] know what [its] location [is]. It's a big boat, a big, big boat. We landed [on the boat], and I said, “Hey, where are we going?” I can give you his name. That's the only thing I can give. His name is Alex.

MS - So Alex is the name of your relative who actually isn't serving in the military but had a higher rank than you.... For the mission, he had a higher rank than you.

JP – Well, when I say rank, there's different levels of when you go to these missions. You don't really follow the rank of the military, but you follow a different rank system. It's a rank system [based] on experience and what you have been through. So I was quite surprised when I saw him with a higher rank than me in this particular mission.

MS – Okay, that's a very important point because that is something I've come across before. William Tompkins was a second-class seaman, but because of his expertise and his abilities, even though he was an 18-year-old second-class seaman, he did these covert missions. And when he was on these covert missions, he had the rank of lieutenant commander. That was back ... around 1943 when he was serving out of Naval Air Station, San Diego. So, his regular rank in the US Navy was as a second-class seaman, but when he was doing these missions, he was taking briefing packets to different bases, and he had the rank of lieutenant commander. So, it sounds like your relative, Alex, had much more experience, and so he had this higher rank [for the mission].

JP - So yeah. Well [what] we also need to understand, Doc, I know you're familiar with this, but ... everybody that goes through these programs they go through these 5 years and back, 10 years and back, 15 years and back, 20 years and back. They gained rank on these years and back, and back and forward. And they gain experience, and they

> gain knowledge—more knowledge than other people. So, I know Tony [Rodrigues] is more familiar with that. He knows more about that information.
>
> MS - Tony Rodrigues did a "20 and back," and he served on ... the planetoid Ceres, for 13 years as a slave, as part of the Dark Fleet merchant ship [fleet].

The point that JP has raised here is an important one. There are many individuals who claim to have participated in "20 and back" programs, whose memories are wiped and they are age-regressed before being returned to civilian life to live out ordinary lives. It's widely assumed that their service is over. But what JP is saying is that they can be reactivated, have their memories restored, and then perform new missions. In such cases, they will regain the memories of all the years they served in their covert missions, thereby leading them to have a high rank. This appears to have been the case with Alex.

> JP - So yeah, there's "20 and back," there's "15 and back", "10 and back", "5 and back." There's a lot of different [number of] years and back [programs], if you get that into your brains.... It's amazing the technology that we have, you know, and it's not out [in the public domain] yet. So, we were on this boat, and they lined us up. There's like twenty other soldiers lined up. Everybody had a mask [on]. I had a mask myself, and we were dressed in like a grayish uniform type of, like sweat piece ... uniforms, and we had gloves. I remember that ... on the ship, there was a triangular craft that was hovering over us. This triangular craft ... came down to the level right next to where the helicopter was, ... right next to the ship over the water. It hovered, and a door came out like the shape of an 'L', and then it spread out and it was on the ship. And it was ... cool because this TR-3B

was following the same movements of the ship in the waves when it connected the L-shape, you know, ramp to it. So it was floating with the ship and connected with the movement of the waves; the movement of the ship. So, I noticed that it connected when it touched the ship. It started doing safety movements. But it was stationary, and the ship was moving. We were watching it coming in. So that was quite interesting. I [had] never seen that before. It came down. I'm gonna explain it one more time. It came down, it connected to the ship, and then it started doing the same movement. So we saw that, and then everybody started going [into the TR-3B] ... It was a bigger TR-3B. It was huge. I noticed that, and I said, "Hey, where the hell are we going? Do you know where we're going?" Nobody knew where we're going. And we sat down and everyone was looking at each other like really scared ...

MS – Yeah, I just wanted to ... repeat that for people that are trying to follow what's happened. So you land on the ship. You're taken there by a Black Hawk helicopter. You land; there's twenty personnel all there, and you're given these OCPs—the ... [Operational] Camouflage Pattern uniforms—you put those on. What other equipment were you given for this mission before you got on to the TR-3B that flew up there?

JP - We did not have any weapons when we went on the triangular ship. They had weapons there for us, already connected to the ships that were part of the inventory of the ship as well. The ship carries a certain inventory that is for the ship itself and for the occupants. When they give you these weapons, they [are] from the TR-3B [inventory]. I don't know if I ever told you this, but they ... when you touch them, everybody's connected. It's like a radio. The grip can sense the heartbeat of your hand and your heart pressure and all that. So, they'll know by you carrying this weapon, and it has a type of GPS. So this weapon that they give you is ...

MS - Like, a smart gun?

JP - Well, it's a really smart, smart gun. It has a kind of sound weapon that you can manipulate the sound to it, and you can make anybody throw up. A second type of ray gun ... you can see in the infrared [with it].... You can see the heat.... You can see when you shoot it. It's like a laser, but it's not like a Star Wars laser type of gun. It's different from [an] M4; it's [got] no bullets involved. It has a battery pack, and this battery pack lasts for days on it and ...

MS - Is it like a microwave gun where you know where you have different settings on it.... [With] one setting you can make people sick, another setting ....

JP – Yeah.

MS - You can make them kind of run because they get [tremendous] heat or whatever?

JP - Or make people turn crazy, in a way like madness.... When it attacks the pineal gland, it changes everything. It's insane technology. It's crazy. We have naval ships ...

MS - I mean, you can literally turn people into mindless zombies. Is that what you're saying?

JP – No, not zombies, but ... they'll just become insane—like, screaming and running all around the place to give their location out.... Say [for example] we're in a wooded area [and] we just spray this weapon out. [Then] we could just hear people screaming out of nowhere, and we know their exact location. It's a cool weapon. I just hope people don't use it in the wrong way. We just have it for protection. So we took the TR-3B, and we landed on this island. I don't know what island this was. It was closer, and I knew it was a cold island. You could see a lot of buildings, military personnel working and all that. This is somewhere in the Atlantic, south Atlantic when you take off from Puerto Rico [in the direction of the] south Atlantic. It took us like an hour to get there with the TR-3B.

MS - So when you say south Atlantic, and it took an hour to get there on the TR-3B from that location somewhere in ... [the] Tampa area.

JP - Not the Tampa area. The Gulf—somewhere in the Gulf [of Mexico].

MS - Somewhere in the Gulf of Mexico? ... So it's southern Atlantic. We're talking off the coast of, like, Argentina or Brazil?

JP - Yeah, but a little bit farther [east], next to like [South] Africa or like more in the middle.

MS – Okay. Kind of like the south Atlantic, right down, kind of like the Falkland Islands? ...

JP - Yeah, we have a couple of islands there that are not showing on maps, on Google Maps, or anything.

They're quite big Islands and probably half the size of Puerto Rico or the size of Puerto Rico. There's islands there that are not shown by Google Maps or any kind of map or any kind of satellite. Quite interesting. There's a lot of islands around like that. They just appeared probably using the same technology that China was doing to create an island, you know, but it's been there for a while. The island ... [has] buildings. They're really, ancient looking.... I don't know if you've ever been to Egypt or Israel, where you see the ancient type of building and how it was built. But the base was in between these buildings and all that. It was kind of cool. And we had other ET races working there, and Nordics working there as well. So, we landed ...

Figure 33. South Atlantic Ocean with islands

MS - So can you explain? ... You land [on this island], and you see these Nordics working on the base. So, we're talking on the surface of the base. You see different ETs, including Nordics working. Is that what happened?

JP - Yeah, we saw Nordics working, and the ship hovered on top. And then it came down, and it dropped all of us off. And then it just zipped out in the blink of an eye. Just left, I said, "Man, why the hell [do] they do that when we ... spend so much time to get here?" ... Everybody was, like, ... cursing out the pilot.... But we were there on that Island, and ... in the middle of the island ... they have this tower that looks like the Egyptian tower that also the White House has. I mean, the Washington ...

MS - The Obelisk.

Figure 34. The Washington Monument (Obelisk)

JP - They had one [obelisk] in the middle, and it was huge. It was a golden color; tan in color. And it had Egyptian writing on it. And we saw a step pyramid there as well, and we were like, "Man, where the

> hell is this place at, like what is this?" And then my family member said, "Hey, follow me. I need to talk to you." So, we went into this tent-looking place where they were briefing people, and I said, "Hey bro, like, what we're doing here? ... what are you doing here?" ... [He says,] "They said that I could be in the mission with you, and we're gonna go underground here." [I say,] "So, what kind of city do they have here?" He says, "Man, it's nothing like on top of the island. All these people that used to live on top of the island, they moved down." And I said, "Hey, but I see Egyptian writings all over!" [He said,] "Because, yeah, these people are Egyptian, and they kept their traditions and all that. Yeah, you're gonna get to know." I said, "Cuz, how many places are like this around you know Earth?" He's like, "Just follow me, man. Just follow me and shut up. Don't say anything!" ... I was totally confused, Doc in the situation, but he told me to follow him.

What JP witnessed lends support to theories about Tartaria—an alleged worldwide civilization that existed in some form up to the 19th century, but all evidence of which has been systematically covered up by the global elite.[107] Furthermore, it has long been theorized by independent archeologists that pyramids were once part of a global energy grid that wirelessly transmitted energy to power homes, cities, and aircraft. Researchers such as David Hatcher Childress found that pyramids contain quartz crystals that generate a piezoelectric effect due to the Earth's natural seismic movement, thereby creating a constant power supply.[108] The famed inventor Nikola Tesla also proposed the creation of a global communication and power grid that would transmit energy from the Earth through large metallic spire towers based on his prototype Wardenclyff Tower.[109] Not only was Tesla's proposal ruthlessly suppressed by bankers and oil industry tycoons, but all evidence of a feasible global wireless power system was destroyed. JP's sighting of both a pyramid and an obelisk/tower on the mysterious island suggests that these were once a node in a global wireless power and communication system, all evidence of which has been destroyed or hidden, as in the case of the island JP's covert team had visited.

> JP - So I followed him, and I saw a familiar elevator—similar to what the donut ship had in the Atlantic Ocean for the ark. And I looked at it and said, "Hey, that's an elevator!" He says, "Yeah, we have a lot of these all over the place." So, we got in the elevator. It was me, him, and two other guys—a total of four people. So, I was like, "Oh, we're going down?" He says, "Yeah, we're going down." And then there was a dog as well that came with us, a Labrador [Retriever]. It was trained really good.... We went down, and then [the elevator] stopped in the middle. It stopped on the floor, and then the two guys and the dog left. And then we kept going down, and the elevator kept going down. We kept going down, and we stopped in this big dome-like place filled with ships. And you could see as far as you can see. It was huge; it was humongous. And my family member, Alex, said, "You see this? This is another spaceport." I'm like, "Whoa, but this is a huge one!" You can see, as far as you can see, Doc, different kinds of ships, similar to what we saw in the last ... [mission] I was telling you about. But this one was like fifty times bigger. Like, it was huge. I was like, "Man, how far down are we?" [Alex said] "Just don't worry about it. Just follow me." So, I'm like, "Bro." But they explained to me what's going on.
>
> MS - So just to clarify, this base that you saw down there in the south Atlantic underneath that island, that's not on any map, that this base was much

bigger ... than the ... spaceport that you saw in that Alabama, Mississippi, Tennessee [border] area? That was a spaceport that used stealth [technology], and craft could come in and out through some kind of light or laser device through the base into the upper atmosphere. But here in the South Atlantic [there is] a much bigger base.... You said 50 times bigger, so that's enormous.

JP - It's huge. So I went with my cousin and we stopped and, you know, we saw this [spaceport]. Then two people approached us. They were pissed off. They were mad, and they grabbed us forcibly, and they started talking this weird language.... They sounded like, “um, a ga ga re, ko ko ...” It sounded similar to that. The sound, I can remember that I got, it [was] like, a ga ga re tu tu rey, you know. They started talking this weird language.

MS - You said there were two of them, but there were twenty of you guys that got off the ship in these uniforms with these special weapons. So ... did these two guys from the base ... stop you? ...

JP – Yeah, these two guys from the underground base were not dressed as us. They had robes on and all that. In the elevator only four of us came down with a dog. They stopped midway; two of them left, and we kept [going down]—me and my family member. We kept going down, and we stopped in this big ass port that you can see as far as you can. And that's when we got approached by these two other people dressed in robes. They started talking this weird language and they grabbed us by force. We did not have our weapons. We left our weapons on top of the island. We went into the elevator without these weapons. He grabbed us by force, and they put us in this box. And we were both there ... until Saturday. We did not eat anything or drink anything; we had to pee in the corner. It sucked. I don't know why they had us there, but we were there for probably 22 hours, around there, [from] Friday to Saturday. We were confused why they had us there.

MS - So this box was like a prison cell. Can you say anything more about it? I mean, what was it like? Clearly a prison cell with the amenities to hold prisoners or was it just like a temporary box shelter? ...

JP - It was like a temporary metal box—a box. It was metal; like the whole thing was metal. Cold as shit. You can hear; you can touch the wall and it was vibrating. I was trying to get the hell out of there. I don't know what was going on. I was touching the wall. I was like, "Why the hell?" I was arguing with my family member, Alex, and I was like, "Why the heck [have] you brought me here?" He says, "Just be quiet, bro, and just be calm; that's it. Don't worry about this." I'm like, "Okay. Well, we're stuck in here. I don't know how long we're gonna be here." ... I was just trying to knock on the walls, trying to do morse code.... I even screamed out loud. I was driving my family member crazy. He was just calm. And they opened up the box because, for one, I was scared for the oxygen to run out for us. It felt tight, and I was already feeling like, you know, dizzy and all that with all the CO^2. And I was worried about not having food. It was crazy. It was a crazy experience. And [after 22 hours] they opened up the door. We were so weak. I was so tired and weak, and I did not want to fall asleep.... My cousin did not want to fall asleep either....

They took us out, and they lined us up. And I could understand what they were saying, "Okay, they fasted enough to see what they needed to see." So, the reason they put us in the box is to ... have us, like, pure without ... food—or something like that. I don't know what the hell they wanted to do with us, with no food and all that. But they just wanted us, like, fasted, you know. I don't know what that has to do with some ET races or, you know, fasting or anything like that, but they wanted us, like, kind of pure. So they took us out, and they drove us in this type of train- ... looking thing that was floating on magnetic freaking tracks. And it floated us to a different location, and it stopped us there.

And there was a Nordic there. He was dressed in silver. He had blue eyes, long white hair—like a whitish, yellowish hair. And he said, "I have to tell you something, and I want you to relay this message." ... I looked at him, and I said, "You made us go through what we went through. Why didn't you tell us that we were gonna go through that? ' He says, "You need to have patience." I'm like, "Oh!" I was stressed out, Doc, about the whole situation. And the Nordic was looking at me. He says, "Soon we're gonna be moving and taking our ships [out through] .. different types of volcanoes and [from] different kinds of bases—military bases around the world. And we want you to know that we're here not to cause harm but just to give protection and to teach. And we're going to start picking up a lot of people and showing them this type of technology, and we're going to share." I asked him, " where are you from?" and he says, "I'm from a place that is way older than you." I don't know what that meant, but he said, “I'm from a place that is older than you.”

MS - That sounds like he's referring to an Inner Earth civilization that is much older than our surface civilization. Our civilization, if you want to technically date it, is probably 6000 years old, going back to the Sumerians, but it sounds like this civilization he belongs to is much older than that.

The Nordic’s reference to their civilization soon using volcanoes to reveal their spacecraft is very significant after the emergence of a video showing a fleet of UFOs coming out of Mexico’s Popocatepetl volcano three months later on August 24, 2023.[110] The video was taken from livecam monitoring of Popocatepetl that is available on a public website. Twenty UFOs emerged from the volcano in a formation that became worldwide news.

Figure 35. Screenshot from video of UFO fleet emerging from Popocatepetl Volcano

JP - Then he gave me a type of crystal—a bluish crystal—and he says, "Take this, and take it back up there. This is your way out." I said, "That's it? I came down here for you to tell me this? You couldn't, like, tell me up there? But I have to come down here?" He said that he is like a 1,200 years old, and that he could not go to the surface yet. But there's others like him around the world that will hit the surface. And I'm like, "Okay. I feel, you know, [you are] special." But I was still, you know, angry. I was still mad, and my cousin was just calm. He was just like nothing happened.

MS – Okay. So that kind of like does make some sense that you are put in that box for nearly 24 hours, because your vibration needed to be cleansed so that when this elder from that Inner Earth civilization met you—he's what, 1,200 years old?—that your vibration wasn't going to be too jarring for him; that it wouldn't be too disturbing. Because I guess that he would need to be protected to a certain extent from people from the surface whose vibration was very strong and maybe jarring or disturbing in some way.

JP – Yeah, but he pissed me more off putting me in this box, you know. He knew I was pissed off by the sarcastic way I was talking to him and all that. My family member, Alex, was like, "Have you talked to these people before?" I'm like, "Yeah. I have talked to different people of different races before, and from different planets as well." And he was shocked that I talked to a different type of people before. The Nordic, he said, "I'm gonna walk you back." And then he started walking us back, but he looked really young. I don't know if he was [1,200 years old]. Why wouldn't he be telling the truth about his age? I don't know, but he really looked ... still young and all that. And I remember him giving me this crystal, and I hold it in my hands, and when you squeeze this crystal, you can see the future! So, it vibrates your whole body, and you can feel the future and all that. I did not see the Moon.... I saw the sky and I saw mountains. I did not see buildings in the distance. I saw futuristic cities flying; building-like structures flying around. It was weird. And then I just gave it to my cousin, and he has it. And the Nordic said, "Remember, what I told you? We're going to be visiting the bases."...

MS - So this vision you had, that crystal device, when you squeezed [it], it gave you a vision, and I'm assuming a vision of the Earth, but one where you saw futuristic cities. The environment was cleaned up—very pristine, very clean, but no Moon. That's interesting because ... I've come across many sources that say that the Moon actually is an artificial body, and it's a control mechanism. And that if the Moon left us, if we got the Moon to leave its orbit, ... that control that it exercises would be gone. And our planetary vibration would be able to rise more quickly.

Immanuel Velikovsky was the first major researcher to cite multiple ancient sources describing pre-lunar cultures in his popular book *Worlds in Collision,* published in 1966. In it, Velikovsky cited Democritus, Anaxagoras, Aristotle, Apollonius of Rhodes, Plutarch, Hippolytus, and Lucian, all of whom described a time when the Earth did not have a Moon.[111] One theory is that the Moon first appeared during Atlantean times and may have been a major factor in its destruction. The Moon has been used ever since as part of a control system by regressive extraterrestrials to monitor and interfere with humanity's evolution. Consequently, once humanity has freed itself of negative extraterrestrial control, there will no longer be a purpose for the Moon. So it would not be surprising to see that in the future, it will be relocated away from the Earth's orbit, just as JP saw through the crystal device.

> JP - Yeah, so that was quite interesting. I don't know how far in the future that was, but ... after he kept talking to us, I felt a lot of peace with this Nordic. There was a lot of Nordics behind him. I remember them, like, just behind him, like, watching him. And so yeah, we went to this mission just to receive that message, and that really pissed me off in a way, you know. I could have gotten that message here at home, but I guess, like you said, maybe I needed to be in a vibrational [harmony] with all the fasting and all that, just to see him, you know. That's understandable now that you said that because they're in a different vibration.
>
> MS - Right, so this Nordic being that you saw, I mean, we're not talking Nordic in the sense of an extraterrestrial. We're talking about Nordic in the sense of someone who's human but looks Nordic and is part of an Inner Earth civilization. They're very ancient, and ... maybe they are working with Nordic ETs and their ships are going to be revealed much more frequently now.
>
> JP - Yeah, I think they've been here for a long time on Earth, but they're ETs. They come and go; they go and come; and come and go. And they're scattered all over the world; inside the world; inside Earth and outside—flying these ships and all that. There's a lot more different ETs flying around. And don't forget about the drones coming out from the arks as well.

That's quite interesting. So we went back on the elevator. We went back up—all the way up—me [and] my family member. The other soldiers that came with us, were nowhere to be found. So, the TR-3B picked us up again, and ... we went out of the atmosphere of Earth. We went around Earth twice; then we went to the location of where the Navy ship was. We got out [and] quickly we got into the helicopter. And [it] quickly took us back to the location. [They] drove us back to where I was parked, and then I [left for home].

It's funny because I texted my family member [Alex] this morning, and I said "Hey, that was freaking cool." And he's like, "What are you talking about?" [It's] like he doesn't know [anything] about it. [It's] like nothing happened to him. So that was quite weird. Maybe he didn't wanna be part of disclosing or anything like that, or he's being watched. But I tried to text him. I tried to call him, and every time I talk about the situation, he says that I'm crazy and that he doesn't know what I'm talking about.

MS - That's very interesting. But this family member arranged this mission for you. I mean ... it was done under his authority. So that is very interesting.... He could be just kind of like maintaining secrecy, or maybe his memories were wiped. After each mission, his memory is wiped or something. It's very strange.

JP - That is [strange]. We grew up in the same place. We're close family members, you know, but I never would have thought that he was part of this as well.... He's like a year and a half older than me.... It's quite interesting.

MS - It is [interesting], that is fascinating. Well, I know we're going to be releasing this [interview] around the same time as ... my book about your life—about when you first contacted me in 2008 is coming out. So, it'll come out on June 5 [2023].... That's where I present all of the missions or many of the missions that you've told me about since 2008. So, it's been fifteen years now that you've been telling me about these missions, and you've given me a lot of photos, [and] you've given me some video. And yeah, I've recorded it and ... kept notes of it all. So now it's all in a book form so people that want to learn more about JP's past—when we first began communicating what happened—[can] look at some of the documentation, going all the way back to 2008. That's all [contained in] this new book that I've released which is about [JP's missions] that's called the *US Army Insider Missions* (Volume 1).

JP - It's quite interesting you're doing that for me and for everybody that wants to know about what's really happening. That's really nice of you. I really appreciate you; your job. And I really appreciate what you're also doing for this community. It's funny that you say that because somebody approached me, somebody called me, and asked if you wanted to do a movie about this. I'm like, "I don't know about that.... You have to talk to Doc." ... It is what it is. But that's quite interesting. A lot of people are gonna know about my life story. And I've been telling you [my experiences] for the past fifteen years, and it has a lot of connections with [current events happening] now. Now that we're finding out that there's connections in every part of how this was happening, it's quite interesting.

> MS – Well, it's been quite a journey. Your transition from a civilian where you were having these experiences and then your decision to join the [US] Army so that you could learn more, be exposed to more, and reveal more. So, you've got an incredible mission or life purpose that you are fulfilling in revealing the truth about the extraterrestrial presence [and] about secret space programs... You're very pivotal ... to the full disclosure that is coming to our planet. So, I want to thank you on behalf of my audience, JP, for everything you do and [for] your courage.... This does come with risks ... I want to talk about what's happened to you, but definitely, it's not an easy thing. And so I, again, just want to applaud your courage and dedication to getting the truth out there to the rest of humanity.

What I'm alluding to here are ongoing threats, harassment, and even assassination attempts on JP and his family that have occurred recently in response to him revealing his covert missions. While JP is supported by his superiors in the covert missions he performs, there are other powerful groups that are opposed to his ongoing disclosures. At the close of our update, JP elaborates upon some of the difficulties he has faced.

> JP – Yeah, it's hard, Doc. A lot of people [have] gone through this in the past and in the present.... I have to stay inside my house 24/7 because there's cars following me all over the place and people threatening me. Christ, it's quite tough, you know. You don't know who's who.... I thank God everything is [okay]. I'm getting permission, you know. It's not like I'm not protected. I'm protected by a lot of people. So as long as I get the green light, you know, to talk to you, I feel safe. The moment they say I can't talk to you anymore, that's when I guess I can't.

But so far, I'm getting the green light, not the red light. [There are] certain things that I can talk to you about. Still, there's other things that has been happening to me that I can't [reveal]. I don't have the ... [green] light to tell you about. And it's involving people—a lot of people; certain celebrities.... But everybody's playing a role on certain things that is really hard to talk about. I don't have the green light, yeah, to talk about that. And also, this passes from different countries as well. Brazil has a major story, as well, about this. There's a lot of stories in Brazil that I don't have the green light yet to talk about. And I can't wait [for] when they say, "Okay, you can talk about this; this is coming out. All right, you can talk about this." It's going to be quite interesting when that happens.

And now with this development with my family member being part of this. You know, we do carry the same blood from one part of our family.... So there's something there, you know. And then my father had [an] experience in Puerto Rico as well. I remember telling [you] about this. He saw a big ball of fire coming out from a lake from Puerto Rico when he was younger, and he followed this ball of fire and the ball of fire disappeared in the lake of Puerto Rico. And that experience changed his life totally. And he's [now] working for the government. I can't tell [you] what agency he's working for or who he's working for, but yeah.... You know, when people have [a] history of things happening to them, it keeps following your generations. Yeah, it's tough. But we have to get it out there, you know, and share the love and share the positive energy and the information that will help humanity move forward with the truth. I really appreciate you for what you're doing. You know, you're playing a big role as well, and I appreciate you.

In mid-June 2023, I had the opportunity to speak with JP's father, who shared his experience with the large fireball he saw in Puerto Rico during his youth. It did appear to be some kind of extraterrestrial event that involved missing time. That and other strange phenomena surrounding JP's father during his youth do raise the possibility of intergenerational extraterrestrial contact involving JP's family. Given that his cousin is also involved in covert projects, the possibility is even higher that extraterrestrial contact has been an ongoing phenomenon in JP's family.

Chapter 13

US Military Works with Nordic ETs on Time Travel Research

On June 23, 2023, JP, who continues to serve with the US Army, was taken to an undisclosed location along with five military personnel from different nations who were all multilingual. They met at the designated site with Nordic-looking extraterrestrials who worked with human scientists to develop time travel technologies. In the main room where the multinational team went, there were four-time travel devices that were hemisphere-shaped tunnels with event horizons that could transport a person to the years 2090, 2050, 1940, or 1550.

JP said that his multinational team was interviewed about whether they would individually volunteer to travel to any of the time periods to conduct research on space arks. They were told that they would spend up to 10 years at the location and then be returned to a time shortly after their departure, thereby not unduly disrupting their everyday family life. What follows is the transcript of the interview with grammatical corrections, redundancies removed, and my commentary.[112]

Interview Transcript

Key: MS – Michael Salla; JP – Pseudonym for US Army Soldier

MS - Welcome JP to Exopolitics Today.

JP - How are you doing, Doc? It's a pleasure to be here to share this beautiful message to humanity and to bring out this information. I got the green light, so I'm going to go on and give you the information.

MS – Perfect. So [do] you just want to explain to people what you mean when you say you got the 'green light'?

JP - When I get the green light, it's because the higher-ups told me to talk about the situation. When they say 'red light,' I have to wait a certain time until things happen, until I give you the information.

MS – Right. So you've been sitting on this information for a little while, waiting for that green light.

JP - It happened Friday, okay. So Friday night, Saturday morning around, like at 11 [am], I came back home.

MS - Okay, all right. Well, [it happened] just a couple of days [ago] then, but I'm glad you got the go-ahead. So yeah, tell us about your mission and interview.

JP – Okay. It was a total of five soldiers from different branches. We had Navy, Air Force, [and] Army. We took a white bus, we were in civilian clothing. So we had sneakers; we had jeans; we had regular clothes. They took us [from Florida] to another location. We went to another state, and we flew over there. There's a state in the United States of America—I can't give you the right location because [of] security reasons and because of how advanced this technology is. You know, for security, we can't say the location in this interview. But maybe in the future, some other whistleblower or somebody else will give you the location, or we'll probably talk about this situation.

MS - So you were taken to some location. What happened with the five other personnel?

JP – Well, they were there with me. Everybody spoke a ... different language. We had French speakers; we had Brazilian Portuguese; we had Spanish; we also had a South Korean type of dialect. All languages. The person that talks South Korean also talks Russian and Ukrainian, and that [Korean] language.... Each person spoke two or three languages. Me myself, I speak three languages. As you know, I speak Portuguese, Spanish ... and English, which makes three. It's quite fun to know a lot of languages ... because you can go through different places and talk to different people. Because when you talk in a different language, you can resonate the story in other languages and all that. So it's quite interesting.

JP's point here is important to keep in mind when considering the type of personnel those running the time travel projects would want to recruit and send to different eras. Multilingual military personnel have the advantage of different languages that they can call upon to assist them in a strange new environment and time era. But more importantly, they are able to quickly learn the local language to fit in and adapt. Their military training will likewise help them survive off the land if necessary.

JP - So we went to this place, and it was a big room, and the room was metallic. We went in, and we saw Nordic ETs. When I say Nordic people, I'm talking about they're really pale; they got white hair, [and] blue eyes.... Their skin is really white. And these people actually, you know, believe it or not, they live among us. They sometimes wear makeup or ... [dye] their hair a different color; put contacts [on their eyes], and they go and work in government facilities; or they become a civilian. They become a person in the United States—in different parts of the country; and also in different countries as well. And they're all connected to each other. So, if they communicate with each other, it's like a [Nordic ET] nation integrated into different [Earth] nations. It's quite interesting how they ... still live happily and in harmony together, and they're living in different nations. It's quite interesting how they do that, and [how] they work on doing that. They were pale there. They didn't have makeup or hair [dye] ... or anything like that, but they were also wearing civilian clothes.... I found that quite interesting. They were just wearing regular civilian clothes, just like us.... They had white sneakers and they had, like, white scientist kind of rope [a lanyard] with their ID tags. [The] Nordics, they're all as white as what they were wearing, you know—the shirt and all that.

MS - Were they abnormally tall? Were they thin? Were they both?

JP - They are like 6′ 5″; 6′ 3″—around there, that height. They're more like our height, but you could tell that they're Nordics, you know. They come in different heights ... just like us human beings, you know. But most of the Nordics are really tall. They range up to 6′ 6″. They look like basketball players.... Most of them are tall, but, you know, they have people our sizes as well, 6′ 2″; 6′ 5″. And they're really muscular. Their body is more toned. They

> have less fat ... I guess because of their diet or what they eat. They have less fat in their body, but they're more muscular than us.

There have been many contactees and whistleblowers who have revealed that extraterrestrials live and work among us. In my book, *Galactic Diplomacy: Getting to Yes with ET* (2013), I present extensive evidence concerning extraterrestrials living among us in a range of capacities and professions, and how they are monitored by covert governmental agencies in a way similar to what was fictionally presented in the Men in Black movies. It is, therefore, not a great surprise that some extraterrestrials choose to work with the US military and/or aerospace corporations on advanced technology projects such as time travel.

> JP – Yeah, we were in this room, and [the Nordic ETs] were there. And we saw something really, really interesting that I think a lot of people are going to be interested in hearing this. We saw four different rooms, right. They were metallic in color, and the rooms were oval in shape. You can see into these rooms.... We entered into this big hallway where you see these four rooms. And then on top of these rooms, you can see the dates; they had different dates. So, I asked one of the humans [about these rooms]. He worked for the Air Force. There's also people like that—civilians, [normal] human people working there.
>
> We saw another ET, a different type of ET, and it looked really weird. We knew it was an [extraterrestrial] entity. It was on a type of chair that moved, and he was encased.... He looked like a type of slime or something like that, but he was encased [in something]. And he moved around with this type of, it's not like a wheelchair, but it had like a ball

under it. And the ball moved similar to that Star Wars robot that moved with, like, the ball—that technology. But it was metal. You can still see a type of skin, but it was scaly.... It was a ... [strange] entity, and he used that type of wheelchair to move around and to press whatever. Yeah, it was different. I [have] never seen that kind of extraterrestrial before.

MS - Like he was in some kind of environment suit?

JP – Aquatic. He was aquatic by the way he was looking. So that machine [was] pressurized [to simulate] what his planet feels, you know. It was quite interesting. He was moving out of the machine; you could see [his] little arms coming out. The way he was maneuvering—it was like he's been using it for years. It was really precise, the way he was using the machine. I think he's been here, living or working there for a long time. The way he was moving around, it was like he knew what he was doing. There was another room that had another one working [at] another side, and you could see him rolling back, rolling forward, rolling back, and they got to each other, and they communicated. I don't know how, maybe they communicated by electro-telepathy. And they went back [and forth], I guess, exchanging information to rooms and all that.

And then you had the Nordics. And you had [other] humanoids who ... looked Indian-type, but oriental looking with orange skin and a greenish eye; and the eyelashes on the side were ... [longer] than human ... eyelashes, but it looked human too. If they put makeup on and put [in] contacts or something else, and live on top of where we live, they [would] look

> just like human beings. They'll pass like oriental—like the islanders of Guam—that type of oriental looking [person]. But yeah, I guess, they cut their eyelashes to make it [appear human]. But their eyelashes they grow really long to the sides, and their eyebrows they grow really long, more to the sides. It's different humanoids, you know, that come from different parts of different star systems that work with us as well.

In a series of questions and answers I was able to conduct with Thor Han Eredyon on July 7, 2023, which were relayed through Elena Danaan, I asked about the identity of the extraterrestrials working with the US military on time travel experiments. Thor Han replied as follows:

> This is us. We are working with the Earth Alliance and certain aspects of the military. Your contact JP is working with the good side, and he is used to revealing the truth. These time devices, we have helped the military to develop that because the other [negative] side was developing ... Nebu [Tall Gray] technology related to time travel. You know it has been a time war. And we have helped our friends, our allies on Terra. There are key points in anchoring a timeline. You do not anchor a timeline just on one point but on a web of many points, like a mesh if you want. These dates are dates in the past and in the future of this timeline, to make sure it is anchored, and to make bridges; to create, "quantum", as you name it, links to anchor the timeline. Things are going to change. And these particular points, they are points of weakness, they are bifurcations of time. Time, as you know, is not linear. It is not ephemereal or abstract. Time is something that has no value in the absolute. It is a

> web—like a grid, if you will—and each point on the grid are bifurcations. We need to secure them.[113]

Thor Han's answer is helpful in understanding the reasons why extraterrestrials such as the Galactic Federation of Worlds are helping the US military develop and use time travel technology.

> JP - So these four rooms, they had dates on them, right. And we had the year 2090 in one room; we had the year 2050 in one ... [room]; we had 1940 in one room.... One [room] was going back to, like, 1550s and 1560s. It was going back and forth. So, I guess there they were trying to get to that time. And you can see in these rooms, right. And you could see what looked like a picture, but it looked really real. We were excited but nervous because of what we're seeing... You hear about the "20 and back" and all that, but you don't really see how they do it or where they go. I was asking questions about time travel to these scientists, ... "Hey, so this is where, you know, you go back in time and all that?" He says, "Yeah, this is where we do time travel. I'm not a good fan of time traveling," he was telling me. I said, "Hey, but can you manipulate it, like if you go there, can you change something if you go to that time?" He says, "No, you can go in there like nothing happened, and ... you can't change the outcome ... because it already happened." I was like, "What do you mean already happened?" And then he said, "Like if you go back in time and you go there, that means you went there already. So it already happened; so it doesn't affect anything." I'm like, "Oh, okay. So if you guys go back in time to the future, to these different ... [times], it's not going to affect the timeline?" He's like, "No, because it already happened." I was confused in a way, but it

kind of makes sense because if you go there, [it] already happened or if you go into the past it already happened. So, I don't know. I got a good sense of it. And then I said ... "How can you go to the future or how can you go to the past?"

I was asking questions about this [to] see if it was, you know, legit and all that. And then you see somebody coming back. I saw somebody coming back from 2050. He blurred into existence, and he was wearing ... different clothes. And they [the scientists] take him really fast to another room. They cleanse him; they take his clothes off; they give him different clothes, and he was walking towards a 1550s room. I'm like, "Holy shit. What the hell is this?" Everybody's like, "What the hell? What the heck is that? Holy crap, this is crazy!" So, everybody was just nervous and excited at the same time that we had this, but I was asking, "What are we doing there?" He says, "We're just looking." I said, "This is just to investigate certain things and to see how the future [unfolds]—which people end up where and like."

They have this in other countries, too. I can't tell you the exact country; there's three other countries that have this type of technology, but they use it [in] a different way. Yeah, I was asking, "Okay, so if you enter into a time [destination], right, and time travel has not [been] invented yet, how can you go back into that particular time or forward [in] time?"... He said, "You mean time [travel] was not invented by humans. Now, there's ETs that have invented time travel, maybe hundreds of thousands of years ago. You have to understand that. So, it's not just human beings. [You] see, human beings got a concept of

> time travel.... We have learned the time travel of [capturing] sound, of capturing light, and all that." And I thought of it like it kind of makes sense, you know. People that are going to hear this interview are hearing a voice of the past and a voice that already spoke.... They're going to see an image that was from the past and, you know, if you think about it, it's a type of time travel, but a different type. And we already see it as a norm, and we see it as ... capturing light and capturing sound. But ... if you get into it, it's a type of time travel. You're capturing the past, and you're 're-hearing' the past, and you're 're-seeing' the past. So he put it like that.
>
> He said, "There's ET species that have invented time travel before us, and they have shared their time [travel technology], and we captured the time [travel technology] on Earth.... We can go back even hundreds of thousands of years." I'm like, "Wow, that makes sense." So, humanity only ... invented time travel ... probably [in the] 1940s or maybe early 1900s. I'm not sure when, you probably know more than me about that.

The feasibility of time travel has long been speculated by scientists due to Albert Einstein's Theory of Relativity, first published in 1905, which posited that time moved in reverse with faster-than-light speeds.[114] With the recovery of extraterrestrial spacecraft, it was soon learned that these craft used a form of time travel to be able to navigate the cosmos from different epochs, proving that Einstein's theory was correct. In the late 1950s, an Italian priest, Father Pelligrino Ernetti, discovered a time travel device when experimenting with the sound frequencies of songs chanted by Benedictine monks. Father Ernetti called his device a 'Chronovisor', and with it, he could look into the past to capture sound and light. In this way, they were able to watch and record the crucifixion of Jesus of Nazareth.[115] In my book, *The US Navy's Secret Space Program and Nordic Extraterrestrial Alliance* (2017), I explained how time travel technology was routinely used in secret space programs. All this corroborates JP's experience of seeing the Nordic extraterrestrial scientists assisting the government/military run time travel experiments.

ESCLUSIVO Un giornalista dice: "Ho le prove di un'eccezionale

Inventata la macchina che fotografa il passato

Siamo al di là delle più avanzate ipotesi della fantascienza. Lo conferma un monaco benedettino, padre Pellegrino Ernetti, che insieme a un gruppo di dodici fisici sarebbe riuscito a realizzare un complesso di apparecchiature che consentono di ricostruire immagini, suoni e avvenimenti accaduti centinaia e centinaia di anni fa. Tra l'altro la macchina avrebbe "captato" dallo spazio il vero volto di Cristo mentre era ancora vivo sulla croce. Padre Ernetti dichiara: "Gli americani stanno tentando anche loro di scoprire quello che noi abbiamo già scoperto. Allora avremo la controprova e la conferma dei nostri risultati"

Figure 36. Italian Newspaper story on Father Ernetti's Chronovisor (1972).

> JP - They took us into this room, and they showed us that [time travel technology], and they asked us questions about how we felt when we went to the ark. The ark has this type of technology, and it has a portal that can make it to other arks. And that's a type of time-traveling technology. And it's ancient as well. [It] goes [back] thousands of years ago, you know. I'm like, "Wow, this is insane if we're working with this and all that. I just hope it doesn't fall into the wrong hands...." I was telling the guys ... 'Hey, this is crazy because, yeah, man, I'm not going through that shit." The other guys are like, "I'm not; we're not going through that shit. Hell no, we're

good."... I asked, "Hey, will I totally get my time in? And how does time work over there ... like, if you pass ten years in one of these time [periods]?" They're saying that the years [during the time travel projects] fluctuate every couple of months. They use different years and all that. So it can fluctuate [with] different time frames and all that. Ten years will be like nine or eight hours, depending on what month you go in and what month you come back in between those years and all that. So it could be like nine hours for ten years or two years for one hour. So they measure it like that, and it was quite interesting how time flies over there. They keep the location so they know. Like, say we go to the 1940s or the 2050s. They know the exact location where you're going to end up, and they know the future of that location. So they know that that location is going to be there when you come back. They look at disasters; they look at storms; they look at earthquakes; they look at different things that happen in that time frame where that location is safe in those years for it not to be disturbed. And they use a type of cloaking technology, probably like in the woods somewhere [in a] national forest—those types of technology. And like in a National Forest, you can come out and come in. It's quite interesting, Doc, when I saw this.

So they were asking questions about how I felt [inside] an ark, and I said, "Yeah it felt good. I activated here and there." And the scientist, he was like, "So, you think if we take you to the future or to the past you can still activate these arks? Because they're newer in the past and they're older in the future." And I was like, "This is way above my pay

> grade." I'm like, "I don't know if I'm gonna do this or not."

This passage is very relevant to JP's experience of when he was taken 100 years into the future and found that human survivors were living on giant space arks that had escaped some planetary catastrophe.[116] The remnants of Earth humanity were protected by Nordic extraterrestrials and military forces drawn from surviving national groups. Such an alarming future scenario would naturally be of great interest to contemporary military and political leaders who would want to learn about space arks and their functions, and to prevent such a global calamity from happening in the first place.

> JP - So I felt peace, you know. Like if they gave me the opportunity, I'll do it. But it's quite scary thinking if you get stuck back there because there is a possibility that it closes and it's not safe.... And it could take probably, like, 80 years for them to open that same time frame back, but over here it's, like, probably two or three days. But for me, it would be like ... a long time, like, 30 or 40 years. You know, a lot of shit can happen in that time frame. So that's the scary part about it. And there's a lot of people that have been in these types of missions, and they don't come back. They die of old age in that time frame, but they can't say anything about it. They can't talk about it. And they sign a waiver about it—they make you sign before you go into these missions. And you can't talk about it. I know it probably ... sounds far-fetched, but [not so much] now with all these people coming out—all these whistleblowers—with [information on the] technology of UAPs, UFOs, and all that. These UFOs carry this type of technology of manipulating

gravity, manipulating space and time. And I think people should know that, yeah.

MS – So, what happened in your case? You were offered the opportunity to go to another time to interact with one of the arks. ... It sounds like you said no. So, what happened then?

JP - I told them, like, "If you guys give me the opportunity and give me your word [that] I will come back, you know, [and] not stay over there, I'll do it. And I have to go with the guys, you know. We're gonna go into this together." They say, "No, the ... [largest] group that you can take is three people. Yeah, and you guys can't take anything with you. You guys just try to make contact. You guys come back to the location and keep us updated every other day in your time over there. You guys are going to come back older, and you're gonna see [that] over here only ten hours is going to pass. But over there, it's gonna be like maybe nine years or eight years. So, it's up to you guys, you know. A lot can happen in eight or nine years. There's no medicine ... you can't take anything with you."

MS - So were they offering to take you to what, to 2050? Was that the time period that they were offering to take you? Did they tell you what time period they were going to take you?

JP - Didn't tell me what time period.

MS - I see.

JP - Those are the time periods we saw in these rooms and ...

MS - And you said there were five other people with you, so, you know, were you all given that opportunity?

JP - Yeah.

MS - Did some say yes and others no?

JP - There's another guy; he's like, "Let's get the hell out of here. I'm not doing this shit." There was another guy that was really interested. I guess when you lose a loved one, right, and you have this opportunity coming to you, right, you'll take [it] in a heartbeat. Yeah, I want to see it. I want to see my family members again. Yeah, I want to see my dad again or my mom, you know, they died in an accident. I would love to see them and spend time with them before whatever happened to them happens, you know, or try to stop it. You have that mentality. You got another mentality saying, "No, it's not for me. This is crazy. You guys are full of it. You guys [are] gonna leave us over there, and that's it." I thought maybe this is the way they probably get rid of people sometimes. That crossed my mind, you know, take you to a different time and just [say], "Hey, cool, have fun!". But I saw the person come back. He came back from a five-year mission, and he was ... [gone] only for three hours [in current time]. So that was quite interesting. And he came back with a lot of information—books and books. He had a backpack with books and all that.

MS - So this is one ... of the people from that group of six that you traveled [with]? ...

JP - No, no, a different person.... A different soldier that came back from that time frame 2050.... So that was quite interesting seeing that. It's like you see the place when they see him blurring into existence in our time frame, and you just see him blur, blur in. He just blurs in. It uses like a ... sound vibration, electro ... I don't know what kind of technology. This is crazy technology.

As mentioned earlier, Father Ernetti stumbled onto the Chronovisor technology when experimenting with the recording of sound vibrations of chanting Benedictine Monks in the 1950s.

MS – Okay. You said that there were Nordics that had that time travel technology. So if you went back to the 1550s, for example, then the Nordics that were living at that time, you would approach them and say, "Hey, I'm from the future. I'm here to do a mission..."

JP - I'm sure they have their codes and how to approach and all that. I think once they give you the mission, they give you everything you need to know and who to communicate with within that time frame just to be safe, you know. I'm sure they give you all that information. They just didn't give us the information because we didn't agree [to do it].... They're still interviewing us, you know. It's a process, I guess, of how to receive this type of mission because it's a commitment. You're going to be there for a long time, you know. Yeah, it's a commitment. So, this brought me [to remember] the technology that we have over here, you know, about them knowing everything you know, when they put you in that room.... [Remember] I told you that story?

JP is referring to his mission described in Chapter 11 when he was taken to a military base facility and exposed to technology that would trigger and record past-life memories.

> MS - That's right. Yeah, they put you in that room, and they could see everything that's happening with your life, and [who] we've interacted with or who's going to interact with you.

> JP - So we do have crazy technology, Doc, that people are going to be really excited [about], but it's just too advanced. I guess they're trying to advance humanity really fast to understand this technology, but it's going to be really hard to integrate this type of technology with people nowadays because [of] their mindset. The black hats, you know, they're integrating this type of [limited] mindset. It's so crapped up, you know. It's hard, man. It's hard knowing that we have all this and we can't do anything or share [anything] about it, you know, it's crazy.

> MS – Right, okay. So did you see all four rooms, or did they just tell you about them?

> JP – No, we saw all the four rooms.... You can see all four rooms. [The] 1550s, you can see it's lush; it's green. You can see hills as far as you can, and it's more lush. I think it's the same location at different times, so that's quite interesting.

> MS – Okay, so when you're saying these four rooms, these four rooms are like you walk into that room, and you're in the 1550s in some location, like in the future or in the past that corresponds to that precise

physical location, you know, where you were at that time on Friday?

JP - Yeah.

MS - Okay, so that would have been June 23rd [2023]. So, on June 23rd, you're in this location. If you go into any of those rooms, you would be at that same location but at another time. So in one case, it would be just like green and pastures and all of that.... When you say you saw each of the four [rooms], but you didn't go into them, right?

JP – No, you can see through, you can see it ...

MS - See it through what? Like through a door, or how did you see it?

JP - It's open. It's like a garage door. It's like they're really open. You can see into it, but you can't see when they're coming in and they blur into existence. You can't see them on the other side because time is running differently. Time is faster over there. So you can't really see when anything moves or grows— ... it's blurred, but you see the location. It blurs in and out—like you can see the location, and it's protected by something that is like, not a frame, but it's like, how do you say, like it's like a metal frame. But [has an] oval shape. It has a laser that protects it; a type of laser. You can see the fluctuation of the laser when the other side hits it; you can see the laser. It looks like water, but it's not water. You can see the tank from the other side touching the laser, and you can see the laser. So, you know, when the guy came out, it was a loud noise. It was like rrrrh then everybody went to that room and took them out, and [asked], "How do you feel?" You had a doctor checking his heart. He had somebody else taking his shirt out, putting him into the other room. Another guy [was] bringing [him] different clothes [for his next mission]. It was like a pit stop. Like everybody knew what ... they were doing, you know. Everybody had their role of what happens when they come back out....

MS – Okay. So all four of these different areas were like entering into an open garage, and you mentioned something blurry. So I guess we could call that the event horizon between the present time and that era that you would step through.

JP – Okay. So all of this was all in one big room, but you had like four different areas. Whether you had these event horizons.... You got these rooms, they looked like ... about the size of a garage. They look like that ...

MS – Oh. Kind of like an oval-shaped carport. You're just making a shape that looks like an oval-shaped carport.

JP - And there you have them here, and it's fluctuating right here. You can see in there....

MS - Yeah, okay. So it sounds like it's very similar to that show in the 1960s called The Time Tunnel. I don't know if you ever saw that?

JP – No.

Figure 37. JP moved his hands to depict a hemisphere shaped carport.

MS - They had a like a circular type tunnel where you'd walk in, and you go through that, and you go into another time....

JP - It's like that half-oval shape, and it hugs the floor in the bottom—like smooth; like, really nice. And then the other one is right next to it. And then the other one's right next to it. And the other one's right next to it. And you're just standing ... looking in here, like man, "What the hell?" You're looking at all of them. And then everybody's like walking around, working and checking the date. The dates are right here, on each one of them, so ...

MS – Okay.... [for] people [who] are listening to this, just to describe what you said. It sounds like ... four ... hemisphere carports. Just one by each other with the sign on top saying, you know, 1550s, 1940s ...

JP - I know this shit sounds crazy for a lot of people.... I got the green light to talk about it ... [but] not the location.

Figure 38. Image from the Time Tunnel TV show. Irwin Allen Productions, Twentieth Century Fox Television

MS – Okay. So each of these kind of like garage or carports ... that have that hemisphere shape, like a tube—each one has an event horizon. [Do] you know what's the technology that's creating it? Is there a machine in there that's creating all of this?

JP - I did not see any machine. I saw this shit, like connected to the floor, and I guess the whole floor is the freaking machine because you could feel the vibration on the floor. You could feel you're vibrating. You're like this the whole time.... You're hearing like a hum; like everything is humming.

MS - Okay, all right. So you have that experience. You're given that option of going, and it sounds like most of the six of you, that you declined that offer. So, what happened then?

JP - They talked to us for a little bit. They made us sign some papers to not talk about the location; you know where it is. So we signed ... papers, and we're not going to give the location, you know. It's, I guess, for security reasons. This won't, I guess, harm anybody if somebody grabs it. I don't know what they would use it for because the guy told me once you travel back and forth in time, you already did it before, so it's not going to affect the time frame. So if you meet anybody over there, it's because they don't know if you're from the past or for the future regardless because, you know, you're there for a certain mission, and you're coming back for a certain mission. Like I said ... they'll connect you with somebody from that time frame who has been there for a while already.

MS – Okay. So you connect with someone at the other end, and that would be your way of getting back once you've done your mission.

JP - It was quite interesting to see that place. It was really interesting to see. On the side, I remember seeing couches ... [with] people sitting down. It was like regular couches. On the other side, I saw where the 2090 [device] was. You saw a different type of couch. It was like you sat on it, and it just hugs you. ... You sit in it, and it just hugs you. It's weird, but it was kind of cool. We saw the different outfits that they had. They had different—not costumes—but they had different closets with different shoes;

different like, I guess, what people wear in that time frame. So, when you go in, you have to change. And you have to ask ... [what] clothes that time frame required and all that. So that was quite interesting also to see.

MS – Okay. You mentioned that the primary goal for those opportunities to go into these different time designations was to, like, find the arks. So it sounds like the people within the covert programs are wanting to get as much information as they can about the different arks.... You said there were five others plus you, so each of you kind of had experiences with arks before?

JP - Yeah, I know two of these guys that were with me; the other two I didn't know.

MS - I see. All right. So they're trying to get people to sign up to go into the past or future to learn more about the arks both in the past and future.

JP - They went to the 1550s. But they're saying that the ark is even old-looking right there [in the 1550s]. You know, it probably goes back even more. I don't know how [far] back they can go, but ... it didn't go a couple hundred thousand years back. But, you know, they're really protective of how [far] back they go because they don't know how it looks. They don't know what to expect. What species of animals are alive? What kind of fungi? What kind of diseases they have, you know? In this time frame that they were working on, they know, I guess. There's certain ET races that came back from the future, so they know what to expect. The Nordics know what to expect in that time frame. The other ETs came from the 2050s. They know what to expect from that time frame. We know what to expect in the 1940s and 1500s, you know. As human beings, we know what flags, we know what diseases were in those particular times. So when they tried maybe to go even farther than that ... we don't know what to expect. Because once you go, you're there for a long time. So you don't know, you know, what disease is or ... if your body is even capable of breathing. So that's why they're really careful for that, or they'll probably send—[it's] hard to say this—but probably a dog with a leash, a long metal leash, and keep them there for one hour. Then bring [them] back just to see and study the animal, or maybe a horse. They send them back, or they'll send capsules or types of vehicles over there first. It's big enough for a type of tank or something that holds pressure to go into and then come back out, you know. And I guess they have to do the investigation first.... They don't know if they're falling into water, [or if] they're going into a water [environment]. Things change; time changes things, you know.

MS – Okay. So what happened at the end of the mission, at the end of the interview? [Do] you want to tell us?

JP – Yeah, they took us to another room. We saw different kinds of plants; there were different types of trees that they had in pots. I don't think they were part of Earth because they grew different. There's one that had like a leather texture on it, and it had thick green leaves, like the leaves were really thick. We saw that, I guess it's food. Maybe ... what the Nordics or other ET races eat. They have their own area of [the] cafeteria we went in ... [when] we ate.

They have their ... other location [in the cafeteria]. They have different ... buffet kinds of food. After that, we went out and we took an elevator, and we went back to the surface. And then we just left. We came back, and they just—they're really careful about not giving the location. So I'm gonna respect that.

MS - Okay, well, great. So any final words you want to share ... about these arks? People are probably very interested to know if there's been any developments. I mean, have you heard anything about the arks appearing soon? Are they still in the process of activation? What's going on?

JP - There's a mission, I can tell you that, that [just] happened. I'm just getting the green light to tell you about this mission. We went back into the Atlantic Ark, and something interesting happened. So we're just waiting; we're just waiting to tell you before something else has to happen—I guess before I tell you about this mission.

MS - All right, great. So we can look forward to another update soon once you get the green light to tell us about your, I guess, fourth mission [to the Atlantic Ark]....

JP - I'm sorry about this red light/green light thing, you know, but it's I just have to respect it.... They're really giving me the opportunity to talk about all this. So, I want to really respect that. I love the country I serve. This, for me, is the best country in the world, and I just want to respect that, you know ... I know a lot of people are going to give [me] probably crap because of that, but I have to respect that, you know. Because it is what it is.

MS – Yeah. Well I'm sure—on behalf of a lot of the listeners to this interview—I'm sure people want to thank you for your service.

JP - I'm happy with all these whistleblowers [that] are coming out.... We talked about this, you know, time and time again, that they're gonna come out, and they're gonna talk. And that's what's happening. I'm really appreciative of all these whistleblowers who have the heart to come out. I'm really happy for them. I know most of them hear you interview other people and us talking. And they're working with [Dr. Steven] Greer, ... but I'm really happy for them, you know, that they came out. And there's going to be more. There's going to be more whistleblowers coming out. And more experiences that people are going to have. And more videos [showing] that people are ... interacting with these entities and beings and all that. Because they want to make themselves known to people. It's gonna happen. And like I said before, share a lot of love, and have positive energy about everything.... A lot of negative energies are going around. And we just have to think about what's the end; what's at the end of the rainbow, you know? And grab all that gold and share that gold with everybody with knowledge.... Just be positive, you know, and be happy with each other. Don't do people [any] wrong, you know. Because it's gonna bite you in your butt ... if you do negative things to other people.... That's how I see it. And I just want to encourage everybody to think positively and to share love. That's why I always preach, you know, 'share love and keep to your faith.'

MS – Wonderful. Well thank you. Wise words to finish on. So, thank you again, JP.

JP - No problem, Doc. Thank you for the opportunity, and let's go! Let's do this!

JP's mission to the time travel facility with four distinct periods that personnel can choose to visit is very significant. It shows how 'temporal' or 'time travel research' is being conducted by the US military and corporations to assess future probabilities, especially when it comes to the activation and functions of hidden space arks. Intelligence gathering on space arks in past and future eras appears to be the main objective of the mission that was offered to JP and his team. Regular travel into the four time periods that JP described would also be a very useful way of monitoring any changes made to the timelines in a temporal war involving extraterrestrial factions, which I discussed in *Galactic Federations, Councils, and Secret Space Programs* (2022). Also, we know that extraterrestrials use time travel extensively and can monitor major changes that can have a cataclysmic impact on the rest of the galaxy. Therefore, it is not all that surprising that Nordic extraterrestrials are working with human entities to monitor the different timelines.

Chapter 14

Fourth Mission to Atlantic Space Ark

In his fourth mission to the Atlantic Space Ark submerged in the Bermuda Triangle region, JP describes how he and a team of covert operatives were tasked to find and bring back an important crystal jewel from the ark. When JP's team found the crystal, which looked like a purplish black jewel with white stripes, he and other members felt very emotional and began crying. JP claims the crystal is connected to the emotional matrix of the ark and the frequency grid of Earth. JP felt it was wrong to take the crystal jewel from the ark, but he complied with the mission objective, which was to extract the crystal in order to use it to activate other arks and sacred sites around the Earth. When they carried the crystal jewel out of the ark, he said that the ark itself, including the fish, acted in a reverential way.

JP was told the crystal was very important insofar as it was a key for activating other arks. He felt happy that the people receiving the crystal were the right ones and would look after it. JP further says that while the mission only seemed to last a couple of hours, they were actually gone for two full days. He says that he and other mission members don't remember what happened during the missing time but have begun receiving flashbacks of meeting with extraterrestrials on the ark. What follows is the transcript of my interview with JP with grammatical corrections and commentary.[117]

Interview Transcript

Key: MS – Michael Salla; JP – Pseudonym for US Army Soldier

MS - I'm very happy to have JP back on Exopolitics Today, and he is going to be talking about a fourth mission to the Atlantic Space Ark. For those that may be new to the information, JP is currently serving with the US Army. We can't give any more information about where he's serving and specific dates, but he is active, and he has been on three previous missions to the Atlantic Space Ark, and he has described what has occurred there.[118] So now, he's recently had a fourth mission. Welcome back, JP, to Exopolitics Today.

JP – How're you doing, Doc? It's a pleasure to be here to share this beautiful information.

MS – Yeah, this is really exciting. I know people want to know exactly what is going on with the space arks and that you've now returned for a fourth time [from] there. So tell us ... what happened?

JP - We left from where we're at [an undisclosed military base]. There's a total of six of us—a mixture of military personnel [of] different ranks. We went to the ark location.... We were all in civilian attire, and we had different kinds of GPS systems. We had like a ... different type of [wrist] watch that they gave us. This watch, I think, measured our heartbeat; measured the way we felt. I think it's like a motion [detector] or something that feeds back information to the top part of the location that we were going down to. So yeah, we grabbed a helicopter, we landed on the donut-shaped ship in charge of this particular ark in the Atlantic, and we landed [in] civilian attire. There's a lot of military personnel walking up and down and working on top of this ship. It's really hot once you step on this ship, but it's normal. We got a briefing of what we're going to be doing. The briefing ... [was] about going down to the ark and where we're gonna get a piece of the ark and bring that piece up because they were going to do an investigation on the properties of the ark.

So we got into the elevator, and we were going down. When we were going down, the elevator stopped, and we were stuck there for like an hour, an hour and a half, you know. We were calm. Everything was calm ... [while] we're going down. We know that we have to be in a [peaceful] state of mind, a meditative state of mind, because we're entering like a different—not realm—but a different energy. So, we're already trained to enter like a different state of mind when you enter these arks, you know. Maybe the same way an archaeologist ... enters a place for the first time, like a pyramid or something, you know. You have that state of mind that you're there to learn and you're there to get information. So the location of this type of rock, or this type of thing, that's connected to the ark was on the back part—the south side; [the] left part of the ark. It takes you maybe forty minutes by going through the chambers to go to that particular part. That particular part hasn't been [explored]. People haven't gone there yet. So, we didn't know what to expect.

MS - Can you say anything about the chambers that you walk through to get to that end of the ark? You said it was at one part of the ark, this location where you had to gather material. So you walk through chambers; what did you see in the chambers?

JP - You see different statues. You see different writings of past civilizations that have been through the arks. You see different types of doors that open by different sound frequencies that we have. There's a guy that specializes in sound frequency. Also, some of us have a certain type of DNA that activates certain parts of the ark, and that is quite interesting.... When you go through these arks they light up, and these doors ... just move up, or move to the side. And you keep going ... through these chambers.

MS - So if someone would go on one of these arks, it would be like the interior of a submarine. You've got different compartments, and there's doorways between the different compartments. And either there's a sound machine or frequency machine that gets the doors to open, or someone has the right DNA, and the door opens.... So, you have to do it that way. That's the only way to get through the different sections of the arks that are filled, as you said, with remnants of ancient peoples that were [previously] there for a period of time.

JP - Yeah, and while we're going through these arks, you got to be in a meditative state of mind. You can't be overwhelmed by what you see. The reason we have the watch is [to] measure our heart rate and measuring the feelings that we're feeling. So the ark feels you. It's a different type of time when you enter these arks. Time is not the same. Time is a construct of human beings. In some parts of the arks ... time does not exist. Time is everything; it's connected. Like Earth follows time by the rotation of the Moon that goes around ... the Earth and all that. So time is different in different places. Like, for example, ... it takes Mars 687 days to go around our Sun. So that makes 56 days ... [in] a month if it was Earth. So, time is different everywhere you go. In space, astronauts follow the 24-hour time frame ... [based on] the location of ... [Greenwich, England], not the location of space. So, when you're in space ... time is different.... Time does not exist on these arks.... It's also [the same with] these UFOs/UAPs that you see flying around. Time is not the same. That's why when we see these UFOs making these sharp turns and these fast modes [of travel], we can't explain why they do that because time is different for them. What we perceive as time is totally crazy when you wrap your head around it.

MS - Can you say anything about the meditative mindset that you have to develop for going into the ark or ... accessing any kind of time technology or advanced technology? Were you trained? Were you given instructions on what kind of meditative mind you need to be in? Is it like going into nature and just feeling calm and peaceful but connected?

JP - It comes naturally, because when you enter the ark, you feel, like, a pulsing sensation. So, you follow the same pulse and sensation of what you feel—what the ark feels with you, and what you feel with the ark. You feel connected to the ark. So when you feel that vibration, you connect to it. You ... [align] yourself to that vibration and you breathe differently. You look at things differently. Everything seems slower, like in slow motion, but you're still doing what you're doing. You have to [do] .... a couple of breathing exercises that we go through, similar to people doing yoga.

MS - When you're on the ark, you said there was a beat. Can you describe that beat? What's it like, or [is it] a frequency?

JP - It's like a hum ... a booming hum. It's similar to what a heartbeat would sound like but without the second part of the heartbeat. You know, boom boom; it's just a boom boom. You hear [how] everything is vibrating at the same time.

MS – Okay. So [it’s] kind of like a heartbeat, but everything is humming as well.

JP - Everything feels alive; the walls feel alive. Everything feels like if it was a big organism.

MS – Okay. I just wanted to play something for you just to see if it's in any way similar to that. I just wanted to play something ... for ten seconds, and you just tell me ... whether that's in any way similar ...

[Music Plays]

JP – Yeah, it's similar to that, but it's slower.

MS – Okay. Well, that's interesting because what I just played was a binaural beat for gamma brain waves at 70 hertz. I've got similar things for like 60 hertz and 50 hertz. So that's interesting, it sounds like ...

JP - It affects your pineal gland, yeah—the concentration part of the pineal gland. Yeah, I think I talked about that in certain other missions. When the Aztec Mexicans were entering the ark, everything was slowing down, and they felt that same vibration. That's why they started singing 'A Kuria Matte' because they felt that same vibration, and they felt a happiness that they knew that they were in a special place. So when you enter these arks, you feel like you're in a special place—an overwhelming place ... [where] you feel happy, that you feel connected to. So it's really interesting. So we passed that chamber where that water stays still and stationary, and there were these beautiful fishes in there that were fluorescent. You could probably share a picture of that if you find it in this interview.

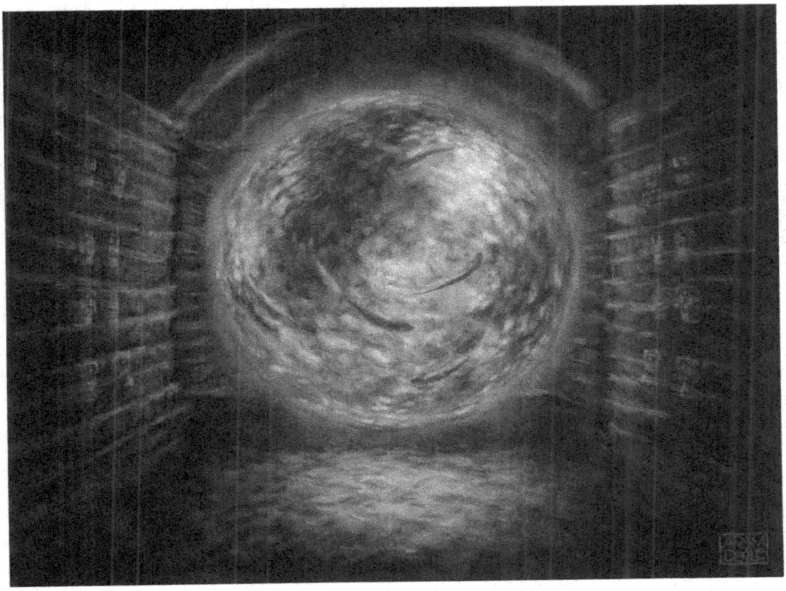

Figure 39. Fish inside of suspended sphere of water in Atlantic Space Ark. Image drawn by Adam S. Doyle.

> We passed that chamber—it's the same fishes.... And we passed through that chamber, through another type of door. And we enter this room, Doc. And when we entered this room, there was a stand-up statue. And this statue looked Indian-like and Buddha-like. It had a statue holding a staff. It was barefooted; it had a rope. And this statue was silver ... and gold in color.... The statue had a third eye, and we looked at it, and [all] the eyes were made of pearls that when you look at [them] ... it sees through you, like, I don't know. Like, it's a different sensation. So, it's a statue with a third eye. We went around it.

The statue appeared to be a guardian or a sentinel of some kind that was placed there to protect ark technologies, especially the device that JP's team was about to take. It's possible that the statue possessed some kind of intelligence and the capacity to stop the mission from proceeding further. However, the fact that the mission proceeded without incident suggests that whatever intelligence was associated with the statue and the ark, had given its permission. This is particularly relevant to the flashbacks that JP and other team members were getting after the mission, which involved events that may have happened during their time in the ark. These events will be discussed later in this chapter.

> JP - One of the guys that were there with us, he was an ex-marine. He went to this spot, and he put his hand down on this particular device [that is part] of the ark. Then a piece of rock with jewels mixed in came out. He said, "This is the rock we need to bring up." And I told the guy, I said, "Hey, wait, if this is part of the ark, why are we bringing it up there?" And he says, "To activate other things around the

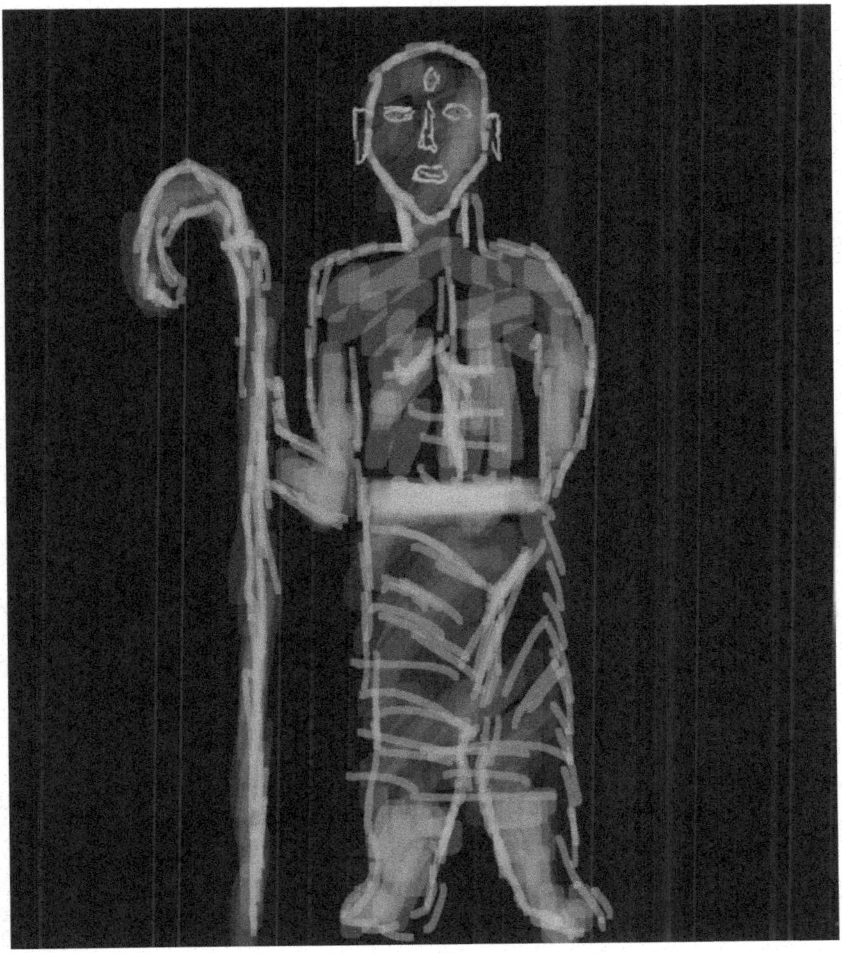

Figure 40. JP's drawing of statue witnessed inside Atlantic Space Ark.

world." And I told him, "I don't want to be part of this because whatever is in the ark, we need to leave in the ark. We can't just take the ark apart and start activating different things." He told me, "In order to activate certain parts in certain temples around the world, we need to bring this jewel with us." And I'm, like, "Man, I just wish we wouldn't, like, touch these things and just leave it where it is because it's part of the ark." He says, "It doesn't matter where this jewel is. It's always going to be part of the ark. The ark feels it, so it's like an extension of the ark." So, he was explaining that this type of rock jewel that we were taking is still felt by the ark because it was [energetically] connected with the ark. So, it was an extension to activate different things in different arks.

So this ark in the ... [Atlantic Ocean] is really important because it activates other things around the world with [this] certain device. So that reminded me of what the Ant King gave us. He knows that seeds can activate different things and help you with health and longevity. So we took it; we put it on this metal capsule. I felt, like, a sense of crying when I ... handled these [objects]—like happiness and crying. You can feel ... a vibration of sadness of what the world was feeling. So, when you touch this thing, you feel like crying. Even talking about it now, you feel like crying. And it is all the negative [stuff] that is happening around the Earth. I think it captures [the frequency of] everything. And I don't think it uses it as energy, but it just captures it, and tries to capture any negative thing that tries to enter the ark, or that's around the ark. So, we grabbed it.

Everybody started getting sad and crying, and we were holding this jewel. And a lot of people in history tried to get this particular rock, this particular jewel.... The militaries around the world is trying to protect this type of jewel. I think ... the higher-ups, have decided to bring it up because a lot of people from different nations, not just ... [United]

States, are trying to go down and try to get this type of jewel out of the ark.

MS - Do you know what it's made of? What kind of crystal? Was it transparent? Was it cloudy? Was it metallic looking?

JP - It was purple, black, and strings of white. But the strings of white were fluorescent and lit up. It's beautiful when you look at it. You're like, whoa. It's like a black jewel [and] you can see through it, like a purplish jewel that you can see through. And then you got white lines that are fluorescent that make the jewel glow and look beautiful.... It looks like a big—not an egg—but like a diamond backward and forward. It has lines of lights that you can see [through] it, and it makes you feel sad. And it makes you feel happy at the same time. It makes you feel what the Earth is feeling, like the sadness. A couple of us couldn't control ourselves, and we just started bawling and crying like babies [while] handling this jewel and ...

MS - So it's connected to the Earth's frequency, like Gaia? ... Some people talk about Gaia as a spirit. So this crystal is somehow resonating with the spirit of Gaia, and you can feel the planet's emotions ...

JP – Yeah.

JP's reference to the crystal jewel making individuals feel what the Earth is feeling suggests that it is linked to the Earth's consciousness field. This takes me to James Lovelock's "Gaia Theory" (aka Gaia Hypothesis) that the Earth is a self-regulating, complex living system that seeks homeostasis or optimal functioning.[119] When the Earth is out of equilibrium due to human activities, then Gaia will take measures to restore homeostasis, such as major Earth changes, pole shifts, etc., which resets the Earth's surface with a dramatic impact on the surface population.[120] The ark's connection to Earth raises the strong possibility that it is linked—through the crystal jewel—to the self-regulating mechanism by which the Earth achieves homeostasis. Thus, the arks will appear at precisely the right time to evacuate the planetary population when Gaia needs to restore itself through Earth changes, which has happened many times in the past, as reflected in historical legends of great floods, pole shifts, etc.[121]

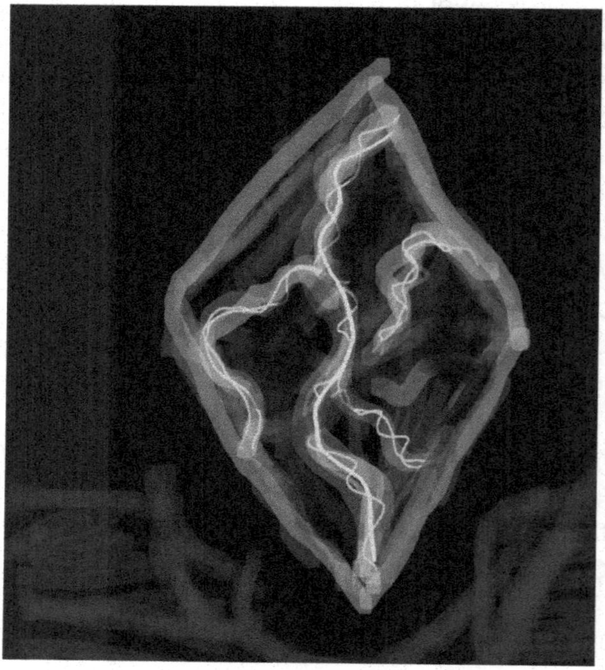

Figure 41. JP Drawing of Jewel extracted from Atlantic Space Ark.

MS - All right. Wow, amazing.

JP - We took [the jewel] and we started traveling back. And when we brought this jewel through the chamber where the where the fishes were, the fish just stood still and started following the jewel. They stopped swimming in the ball of water, and they just respected this type of jewel. And they just looked at it.... We were astonished. We ... felt so good holding this jewel, like if it was something special. So we take it, we bring it back. We go to the elevator, and we start going up the elevator. And when we got [to the top], ... I don't know how much time went by, but it was night. We knew that time was different [in the ark]. [We felt like] a couple of hours had passed or something. And then they told us we were down there in the ark for two days, but it felt like two to three hours.

MS - Was there any kind of protective technology around this jewel? Because it sounds like it performed a very important function for the ark—connecting it somehow with the planet's spirit or energy matrix. Was there any protection mechanism?

JP - Well, they put this capsule in a metal capsule, and it had like ... bulletproof glass; quite heavy. It was interesting. It was a capsule that ... you put the jewel in there, and it's protected. But you can still feel [it] though; you could feel the energy of it. Well, that was interesting... When we went up there, it was night, and there were other ships in the distance that were talking with each other with lights, like Morse code, ... talking to each other. There were ships from different nations. I don't know what nations were there, but there were probably fifteen different ships surrounding the donut-shaped ship that we're in. And they were just communicating back [and forth], and I was saying, "Hey, what's going on?", since we didn't know. We

> have other countries here. They didn't want to tell me what other countries were there. They had helicopters going left to right, communicating with each other. We had jets flying up and down.

It appears that the mission of retrieving the crystal jewel from the Atlantic Space Ark was of interest to multiple nations that were observing the unfolding mission. JP had earlier referred to the crystal jewel as an activation key. The jewel's ability to activate space arks and ancient technologies found in temples worldwide would have naturally aroused much international interest. It's very likely then that one of the mission objectives was to coordinate with other nations in finding and activating space arks and related technologies found in temples all over the world. If so, then this would suggest that the Earth Alliance is coordinating some kind of global disclosure event concerning space arks and associated technologies.

> JP - When we handed over [the jewel], there were people that looked different, they're taller. They took it to this room, and we felt like we had to protect this jewel and see who the hell was going to receive this jewel because we didn't want anything [bad] to happen to it. So we went into this room, and there were people dressed in ... hazmat suits, and they took the jewel. They put it on this gold platter, and the jewel just stood up by itself. [It was] similar to the Earth magnetic [toy] ... that floats, like that. Something like that with magnetics. It did something like that; it started floating up.

JP is here referring to a floating sphere of the Earth that is suspended in the air by a magnetic field generated by a metallic base. These floating spheres are popular gifts that are based on magnetic levitation technology, which uses magnets to create the levitation effect. It's possible, therefore, that the jewel generated a magnetic field or that some other levitation principle was in effect when it interacted with the gold platter as described by JP.

> JP - So, these people in Hazmat they're a little bit taller than us.... I didn't feel that they were human.... I think they were Nordic because [I saw] their faces. They had reddish lips, ... a white, pale face. They had blue eyes, but they had hazmat suits. We did not have hazmat suits. I don't know why they had hazmat suits. I don't know. So, they took us out of the room and took us to another room with a couple of scientists asking us, "What did we feel when we were carrying it?" We told them everything, "Hey, we felt sad, we felt an energy, we felt ...". We were just saying what was happening in the ark, and then they asked, "Do you remember anything else? You know, how long you were there?" And that's when they told us that we were there, like, for two days. And we did not remember being there more than two ... [hours]. We didn't feel tired. We didn't feel anything. And they said, "Yeah. You guys were down there for two days. So, what happened? We'd lost communication with you guys!" It felt like we talked to them, like, half an hour.... [They were] saying that we lost connection for two days. So, in between, I don't know what happened to us. I think something special happened to us six. I think somebody from those six, they're gonna come out soon [and reveal this] to the public. So, I'm excited by that.
>
> MS - Can you share when this visit to the Atlantic Space Ark happened? Was it around the July 4 weekend? Was it before that, after that?
>
> JP - It was in June. It was, like, before that mission ... [where] we went to that place where the time was

different. Remember I told you that there was a mission before? It was somewhere around June; the middle of June.

MS – Okay. That [was the] time travel mission [see previous chapter].... So that was on June 23rd that you went on that time travel mission. This happened after that, just a few days after that. Is that right?

JP - Before that, I remember I told you that we had a mission to the ark that I was waiting [for] the green light to tell you ... I hadn't got the green light for this mission to tell you [yet], but I just felt like telling you because it was a beautiful experience ... I'll probably get in trouble by telling you.... They're telling me not to talk, you know. They're really getting on to me not to talk no more.

MS – So you're telling me that you've been pressured—you're getting some pressure. So feel free to share anything you want about that.

JP – Yeah, this is, you know, when things start getting close. When the truth starts getting revealed to everybody ... they want to stop it.

MS - I remember you telling me about the time travel mission that you've got a bit of blowback for ... releasing that information.

JP – Yeah, they didn't want that to come out, but, you know, I got the green light to say certain stuff about it. So I did .... The studies are out there, man. All this stuff is true. The people gotta, you know, do more research about it.... Just study the life of Tesla.... What is the atomic bomb? And people will get close to [understanding] what is time travel, or a construct of where you're at in a certain time or in a certain location. Yeah, it's tough, Doc, you know. Talking about all this and being followed and getting threatened, you know, with your life.

MS - So I just want to kind of recapitulate here that over the years in working with you, I've found that there was always a faction that was opposed to you revealing anything; [a faction] that was opposed to you releasing photos or videos or talking too much about this. That's been a constant, but after you joined the military, it seemed to kind of stop for a while. But now it's picking up because you're talking again; revealing missions. And this faction that wants you to ... go quiet, they ... are concerned over the [fast] pace that information is now coming out...

JP - Also, for people to understand, ... we've been talking about this for a long time—for ... [fifteen] years already. And now all these whistleblowers are coming out.... I'm really happy that's happening, but that's just triggering ... the bad faction people... Look at the news ... [at] all that's happening. And now, with the book out and a lot of people knowing about what's happening, I've been threatened a lot. But, you know, I have people protecting me. I believe that a lot of people are protecting me; protecting you; protecting every other person who is giving [out] information, because good will prevail and evil will be no more. So, we have to understand that. And we have to share love, and we have to share who we are.... If people do go away, you know, just keep sharing love; keep sharing positivity. All this is gonna come out, regardless if they want it to or not. It's the right thing to do.... Some things can't come out. I know a lot of people are probably gonna give me crap about this, but there's some things that can't come out yet, because it could be harmful to everybody—depending on who uses what, what technology uses what. So I understand some parts of that, but there's things that people just need to know. What you see is not what is really there, you know, it's a construct. When people realize that ... a lot of people are opening their eyes now, Doc. A lot of people are knowing what's really happening, you know.

MS – Well, I want to thank you for your courage in continuing to put out this information, and that's... despite the kind of pressures that you've been facing. And we don't want to go too much into those details, but you are facing the consequences for your actions. So yeah, I want to thank you for making the sacrifice because it's a big thing... You've got a career; you've got a family; and to keep talking about these things does put pressure [on you], and there's risk involved. So yeah, I want to thank you on behalf of everyone that's listening to this.

JP - Appreciate it, ... I know sometimes we go back and forth about what we talk about, but sometimes we have to let things out, you know. So when they were briefing us about what we felt with the jewel, a type of helicopter that I haven't seen before came and landed. It had the propellers on top, and then the propeller twisted up and went back, and it could just jet out. So I haven't seen that vehicle before. I don't know who does it or who makes it, but I think the jewel went on to [the helicopter] and left, [since] I felt the sadness leave. So, I think they're going to investigate what this jewel holds, or they're going to take it to a different place to activate something else. So it's probably a type of key. We were talking about it with the guys heading back home, "Hey, I think that's a type of key to activate other, probably, other arks." They're gonna probably put it in other arks and activate them more. You know, I think that jewel is really important. And I think they're going to protect it the most they can, Doc. I felt peace with the people we gave it to, a sense of happiness. And now my prayers are with them that have the jewel, you know. I hope they do what they need to do to activate whatever they need to activate. And I hope they'll be safe by doing it.

We came back on the [Black Hawk] helicopter. [We put on] civilian clothes, and after that, we went home, and everybody started calling each other. And we started getting flashbacks in our dreams on the lost time. My flashbacks that I was getting, ... I felt like I was in a white hallway, and there were a lot of people there. Different races of ETs were there, and everybody was talking to each other. But it's like little flashes here and there that we were, like, in a big hallway—a big white hallway with a lot of different ETs talking to each other. So, I don't remember as much, but that's what happened.

MS - When you say you had a flashback and you remember seeing all these different ETs talking to ... one another, is that a flashback to something that happened in the ark? Or [was it] some other incident?

JP - Well, that missing time in the ark—those two days that we were in there—all six of us were getting flashbacks of what happened. Everybody was talking about a similar thing; about being in this room or hallway; a wide hallway with a lot of different types of ETs talking to each other.

MS - So that may have actually happened while you were on the space ark. That there were ETs there, and something happened, and your memory was removed. It's missing time, but you're getting flashbacks.

JP and the other soldiers' flashbacks of meeting extraterrestrials on the space ark during the extraction of the crystal jewel are very significant. It means that extraterrestrials were aware of the mission's objective and nevertheless allowed the extraction process to go ahead. Given that the crystal jewel is a key for activating other arks and technologies, the extraterrestrials saw the mission as being in alignment with the ark's ultimate purpose. Since JP and his team witnessed an international flotilla around the donut-shaped naval ship at the end of their mission, it's reasonable to conclude that the crystal jewel would be used to activate other arks and ancient technologies in different countries in a way that indicates extensive international cooperation. This suggests that the extraterrestrials consider greater international cooperation over how the arks are activated and used as something that is aligned with their overall purpose. This is important as the arks can be used either to rescue a significant portion of humanity during a global catastrophe or to assist humanity in attaining a higher level of technological development. Our interview concluded as follows:

MS - Fascinating, okay. So any final words you want to share with the audience about this mission?

JP - Just share love. I always say that because this is the right thing to say, you know. Don't have negativity in your life. Be nice and be kind to people.

A lot more people are gonna come out—like I keep saying—with different experiences. A lot more whistleblowers are going to come out about different situations in the military, and in the civilian sector. Now politically outspoken figures are going to be coming out, saying that, "Hey, this is true. This is happening." We just have to be ready and share love, and accept it, and open our hands for this type of disclosure, because they're coming back. And we just have to be ready. They're coming back.

Conclusion

There is a significant difference between JP's covert mission destinations described in Volume 1 versus Volume 2 of *US Army Insider Missions*. Of the six missions described in Volume 1 that took place after JP joined the US Army in late 2019, three were to off-planet locations, while three took place on Earth. The off-planet missions were conducted under the aegis of US Space Command, which is led by General James Dickinson, who is responsible for integrating all US military assets for space operations that take place above an Earth altitude of 60 miles (100 kilometers). JP's terrestrial missions to the Atlantic Space Ark and a nearby undersea city complex in the Bermuda Triangle were presumably conducted under the control of US Northern Command, which is led by General Glen VanHerck.

In contrast, in Volume 2, only one of JP's missions was conducted under the aegis of US Space Command, which was to the Moon to gain access to an ancient space ark connected to an underground civilization of Ant people that JP had previously visited. Another off-planet mission was with a Nordic space convey to resupply extraterrestrial colonies on Ganymede and Europa, and did not involve Space Command. The remaining ten missions were to terrestrial locations such as underground civilizations, spaceports, or underwater locations. Nine of these were under the US mainland or surrounding ocean, while only one was to a non-US geographical location —an unknown island in the South Atlantic. The nine US-territorial missions would again presumably have been under the control of General VanHerck's US Northern Command.

What I want to bring to the reader's attention are three factors that help explain the overall context for JP's missions and how these relate to a covert disclosure process that appears to be underway. First, US Space Command was given the lead role for coordinating Earth's spacefaring nations in taking control of our solar system under the Jupiter Accords, as I described in *Galactic Federations, Councils and Secret Space Programs* (2022). General Dickinson would consequently have a significant role in ensuring greater military and civilian cooperation in space through initiatives such as the Artemis Accords, which by early August 2023 involved bilateral agreements between the space administrations of the US (NASA) and 27 other countries.[122]

Second, in January 2023, a comprehensive disclosure plan was allegedly delivered to General VanHerck, which had been developed with the cooperation of the Galactic Federation of Worlds. Elena Danaan claims she witnessed the handover of the plan through the eyes of Thor Han Eredyon, a Galactic Federation representative, who personally delivered the plan to an underground facility in the Blue Ridge mountains.[123] What lends credence to her remarkable claim is that Danaan recognized VanHerck from a list of 44 4-star generals found on Wikipedia at the time.[124] She also recognized the surrounding mountainous terrain as consistent with a view from the Raven Rock Mountain Complex, which we later discovered is used as a Continuity of Government facility controlled by the US military. In a Continuity of Government emergency, VanHerck's Northern Command would be in charge of the US until civilian leadership could be restored. If such a disclosure plan was delivered, then that would place General VanHerck in charge of unveiling the disclosure process that involves a great number of classified projects and facilities that are both off-planet and in hidden terrestrial locations. The possibility that such disclosures could lead to a Continuity of Government emergency is very real, which would explain VanHerck's involvement with a UFO disclosure plan.

Third, on June 16, 2023, General VanHerck released an extraordinary public criticism of an announcement by US Space Command that contained comments from General Dickinson. According to VanHerck, an "incredibly misleading" statement was made by Space Command.[125] VanHerck went on to say: "When you

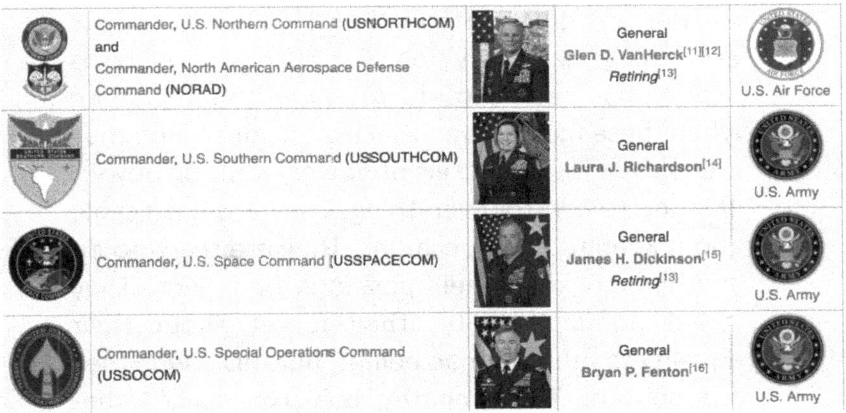

	Commander, U.S. Northern Command (**USNORTHCOM**) and Commander, North American Aerospace Defense Command (**NORAD**)		General **Glen D. VanHerck**[11][12] *Retiring*[13]	U.S. Air Force
	Commander, U.S. Southern Command (**USSOUTHCOM**)		General **Laura J. Richardson**[14]	U.S. Army
	Commander, U.S. Space Command (**USSPACECOM**)		General **James H. Dickinson**[15] *Retiring*[13]	U.S. Army
	Commander, U.S. Special Operations Command (**USSOCOM**)		General **Bryan P. Fenton**[16]	U.S. Army

Figure 42. Extract from a list of 44 active duty 4-star generals on Wikipedia, recorded on Aug 25, 2023

have somebody from Space Command saying: "So, we've owned the missile warning mission since Space Command stood up,' is totally deceiving and incorrect." [126] VanHerck next went on to make the following enigmatic statement: "As Santa goes around the globe, Space Command provides domain awareness to me to track Santa and provide warnings to all the kids around there of where Santa is and what time he's going to show up at their house."

Ostensibly, these criticisms involved jurisdiction over tracking nuclear missiles. Vitally important, "Santa Claus" is a euphemism used by NASA and the Pentagon for UFOs, as multiple whistleblowers have revealed.[127] VanHerck's criticisms boiled down to a power struggle over who has overall authority over underground civilizations and facilities under the United States and adjacent ocean waters. Is it Northern Command, as these locations clearly fall under its jurisdiction, or Space Command, because there is a significant amount of space travel both to and from these facilities?

In my series of questions and answers I conducted with Thor Han Eredyon on July 7, 2013, which were relayed through Elena Danaan, I asked about the power struggle between VanHerck and Dickinson. Thor Han's response was:

> I haven't met Dickinson; I have met VanHerck. VanHerck is a very proud man. He likes to control everything. He is very good for his position. This is why he has been chosen. You need to understand when these men arrive at such a responsibility; they are chosen for their skills of power, wanting power, wanting to control everything. They are despicable about keeping their positions. They are ready to do anything to keep their positions of power. They forget about humility. They forget about their equality to other human beings, but this is why they are chosen. The empathy is very weak. I met VanHerck; he is a very proud man and very efficient in his work. This is why he was chosen. And I can understand struggles for power, but this is ridiculous; they should all work together. We tried to advise them, but they did not listen. They need to work together. These two organizations are meant to work together. These human games should stop.[128]

Thor Han's answer reveals some ugly truths about powerful US military leaders in charge of negotiations and relations with extraterrestrial visitors. VanHerck and other senior military leaders are chosen for their ability to wield power, authority, and control over every aspect of a military environment that aligns with the goal of achieving full spectrum dominance. Empathy and equality are secondary or missing human qualities in such leaders; nevertheless, VanHerck and similar military leaders are in charge of the disclosure process for our planet.

If General VanHerck and Northern Command have been given authority to implement a disclosure plan designed with the input of extraterrestrials, then that would explain the difference in JP's mission targets. It suggests that a decision has been made to focus JP's missions on underground and undersea facilities, particularly those under the jurisdiction of US Northern Command.

JP's superiors are allowing his information to be relayed out for public dissemination, which makes him part of the covert disclosure plan that is underway. This official approval suggests that disclosure of JP's missions is to help the general public understand what's coming and to prepare Americans for the tremendous psychological shock of the official disclosure of extraterrestrial life, non-surface civilizations, and reverse-engineered spacecraft.

At the time of writing, a historic UFO (UAP) meeting has taken place on July 26, 2023, in the US House of Representatives Oversight and Accountability Subcommittee for National Security.[129] For the first time, a whistleblower, David Grusch, revealed the existence of multiple classified reverse engineering projects taking place at corporate facilities. Grusch spoke of up to 40 highly credentialled witnesses with need-to-know access to classified programs related to non-human life and technology who could testify before Congress about the reverse engineering programs, and also share documents and photos of these programs. Significantly, an investigative reporter, Michael Schellenberger, confirmed that highly credentialled whistleblowers are prepared to come forward to corroborate the existence of reverse engineering programs involving between 12 to 30 recovered non-human spacecraft.[130] Grusch's revelations and Schellenberg's findings substantiate JP's assertions from earlier in 2023 regarding highly credentialled whistleblowers coming forward soon with documents and photos of classified UFO-related projects.

Critically, as a result of Grusch and other witnesses' testimony about the reverse engineering of non-human technologies to US Senate Defense and Intelligence committees, a UAP Disclosure Act for 2023 was unanimously adopted by the US Senate as an amendment to the National Defense Authorization Act for 2024.[131] The Amendment contains many provisions that will expedite the release of UFO records (25 years after their creation) through a Review Board set up to work with the National Archives that will report directly to the US President. Crucially, Eminent

Domain will be asserted over all materials related to recovered UAP technologies, thereby ensuring that corporations cannot simply deny the Review Board access to what's in their possession.

JP's disclosures are groundbreaking and appear to be part of a covert disclosure plan supported by senior military officials wanting to acclimate civilians to the extent to which relations with underground non-human civilizations such as Ant People, Inner Earth Nordic colonists with extensive spaceports, and technology exchanges with underwater civilizations are occurring. It is not coincidental that JP is being allowed to participate in, and publicly reveal his classified missions to secret underground and underwater facilities, at the same time as other more highly credentialled whistleblowers are coming forward to speak about related facilities. What JP's missions reveal is that not only do reverse engineering programs of non-human technologies exist, but they have succeeded to varying degrees, and involve cooperation with non-human life, both extraterrestrial and Inner Earth or underwater civilizations.

JP's final mission discussed in this book is arguably the most critical of all his missions to date. This mission revealed that a multinational alliance of nations is coordinating to harness the crystal jewel device extracted from the Atlantic Space Ark, which is a key to activating other arks and ancient technologies found around the world. This international initiative is happening with the assistance of extraterrestrials associated with the Atlantic Space Ark desiring to accelerate the global activation process and thereby awakening humanity to the reality of galactic life visiting our planet. Consequently, JP's 4th mission to the Atlantic Space Ark appears to be a critical feature of a comprehensive disclosure plan coordinated between extraterrestrials and military leaders at the Raven Rock Mountain Complex in January 2023. In conclusion, there is good reason to be confident that a series of officially coordinated disclosure announcements are about to take place around the planet revealing the extent to which non-human life and technology exists, and how these are to be shared for the common benefit of all humanity.

Acknowledgements

I am deeply grateful to JP, who has confided in me his incredible extraterrestrial and secret space program experiences for 15 years and given me photos and videos of the different types of antigravity ships and orbs he has encountered. After joining the US Army, he has continued to share his direct experiences in covert space operations and ark missions. Despite the risk of an official reprimand and financial risk, he has continued to share much sensitive information, which speaks volumes about his courage and commitment to full disclosure of UFOs, ancient civilizations, and extraterrestrial life.

I greatly appreciate Adam S. Doyle for creating the incredible cover that incorporates four scenes from JP's missions. Thank you Adam also for creating the illustrations of the underground spaceport, one of the Ant People and for the fish inside a liquid sphere.

I am also very grateful to Duke Brickhouse, whose proofreading and suggestions were extremely helpful in producing the final version of this book.

Finally, my heartfelt gratitude goes to my soulmate, Angelika Whitecliff, whose enthusiastic encouragement and wise counsel were instrumental in my writing, editing, and design of this book.

Michael E. Salla, Ph.D.

About the Author

Dr. Michael Salla is an internationally recognized scholar in global politics, conflict resolution and U.S. foreign policy. He has taught at universities in the U.S. and Australia, including American University in Washington, DC. Today, he is most popularly known as a pioneer in the development of the field of 'exopolitics'; the study of the main actors, institutions and political processes associated with extraterrestrial life.

Dr Salla has been a guest speaker on hundreds of radio and TV shows including Ancient Aliens, Coast to Coast AM, and featured at national and international conferences. His Amazon bestselling *Secret Space Program* book series has made him a leading voice in the Truth Movement, and over 5000 people a day visit his websites for his most recent articles. He is also the host of the popular podcast *Exopolitics Today* with over 150,000 YouTube subscribers.

Endnotes

---

[1] https://www.democrats.senate.gov/imo/media/doc/uap_amendment.pdf (accessed 7/30/2023).

[2] David Grusch's opening and closing statements at a hearing held by the National Security Subcommittee of the House Oversight Committee is available online at: https://tinyurl.com/2ns45ar4 (accessed 7/30/2023).

[3] See US Navy, "Establishment of Unidentified Aerial Phenomena Task Force," https://www.navy.mil/Press-Office/Press-Releases/display-pressreleases/Article/2314280/establishment-of-unidentified-aerial-phenomena-task-force/ (accessed 8/27/2023).

[4] See "Juan Ponce de Leon," https://www.history.com/topics/exploration/juan-ponce-de-leon#fountain-of-youth (accessed 2/19/2023).

[5] Interview originally published in audio form on October 6, 2022, see Michael Salla, "Mission to Underground Civilization in Florida and a Gift for Humanity," https://www.youtube.com/watch?v=IYUvY0xlTWQ (accessed 1/20/2023).

[6] See Edgar Rothschild Fouche, "Secret Government Technology," https://www.bibliotecapleyades.net/ciencia/ciencia_extraterrestrialtech08.htm (accessed 1/20/2023).

[7] For a detailed discussion of the TR-3B in terms of its development and deployment, see the *USAF Secret Space Program: Shifting Extraterrestrial Alliances* (2019).

[8] For sources of native American legends about the Ant people, see "Native American Ant Mythology," http://www.native-languages.org/legends-ant.htm (accessed 1/20/2023).

[9] See "Rosewood: The Tree that Bleeds – BBC (2020)" https://naturedocumentaries.org/19229/rosewood-tree-bleeds-bbc-2020/ (accessed 2/19/2023).

[10] Book of Genesis, Tree of Life Version, Chapter 2, verses 9,16 & 17: https://www.biblegateway.com/passage/?search=Genesis%202&version=TLV (accessed /30/2023).

[11] "Top Secret Disclosure Speakers share their Intel for the Galactic & Spiritual Informers Connection!" https://youtu.be/PPGeq9XVVAI?t=1447 (accessed 1/20/2023).

[12] I discussed this incident in *US Army Insider Missions*, Volume 1, pp. 235-42.

[13] See *US Army Insider Missions*, Volume 1. Chapter 15.

[14] "How and why do fireflies light up?", Scientific American,

https://www.scientificamerican.com/article/how-and-why-do-fireflies/ (accessed 7/30/2023).

[15] See Michael Salla, "Awakened Stasis Giants Secretly Located & Imprisoned by Global Elite," https://exopolitics.org/awakened-stasis-giants-secretly-located-imprisoned-by-global-elite/ (accessed 7/30/2023).

[16] Interview originally published in audio form on October 20, 2022, see Michael Salla, "2nd Mission to Underground Civilization in Florida & the missing Gift for Humanity https://exopolitics.org/2nd-mission-to-underground-civilization-in-florida-the-missing-gift-for-humanity/ (accessed 1/21/2023).

[17] See Dick Allgire, https://twitter.com/CryptoViewing/status/1658217212514017296 (accessed 7/31/2023).

[18] See "Which Members of The Royal Family Are Freemasons?" https://masonicfind.com/freemasonry-the-british-monarchy (accessed 7/31/2023).

[19] See James Bickerton, "Prince Philip's secret life as Freemason – Duke's work in tight-lipped society remembered," https://www.express.co.uk/news/royal/1421098/Prince-Philip-news-Duke-of-Edinburgh-dead-Freemason-Windsor-Castle-Queen (accessed 7/31/2023).

[20] Radu Cinamar, *Translyvania Sunrise* (Skybooks, 2011)

[21] See Paul Wallis, *Escaping from Eden: Does Genesis Teach that the Human Race was Created by God or Engineered by ETs?* (Axis Mundi Books, 2020).

[22] Cited from the official website of Ponce De Leon Springs State Park: https://www.floridastateparks.org/parks-and-trails/ponce-de-leon-springs-state-park (accessed 1/21/2023).

[23] The Roundtable discussion was released on October 31, 2022 with the title: "Sleeping Giants, Return of Enki & Saturn Moon Crash: Roundtable Discussion" https://exopolitics.org/sleeping-giants-return-of-enki-saturn-moon-crash-roundtable-discussion/ (accessed 2/24/2023).

[24] See Michael Salla, "7 Sleeping Anunnaki Scientists are Awakening," https://exopolitics.org/7-sleeping-anunnaki-scientists-are-awakening/ (accessed 8/12/2023).

[25] See Mathew LaCroix, *The Stage of Time: Secrets of the Past, the Nature of Reality, and the Ancient Gods of History* (2019).

[26] See Michael Salla, "Is Pentagon using MOAB bombs against Giants hidden in Afghanistan?" https://exopolitics.org/pentagon-moab-bomb-giants-afghanistan/ (accessed 2/23/2023)

[27] This chapter is an expanded version of an article first published on November 9, 2022, titled "Recovering Stolen seeds from a Tree of Life & activation of a

sleeping giant in Iraq," https://exopolitics.org/recovering-stolen-seeds-from-a-tree-of-life-and-activating-a-sleeping-giant-in-iraq/ (accessed 2/24/2023).

[28] See Michael Salla, "Secret Diplomatic Mission to Underwater Cities in Atlantic Ocean," https://exopolitics.org/secret-diplomatic-mission-to-underwater-cities-in-atlantic-ocean/ (accessed 2/24/2023).

[29] Interview originally published in audio form on November 9, 2022, "Recovering Stolen seeds from a Tree of Life & activation of a sleeping giant in Iraq," https://exopolitics.org/recovering-stolen-seeds-from-a-tree-of-life-and-activating-a-sleeping-giant-in-iraq/ (accessed 2/20/2023)
see Michael Salla, "2nd Mission to Underground Civilization in Florida & the missing Gift for Humanity https://exopolitics.org/2nd-mission-to-underground-civilization-in-florida-the-missing-gift-for-humanity/ (accessed 1/21/2023).

[30] See Zhi-Ping Zhang, et al., "Double sperm cloning (DSC) is a promising strategy in mammalian genetic engineering and stem cell research," https://pubmed.ncbi.nlm.nih.gov/32894201/ (accessed 2/24/2023).

[31] See David Jacobs, *The Threat: Revealing the Secret Alien Agenda* (Simon & Schuster, 2008).

[32] For more details, see "Military TDY: Temporary Duty Assignment Explained," https://www.operationmilitarykids.org/military-tdy/ (accessed 2/25/2023).

[33] See Clifford Stone, *Eyes Only - The Story of Clifford Stone and UFO Crash Retrievals* (Self-published, 2012).

[34] See Michael Salla, "An Exopolitical Perspective on the Preemptive War against Iraq https://exopolitics.net/Study-Paper2.htm (accessed 8/1/2023).

[35] JP's information was first published on November 9, 2022, see Michael Salla, "Recovering Stolen seeds from a Tree of Life & activation of a sleeping giant in Iraq," https://exopolitics.org/recovering-stolen-seeds-from-a-tree-of-life-and-activating-a-sleeping-giant-in-iraq/ (accessed 2/25/2023).

[36] See Michael Salla, "Joint US China Mission to Giant ET Space Ark under Atlantic Ocean," https://exopolitics.org/giant-et-space-ark-under-atlantic/ (accessed 2/25/2023).

[37] See Michael Salla, *Exopolitics: Political Implications of the Extraterrestrial Presence* (Dandelion Books, 2004).

[38] See *US Army Insider Missions*, Vol 1, Ch 12.

[39] Interview originally published in audio form on November 30, 2022, see Michael Salla, Nordic ET Supply Missions to Ganymede & Europa's Secret Underground City," https://exopolitics.org/nordic-et-supply-missions-to-ganymede-europa/ (accessed 1/21/2023).

[40] JP describes some of his experiences with Shien in *US Army Insider Missions*, Vol 1, chapters 3 and 4.

[41] "King Matjaž," https://thezaurus.com/king_matja%c5%be/ (accessed 1/27/2023)
[42] See Radu Cinamar, Transylvanian Sunrise (Sky Books, 2009)
[43] See Michael Salla, "A Conversation with Thor Han Eredyon on Colonization of Pleiades & Earth Liberation," https://exopolitics.org/a-conversation-with-thor-han-eredyon-part-1/ (accessed 1/27/2023)
[44] For a detailed history of the Errahel and Taal, see Elena Danaan, *A Gift from the Stars* (2020).
[45] Interview originally published in audio form on January 14, 2022, see Michael Salla, "Visits to King of Ant People and Ancient Moonbase," https://exopolitics.org/visits-to-king-of-ant-people-and-ancient-moonbase/ (accessed 1/23/2023).
[46] JP later clarified that the handgun he and the seven others carried was in fact another caliber handgun that he was not allowed to publicly reveal.
[47] See David Paulides, "Missing 411-North America and Beyond: Stories of people who have disappeared in remote locations of North America and five other countries" (Createspace, 2013).
[48] See "What is the average percentage of water in the human body?" https://www.medicalnewstoday.com/articles/what-percentage-of-the-human-body-is-water#percentage-chart (accessed 1/24/2023).
[49] See Masuru Emoto, *The Hidden Messages in Water* (Atria Books, 2005).
[50] JP's mission to the Moon Space Ark is discussed in *US Army Insider Missions,* Vol 1, Ch 14.
[51] See Philip Corso, *The Day After Roswell* (Pocket Books, 1997).
[52] Interview originally released as "JP Mission to Underground Civilization & Nordic Spaceport" https://exopolitics.org/jp-mission-to-underground-civilization-nordic-spaceport/ (accessed 6/12/2023).
[53] Radu Cinamar, Inside the Earth- The Second Tunnel (Sky Books, 2019).
[54] Incident is discussed in Michael Salla, *US Army Insider Missions*, Vol 1, pp. 128-35.
[55] See US Army Insider Missions, p. 247.
[56] See US Army Insider Missions, pp. 291-307.
[57] The Jupiter Accords were discussed in Michael Salla, *Galactic Federations, Councils and Secret Space Programs* (2022) pp. 137-58.
[58] See Jared Gans, "Five things to know about the Iran-Saudi deal brokered by China," https://thehill.com/policy/international/3895412-five-things-to-know-about-the-iran-saudi-deal-brokered-by-china/ (accessed 8/2/2023).
[59] See "What Was Discovered in Kincaid's Cave in the Grand Canyon?"

https://wheninyourstate.com/arizona/wont-believe-one-man-discovered-grand-canyon/ (accessed 6/14/2023).

[60] Interview originally released as "JP Mission to Ancient Artifacts & Civilizations found in Grand Canyon," https://exopolitics.org/jp-mission-to-ancient-artifacts-civilizations-found-in-grand-canyon/ (accessed 6/14/2023).

[61] Wikipedia, Golden Plates, https://en.wikipedia.org/wiki/Golden_plates (accessed 6/15/2023).

[62] In *Galactic Federations, Councils and Secret Space Programs*, I discuss how an Intergalactic Confederation called the Seeders or 24 Civilizations, begins human genetic experiments on different worlds in multiple galaxies.

[63] See "Concept of Collective Unconscious at Jung": https://carl-jung.net/collective_unconscious.html (accessed 6/15/2023).

[64] See Abraham (Avi) Loeb and Sean M. Kirkpatrick: "Physical Constraints on Unidentified Aerial Phenomena," draft version March 7, 2023, https://lweb.cfa.harvard.edu/~loeb/LK1.pdf (accessed 6/16/2023).

[65] Interview was first published as "JP Update on Ancient Library at Military Base Revealing History of Arks on Earth," https://exopolitics.org/jp-update-on-ancient-library-at-military-base-revealing-history-of-arks-on-earth/ (accessed 6/16/2023)

[66] Transcribed from podcast clip found at: "Tucker Carlson shares bizarre tale of troops dying from UFO encounters," https://www.militarytimes.com/off-duty/military-culture/2023/03/16/tucker-carlson-shares-bizarre-tale-of-troops-dying-from-ufo-encounters/ (accessed 6/30/2023).

[67] See Michael Salla, *Galactic Federations, Councils and Secret Space Programs,* pp. 105-24.

[68] Abraham (Avi) Loeb and Sean M. Kirkpatrick: "Physical Constraints on Unidentified Aerial Phenomena," draft version March 7, 2023, https://lweb.cfa.harvard.edu/~loeb/LK1.pdf (accessed 6/16/2023).

[69] See Leonard C. Levin, *Report From Iron Mountain on the Possibility and Desirability of Peace* (Dial Press, 1967)

[70] See Michael Salla, https://vimeo.com/ondemand/alienfalseflag (Vimeo, 2021).

[71] NBC News, "NASA panel studying UFO sightings says stigma and poor data pose challenges." https://news.yahoo.com/nasa-panel-studying-ufo-sightings-201913754.html (accessed 6/30/2023).

[72] Leslie Kean and Ralph Blumenthal, "Intelligence Officials Say U.S. Has Retrieved Craft of Non-Human Origin," https://thedebrief.org/intelligence-officials-say-u-s-has-retrieved-non-human-craft/ (accessed 6/30/2023).

[73] Michael Shellenberger, "US Has 12 Or More Alien Spacecraft, Say Military And Intelligence Contractors,"

https://public.substack.com/p/us-has-12-or-more-alien-space-craft (accessed 6/30/2023).

[74] I described the harassment experienced by JP in *US Army Insider Missions,* Volume 1, pp. 140-42.

[75] See Douglas Dean Johnson, "Unidentified Anomalous Phenomena": A look at the UAP-related provisions of the final FY 2023 National Defense Authorization Act (H.R. 7776)": https://douglasjohnson.ghost.io/uap-related-provisions-of-the-final-proposed-fy-2023-national-defense-authorization-act/ (accessed 6/30/2023).

[76] See Michael Salla, "Secret Mars Colonies Trade with up to 900 Extraterrestrial Civilizations," https://exopolitics.org/secret-mars-colonies-trade-with-up-to-900-extraterrestrial-civilizations/ (accessed 7/1/2023).

[77] NBC News, "NASA panel studying UFO sightings says stigma and poor data pose challenges."
https://news.yahoo.com/nasa-panel-studying-ufo-sightings-201913754.html (accessed 6/30/2023).

[78] Original interview published on May 4, 2023, "JP Mission to Underground Spaceport in US Southeast" https://exopolitics.org/jp-mission-to-underground-spaceport-in-us-southeast/ (accessed 5/16/2023).

[79] "Caves of Alabama," https://encyclopediaofalabama.org/article/caves/ (accessed 7/1/2023).

[80] AP, "US Space Command site to be located in Huntsville, Alabama," https://tinyurl.com/3xesxzz7 (accessed 7/1/2023).

[81] Leslie Kean and Ralph Blumenthal, "Intelligence Officials Say U.S. Has Retrieved Craft of Non-Human Origin," https://thedebrief.org/intelligence-officials-say-u-s-has-retrieved-non-human-craft/ (accessed 6/30/2023).

[82] I discuss JP's sightings and photos of flying triangles and rectangles in US Army Insider Missions, Volume 1.

[83] See Christopher Sharp, "Bombshell Letter Reveals Canadian Politician's Concerns Of Covert UFO Programs Involving Canada And Five Eyes Alliance," https://www.liberationtimes.com/home/bombshell-letter-reveals-canadian-politicians-concerns-of-covert-ufo-programs-involving-canada-and-five-eyes-alliance (accessed 7/1/2023).

[84] See Michel Salla, *The US Navy's Secret Space Program & Nordic Extraterrestrial Alliance* (Exopolitics Consultants, 2018) pp. 165-80.

[85] Huanzheng Zhu, et al., "Multispectral camouflage for infrared, visible, lasers and microwave with radiative cooling,"
https://www.nature.com/articles/s41467-021-22051-0 (accessed 7/4/2023).

[86] See Michael Salla, "Contact with Nordic Alien in USAF Uniform whose Spacecraft was Photographed,"

https://exopolitics.org/contact-with-nordic-alien-in-usaf-uniform-whose-spacecraft-was-photographed/ (accessed 7/12/2023).
[87] See "Project Bluebeam about to be unleashed according to former FBI Special Agent," https://exopolitics.org/project-bluebeam-about-to-be-unleashed-according-to-former-fbi-special-agent/ (accessed 7/12/2023).
[88] See Michael Salla, "Navy Insiders Corroborate Secret Antarctic Space Fleet & Mission to Oumuamua" https://exopolitics.org/navy-insiders-corroborate-secret-antarctic-space-fleet-mission-to-oumuamua/ (accessed 7/12/2023).
[89] I discussed how US Space Command was given this responsibility in *Galactic Federations, Councils and Secret Space Programs* (2022) pp. 137-58.
[90] See Theresa Hitchens, "SPACECOM takes over missile defense ops from Strategic Command," https://breakingdefense.com/2023/05/spacecom-takes-over-missile-defense-ops-from-strategic-command/ (accessed 7/13/2023).
[91] Theresa Hitchens, "NORTHCOM's head sets record straight on missile defense boundaries with SPACECOM," https://breakingdefense.com/2023/06/after-confusion-gen-vanherck-says-he-has-the-conn-for-homeland-missile-defense-santa-tracking/ (accessed 7/13/2023).
[92] See Stacy Liberatore, "Nasa used Santa Claus as a codename for THREE UFOs spotted during the lunar landings, claims former employee," https://www.dailymail.co.uk/sciencetech/article-3373636/Nasa-used-Santa-Claus-codename-THREE-UFOs-spotted-lunar-landings-claims-former-employee.html (accessed 7/13/2023).
[93] The webinar, "Orbs, Space Arks and Motherships – Why the Deep State Fears Them" is available at: https://vimeo.com/ondemand/orbsspacearksmotherships (accessed 7/12/2023).
[94] Interview first published in audio form on May 18, 2023, as "Tracking Past Life Memories to Find Space Ark Crews," https://exopolitics.org/tracking-past-life-memories-to-find-space-ark-crews/ (accessed 7/15/2023).
[95] See "Bay of Fundy Tides: The Highest Tides in the World!" https://www.bayoffundy.com/about/highest-tides/ (accessed 7/15/2023).
[96] See US Army Insider Missions: Space Arks, Underground Cities & ET Contact (Exopolitics Oonsultants, 2023), pp. 291-308.
[97] I discussed the Raven Rock Mountain Complex meeting in "ET Disclosure being planned now at an underground Blue Ridge Mountains Complex," https://exopolitics.org/et-disclosure-is-being-planned-now/ (accessed 7/16/2023).
[98] See Zamone Perez, "Pentagon UFO chief says alien mothership in our solar system possible," https://www.militarytimes.com/off-duty/military-

culture/2023/03/09/pentagon-ufo-chief-says-alien-mothership-in-our-solar-system-possible/ (accessed 7/16/2023).
[99] Brad Steiger, *Gods of Aquarius* (Harcourt Brace Jovanovich, 1976).
[100] See https://www.alittlesparkofjoy.com/star-seed/ (accessed 8/4/2023).
[101] See Law of One 12:26. https://www.lawofone.info/s/12#26 (accessed 8/4/2023).
[102] "King Charles Coronation: What Is It REALLY About?" https://youtu.be/S5UOekp2Vwo (accessed 7/16/2023).
[103] David Icke, *The Biggest Secret* (Ickonic Enterprise, 2015) pp. 302-303.
[104] The interview was originally published in audio form on June 5 as "JP Update – Visit to Massive Spaceport under an unknown South Atlantic Island" https://exopolitics.org/jp-update-visit-to-massive-spaceport-under-an-unknown-south-atlantic-island/ (accessed 7/17/2023).
[105] The Roundtable discussion was published in audio form as, "Sleeping Giants, Return of Enki & Saturn Moon Crash: Roundtable Discussion," https://exopolitics.org/sleeping-giants-return-of-enki-saturn-moon-crash-roundtable-discussion/ (accessed 7/17/2023).
[106] JP is referring to links to the different articles, photos and interviews that have been published online, the original versions of which are available online at: https://exopolitics.org/jp-articles-photos-videos/ (accessed 7/17/2023).
[107] See James Lee, *The One World Tartarians: The Greatest Civilization Ever To Be Erased From History* (2022)
[108] See David Hatcher Childress, *Technology of the Gods: The Incredible Sciences of the Ancients* (Adventures Unlimited Press, 2000).
[109] See "Tesla's Tower at Wardenclyffe," https://teslasciencecenter.org/history/tower/ (accessed 7/18/2023).
[110] See "UFO Fleet Takes Flight from Popocatepetl Volcano," https://www.latest-ufo-sightings.net/2023/08/ufo-fleet-takes-flight-from-popocatepetl-volcano.html (accessed 9/13/2023).
[111] See "The Earth Without the Moon," https://varchive.org/itb/sansmoon.htm (accessed 7/19/2023).
[112] The interview was originally published in audio form on June 23 as "JP Update – US Military working with Nordic ETs in Time Travel research on Space Arks," https://exopolitics.org/us-military-working-with-nordic-ets-in-time-travel-research/ (accessed 7/25/2023).
[113] "A Conversation with Thor Han Eredyon on Colonization of Pleiades & Earth Liberation," https://exopolitics.org/a-conversation-with-thor-han-eredyon-part-1/#transcript (accessed 7/25/2023).
[114] See J. Richard Gott, *Time Travel in Einstein's Universe: The Physical Possibilities of Travel Through Time* (Mariner Books, 2002).

[115] See Marco Margaritoff, "The Legend Of The Chronovisor, A 'Time Machine' Hidden In The Vatican," https://allthatsinteresting.com/chronovisor (accessed 7/25/2023).
[116] See *US Army Insider Missions: Space Arks, Underground Cities & ET Contact,* Volume 1 (2022) pp. 121-23.
[117] The interview was originally published in audio form on July 21 as "JP Update – 4th Mission to Atlantic Space Ark," https://exopolitics.org/jp-update-4th-mission-to-atlantic-space-ark/ (accessed 7/21/2023).
[118] JP's three previous missions to the Atlantic Space Ark are discussed in Volume 1 of *US Army Insider Missions: Space Arks, Underground Cities & ET Contact* (Exopolitics Consultants, 2023).
[119] James Lovelock and Lynn Margulis first introduced "the Gaia Hypothesis" in their paper, "Atmospheric homeostasis by and for the biosphere: the gaia hypothesis," in Tellus (Volume 26, 1974 – Issue 1-2). Available online at: https://www.tandfonline.com/doi/abs/10.3402/tellusa.v26i1-2.9731 (accessed 8/6/2023).
[120] For discussion of pole shifts see Charles Hapgood, *Earth's Shifting Crust: A Key to Some Basic Problems of Earth Science* (Pantheon Books, 1958)
[121] I discuss these ancient stories of floods, earth changes and arks involved in planetary evacuation in a webinar, "Extraterrestrial Seeders, Space Arks & the Great Reveal,"
https://vimeo.com/ondemand/etseedersspacearks (accessed 8/6/2023).
[122] For full list of Artemis Accords signatories and its contents, visit https://www.nasa.gov/specials/artemis-accords/index.html (accessed 8/25/2023).
[123] I first discussed Elena Danaan's recollections of the meeting between Thor Han Eredyon and General VanHerck in "ET Disclosure being planned now at an underground Blue Ridge Mountains Complex," https://exopolitics.org/et-disclosure-is-being-planned-now/ (accessed 8/25/2023).
[124] See "List of active duty United States four-star officers," https://en.wikipedia.org/wiki/List_of_active_duty_United_States_four-star_officers
(accessed 8/25/2023).
[125] Theresa Hitchens, "NORTHCOM's head sets record straight on missile defense boundaries with SPACECOM,"
https://breakingdefense.com/2023/06/after-confusion-gen-vanherck-says-he-has-the-conn-for-homeland-missile-defense-santa-tracking/ (accessed 8/7/2023).
[126] Theresa Hitchens, op. cit.
[127] Stacy Liberatore, 'Nasa used Santa Claus as a codename for THREE UFOs spotted during the lunar landings, claims former employee,"

https://www.dailymail.co.uk/sciencetech/article-3373636/Nasa-used-Santa-Claus-codename-THREE-UFOs-spotted-lunar-landings-claims-former-employee.html (accessed 8/7/2023).
[128] "A Conversation with Thor Han Eredyon on Colonization of Pleiades & Earth Liberation," https://exopolitics.org/a-conversation-with-thor-han-eredyon-part-1/#transcript (accessed 7/25/2023).
[129] See "WATCH: Whistleblower tells Congress the U.S. is concealing 'multi-decade' program that captures UFOs," https://www.pbs.org/newshour/politics/watch-live-house-oversight-committee-probes-ufos-and-wider-implications (accessed 8/7/2023).
[130] See Michael Shellenberger, "US Has 12 Or More Alien Spacecraft, Say Military And Intelligence Contractors," https://public.substack.com/p/us-has-12-or-more-alien-space-craft (accessed 8/7/2023).
[131] The UAP Disclosure Act of 2023 is available at: https://www.democrats.senate.gov/imo/media/doc/uap_amendment.pdf (accessed 8/7/2023).

Index